Rural Reconstruction and Development

PRAEGER SPECIAL STUDIES IN
INTERNATIONAL ECONOMICS AND DEVELOPMENT

Rural Reconstruction and Development

A MANUAL FOR FIELD WORKERS

Y. C. James Yen
Gregorio M. Feliciano
and the Joint Staffs of the
International Institute of Rural Reconstruction
and the
Philippine Rural Reconstruction Movement

Edited by
Harry Bayard Price

FREDERICK A. PRAEGER, Publishers
New York · Washington · London

The purpose of the Praeger Special Studies is to make specialized research monographs in U.S. and international economics and politics available to the academic, business, and government communities. For further information, write to the Special Projects Division, Frederick A. Praeger, Publishers, 111 Fourth Avenue, New York, N.Y. 10003.

FREDERICK A. PRAEGER, PUBLISHERS
111 Fourth Avenue, New York, N.Y. 10003, U.S.A.
77-79 Charlotte Street, London W.1, England

Published in the United States of America in 1967
by Frederick A. Praeger, Inc., Publishers

All rights reserved

© 1967 by the International Institute of Rural Reconstruction

Library of Congress Catalog Card Number: 67-13863

Printed in the United States of America

PREFACE

No true citizen of the world can fail to be troubled by the grim reality that nearly 1,700 million people living in the villages and hamlets of Asia, Latin America, and Africa are "eating bitterness." They are eating the bitterness of hunger and ignorance, disease and helplessness. For generations, they have been victims of indifference and neglect and, too often, of exploitation and oppression.

A vast majority among them are caught in a cycle of frustration and misery from which they do not know how to extricate themselves. What they lack, in most cases, is not native intelligence or the will to work, but opportunity, especially the opportunity to learn.

They do not have the fairly simple knowledge and the fairly simple technical skills they require in order to start their long climb toward economic security, dignity, health, and responsible citizenship. They need help in acquiring this knowledge and these skills, and we, the privileged among their fellow countrymen and in the wealthier nations, have only begun to learn how to give it to them. With all our vaunted advances in science and technology, and all the tools of education and communication now available to us, we are not yet closing the yawning gap between the poor and the rich in most of the developing societies, or that between the poor nations and the rich nations. Indeed, instead of shrinking, these gaps are growing wider.

One thing we can be sure of is that this problem will not go away if, preoccupied with our own concerns, we simply ignore it. Vast populations growing faster than their ability to produce food and other essentials, expanding gulfs between the privileged and the despairing, and mounting discontent among hundreds of millions who are not willing to wait indefinitely for a fair deal--all of these things are bad news for the entire human race.

An easy escape, for citizens with a conscience,

is to leave such huge problems to governments. It would even be a rational escape if governments, alone, could cope with them; or if private citizens were, in fact, powerless to do anything effective about them. But neither of these "ifs" will stand up under scrutiny.

To be sure, a great part of the financial investment needed, and most of the work required to cope with these huge problems, can only be accomplished through instrumentalities of government. But the job is too big for governments alone. There are many essential things that governments, in their present stage of development, cannot do. There are other essential things that governments, as now constituted and administered, will not do.

There are significant ways in which private citizens who have the desire to do so can complement and supplement the activities of their governments. There are also important ways in which private citizens, effectively organized, can help to change the climate of opinion in their own countries. They can increase the general awareness of what can be done, and how, with available means. They may be able to stimulate their governments to undertake more effective policies and actions, and then to give them some of the popular support they need in taking such actions.

These are not theories, but demonstrated facts--facts that are of special interest to alert citizens who want to do more than wring their hands and analyze their reasons for despair. These demonstrated facts are illustrated in the more than forty years of experience on which this book is based.

It is the experience, first, of the Chinese Mass Education Movement, founded and led by Dr. Y.C. James Yen, which evolved in a few years from a literacy campaign into a rounded, integrated, dynamic rural reconstruction program. This program, during the twenties, thirties, and forties, had a remarkable impact in China and stirred considerable interest in other parts of Asia. It was also instrumental in the establishment of the Joint Commission on Rural Reconstruction (JCRR), which has played such a vital role in the economic and social development of Taiwan (Formosa).

It is the experience, second, of the Philippine Rural Reconstruction Movement (PRRM), which, since 1952, has shown that the lessons learned in China can be applied, and added to, in a new setting. It has shown that in the new setting, moreover, a sizable pilot program could be successfully launched, under private auspices; that in carrying forward that program, a unique pattern of organization and operations could be created, tested, and refined; and that a program so conducted could have a profound effect not only in the rural areas, but in their influence upon the society, and the government, of a developing nation.

It is a kind of experience that is now beginning to be repeated, in appropriately modified ways, in other developing countries, with encouragement and assistance from the recently established International Institute of Rural Reconstruction (IIRR), of which Dr. Yen is President.

The present volume, which seeks to recapture many practical aspects of this long, continuous experience, may be of interest to social scientists, research workers, and students concerned with problems of agrarian development in their own or other emerging nations; to planners and administrators of rural programs--governmental and private; to influential citizens of many developing nations who want to do something about the poverty and misery of the people in their countries' rural areas; and to persons responsible for the planning and conduct of foreign aid programs. It is hoped that readers from each of these groups will find here information, ideas, and insights that will be of value to them, notwithstanding the fact that the arrangement of the materials is primarily for a special category of personnel.

As the title suggests, this manual is organized and designed principally as an aid to field workers in rural reconstruction and development. Those who have cooperated in preparing it have a clear conception of the type of person to whom it is primarily addressed. He (or she) is an educated, highly motivated young man or woman who, after previous months of broad, intensive training,

> lives and works full-time in a village, normally boarding with a farm family;

wins acceptance and trust in the community, and comes to know its people well;

as a friend, consistently respects their dignity, their intelligence, and their unrealized potentialities;

learns to serve as an effective bridge between them and the outer world of science and technology that has so much to offer them, but about which they know so little;

learns, too, how to give the village people--men, women, and youth--skillful leadership, counsel, and assistance in mobilizing their own efforts through self-help programs; and,

while living a rigorous life in Spartan surroundings, separated much of the time from colleagues and intimate friends, is able to withstand moments of loneliness and discouragement.

Young men and women answering this description have for years been the front-line workers of the Philippine Rural Reconstruction Movement. Without them, the movement could never have achieved the results that it has. This manual is for them and their future associates. It is also for young men and women in other lands who are doing, or will do, similar vital work among the rural peoples of their own countries.

Too often, the insights and the practical lessons gained from difficult rural development work remain unrecorded. As a result, new programs, instead of building on what has already been learned, must start again from scratch, repeat the same mistakes, and learn the same lessons all over again.

This is not rational, but it is understandable. The best people "on the firing line" in rural development work are naturally anxious to see results in terms of tangible benefits to the village folk, and in the growth of the people's own efforts to improve the lot of their families and communities. The pursuit of these goals is uphill, demanding work. For those engaged in it, there are not enough hours in the day. When working under these conditions, it is difficult to stop and formulate systematically the practical lessons being learned day by day. It is still more difficult for workers who are primarily activists to summon the extra effort required to put their findings into writing. It may be of interest, therefore, to indicate briefly how this manual came to be written.

In October, 1963, when Mr. Feliciano took charge of the Philippine program, he visited scores of villages and PRRM personnel throughout the countryside. Discussions with the workers brought out many practical difficulties, mainly social and sociological, with which they were contending, each in his own fashion, with varying degrees of success.

These problems seemed so widespread that a decision was made to convene two conferences of the entire staff to discuss and compile what were loosely referred to as "social approaches to rural reconstruction problems." About fifty distinct problems were identified, then discussed in small groups. Case studies were prepared and presented. "Solutions" were solicited and debated. The findings of each group were then placed before a general assembly of the whole staff for scrutiny and comment.

The net result was a collection of useful information and approaches to problems, which far exceeded expectations. For example, with reference to a somewhat sensitive problem of how to identify the illiterates in a Filipino village, twenty-six practical, tested methods were recorded.

Dr. Yen had long felt that a comprehensive analysis of the PRRM operation would be valuable both to members of the PRRM staff and to those from other countries who would soon be coming to the International Institute of Rural Reconstruction, for leadership training, using the PRRM field operation as a practical training base.

Faced with this prospect, members of the joint staffs of IIRR and PRRM went to work. A first step was to review critically all of PRRM's previous training programs for new staff members. Second, the Senior Staff members were asked to prepare new lecture notes and working papers, making full use of the findings of the general conferences mentioned above. Third, these notes and papers were reviewed and discussed during a third general conference. Finally, each department was asked to write a comprehensive manual, in its field, for use during the forthcoming period. During the next six months, the manuals listed below were produced in English, and translated into Spanish.

1. Manual on Field Operations, prepared by Dr. Juan Flavier, then Deputy Director of Field Operations, with the advice of the Director, Mr. Ernesto Rigor, and the assistance of field assistants and team captains.

2. Manual on Plant Production, prepared by Mr. Rigor, with the assistance of Laurito Arizala.

3. Manual on Animal Production, prepared by Dr. Rufino Gapuz, with the assistance of Bartolome Rebollido.

4. Manual on Cooperatives, prepared by Mr. Angel P. Mandac, with the assistance of Roger Bañas.

5. Manual on Rural Industries and Vocational Arts, prepared by Mr. Rigor, with the assistance of Mrs. Josefina S. Corral and Reynaldo de la Torre.

6. Manual on Education, prepared by Mr. Arcadio G. Matela, with the assistance of Damaso Cabacungan (Literacy and Literature), Mrs. Rosalina F. Calairo (Folk Drama), and Norma Callanta (Folk Music and Dancing).

7. Manual on Village Self-Government, prepared by Atty. Enrique Claudio, with the assistance of Mrs. Maria M. Reyes.

8. Manual on Health, prepared by Dr. Eduardo E. Agustin, with the assistance of Dr. Jacinto Gotangco.

9. Manual on Model Farm Families, prepared by Mr. Matela, with the assistance of Mr. José Totaan.

10. Manual on Model Villages, prepared by Dr. Flavier, with the assistance of Mr. Menandro S. Pernito.

Dr. Pablo N. Mabbun, PRRM chief of research, and Mrs. Josefa Jara Martinez, consultant on training, cooperated in the planning and editing of these manuals.

Virtually all members of the IIRR and PRRM staffs (see Appendix A) contributed to the manuals, directly or indirectly, through the presentation of recorded experiences, the working up of case studies, and active participation in the general conferences mentioned earlier.

The ten manuals and their attachments, when completed, came to over 2,000 typed manuscript pages, or more than four times the length of this volume. The material was too bulky and repetitious for efficient use. It was decided that a single, consolidated manual would be desirable. The most essential material in the ten specialized manuals, therefore, was condensed, revised, and rewritten, and an introductory chapter was added. Each section, when completed, was submitted to appropriate IIRR and PRRM officers and staff members for critical review, to make certain that it reflected faithfully their field experiences, as well as the philosophy and principles of both organizations. It may be mentioned, parenthetically, that at many points in this book, the word "he" is used, for the sake of brevity, when "he or she" would be more accurate. This is especially true when the text refers to rural reconstruction workers (RRWs) and technical assistants, at least half of whom are women.

The reader will find in the manual many references to technical facets of the work. These are, of course, basic. But the principal emphasis is on "social approaches" to rural reconstruction. There are two reasons for this.

One is that technologies are advancing rapidly. It is a responsibility of the technical experts and their associates to keep abreast of new developments in their respective fields, and to make available to users of the manual additional up-to-date technical information they need. This can be done through basic and on-the-job training, and through special memoranda or selected literature that the layman can understand.

The second reason is that PRRM, as an experimental movement, has directed its attention mainly to the human and social aspects of development, and to the creation of a dynamic, integrated program in which the village people take a very active part. It is in these activities that PRRM has acquired its most distinctive and valuable experience to date.

Those who have worked in broad-scale rural reconstruction programs know the folly of being dogmatic about detailed methods and approaches. A feeling, at times, that a good deal has been learned is apt to be followed by a realization that it is only a beginning of all that needs to be learned, through firsthand experience, in a vast and relatively new field of human endeavor. No manual could possibly provide "all the answers." This one does not attempt to say the last word on any subject.

It is a recapitulation of experience to date--a book to be mastered and then used, not slavishly but with discrimination. The field worker should not simply lean on it, as on a crutch. It would be better to think of it as a kit of tools--or techniques. When he becomes thoroughly familiar with them, he can then select and use the ones that seem most suitable for forwarding a specific project or for meeting a particular situation. If he is a field worker in a country other than the Philippines, he will need to think alertly and creatively about ways in which this manual might need to be modified for successful use in a different socio-economic setting. It is the hope of the authors that, used in these ways, the manual will become a valuable resource and reference work for both new and experienced field workers.

It is intended, also, to be a stimulus to the worker's thinking and experimentation. There is always a need for the staff member's own intelligence, initiative, and judgment. One worker here, and another there, will discover that there are new and perhaps better ways of meeting a problem, or of conducting a particular project. The result of his experimentation, whether good or bad, will be reported. If it seems promising, other workers will try out the new approach to ascertain whether, for them, it really does work better than the old. This is how the social approaches and techniques presented in this manual have evolved. It is how they will continue to evolve, with further innovations developed and tested by growing numbers of participants in rural reconstruction programs around the world.

It is hoped that parts of the manual may prove useful to leaders of various types of organizations engaged in rural activities, as well as to numerous individuals--including school teachers, agricultural extension workers, health personnel, cooperative supervisors, and perhaps priests or ministers--who are now working, or expect to work, in rural areas.

All field workers and supervisors who use this manual are urged to keep a record of their ideas on how it can be improved. If this is done, and if ideas are then exchanged freely, it should be possible within a few years to produce a revised manual that is greatly enriched by fresh insights and widening experience.

Harry Bayard Price
Director
Technical Cooperation
and Publications

CONTENTS

	Page
PREFACE	v
ABBREVIATIONS AND CONVERSION RATES	xx

INTRODUCTION

Chapter

1 RURAL PROBLEMS IN THE DEVELOPING NATIONS   1

    Asia, Africa, and Latin America   1
    Food and Population   2
    Education   9
    Health   11
    Citizenship   13

ORIENTATION

2 INTERNATIONAL INSTITUTE OF RURAL RECONSTRUCTION AND PHILIPPINE RURAL RECONSTRUCTION MOVEMENT
   by Y.C. James Yen, President, IIRR   19

    Philippine Rural Reconstruction Movement   19
    National Pattern of Rural Reconstruction   22
    International Institute
      of Rural Reconstruction   26
    Centers of Excellence
      in Rural Reconstruction   31

3 PRRM ORGANIZATION, PLANNING, AND ADMINISTRATION
   by Gregorio M. Feliciano, President, PRRM   33

    Organization   33
    Planning   37
    Administration   40

OPERATIONS

4 FIELD OPERATIONS ... 61

    Field Workers and Their Jobs ... 61
    Guidelines for Rural Reconstruction
      Workers (RRWs) ... 70
    Guidelines for Field Operations
      Administrative Personnel ... 95

FOUR-FOLD PROGRAM IN ACTION

I. LIVELIHOOD

5 AIMS AND SCOPE OF THE LIVELIHOOD PROGRAM ... 105

    General Features ... 106
    Change and Growth ... 112

6 PLANT PRODUCTION ... 115

    Emphases in Plant Production Program ... 116
    Improving Rice Culture ... 116
    Expanding the Production
      of Secondary Crops ... 127
    Stimulating Homelot Gardening ... 133
    Developing Extension Farms
      and Plant Nurseries ... 135
    A Seed Bank in Every Barrio ... 140
    Composting ... 147
    Making Farmers' Classes Effective ... 149

7 ANIMAL PRODUCTION ... 155

    Emphases in Animal Production Program ... 155
    Hatching of Purebred New Hampshire
      Eggs by Native Hens ... 156
    Caponization of Cockerels ... 157
    A Purebred Boar for Each Barrio ... 158
    Raising Breeding Sows
      for Upgrading Purposes ... 161
    Raising Fattening Hogs for Market ... 163
    Mass Vaccinations of Livestock ... 164
    Special Training Courses and Seminars ... 166

8 COOPERATIVES ... 167

    PRRM-Sponsored Credit Unions ... 168
    Promotion of Credit Cooperatives ... 169

	Organization and Education	170
	Administration and Management	171
	Supervision	172
	A Look Ahead	176
9	RURAL INDUSTRIES AND VOCATIONAL ARTS	178
	Rural Industries	178
	Vocational Arts	182
10	THE MINIMUM ADDITIONAL INCOME (MAC) PROJECT	190
	Six Ways of Increasing the Family Income	190
	Setting an Attainable Target	191
	The MAC Project	191
	Farmer's Income Record	194

II. EDUCATION

11	HUMAN DEVELOPMENT AND THE FOUR-FOLD PROGRAM	201
	Education for Whom?	201
	Education for What?	203
	Education and Development	204
	PRRM Education Department	205
	Education and the Four-Fold Program	206
12	LITERACY AND LITERATURE	208
	Illiteracy in the Philippines	208
	PRRM Literacy Program	209
	A Look Ahead	225
13	CULTURAL AND RECREATIONAL ACTIVITIES	228
	Folk Dancing	229
	Folk Music	236
	Drama	239
	Other Recreational Activities	243

III. HEALTH

14	SCOPE OF THE PRRM HEALTH PROGRAM	247
	The Rural Health Problem	247
	The PRRM Health Program	249
15	HEALTH CENTERS, HEALTH WORKERS, MOTHERS' CLASSES	251

	The Barrio Health Centers	251
	Auxiliary Health Workers	259
	Mothers' Classes	264
16	ENVIRONMENTAL SANITATION, IMMUNIZATION	271
	Environmental Sanitation	271
	Immunization	279
	Recurring Problems	281

IV. VILLAGE SELF-GOVERNMENT

17	BACKGROUND AND AIMS OF THE SELF-GOVERNMENT PROGRAM	287
	Evolution of Village Self-Government in the Philippines	287
	Self-Government in the PRRM Four-Fold Program	289
18	ORGANIZING AND ACTIVATING BARRIO ASSOCIATIONS	290
	Organizing a Barrio Association	291
	Activating the Barrio Associations	295
	Revitalizing Barrio Associations	303
19	ACTIVATING THE BARRIO GOVERNMENT MACHINERY	307
	Establishing Friendly Relations	307
	Training of Barrio Officials	308
20	CITIZENSHIP EDUCATION AND LEADERSHIP TRAINING	312
	Citizenship Education	312
	Leadership Training	314

V. JOINT PROGRAMS

21	THE MODEL FARM FAMILY	321
	The Program	321
	Implementing the Program	327
	Evaluating Progress	343
	Recognition Day Program	361
22	MODEL VILLAGES	363
	Background	363

Criteria for a Model Village and Maximum Attainable Scores	365
Implementing the Program	371
Recording and Rating of Progress Achieved	374
Progress Report for Model Barrio	375
Rating Sheet for Model Barrio Development	382
Rating Guide for Model Barrio Development	384
Modified Model Barrio Rating Guide for Hacienda Barrios	396
Projection of Goals for Model Village Development	397

APPENDIXES

A	IIRR AND PRRM PERSONNEL WHO PARTICIPATED IN PREPARING THIS MANUAL	417
B	FILIPINO AND TECHNICAL TERMS	423

ABBREVIATIONS

IIRR - International Institute of Rural Reconstruction.

IRRI - International Rice Research Institute, Los Banos.

PACD - An executive agency of the Philippine Government directed by the Presidential Assistant for Community Development.

PRRM - Philippine Rural Reconstruction Movement.

RHU - Rural health unit, in a municipality.

RRMA - Rural Reconstruction Men's Association, in a barrio.

RRW - Rural Reconstruction Worker.

RRWA - Rural Reconstruction Women's Association, in a barrio.

RRYA - Rural Reconstruction Youth Association, in a barrio.

CONVERSION RATES

Caban, cavan - 25 gantas or 2.13 bushels.

Ganta - 8 chupas, or 2.72 dry quarts.

Hectare - 2.471 acres.

Peso - approximately $0.26, in 1966.

INTRODUCTION

INTRODUCTION

CHAPTER 1 — RURAL PROBLEMS IN THE DEVELOPING NATIONS

A brief but broad look at rural problems in the newly developing parts of the world may help us to view specific programs in better perspective, and to discern more clearly their distinctive features and possibilities.

ASIA, AFRICA, AND LATIN AMERICA

Half the people on earth now live in relatively isolated villages and hamlets strewn across the vast continents and neighboring islands of Asia, Africa, and Latin America. They comprise not only the largest, but also the most rapidly growing, segment of the world's population.

Among these rural peoples are enormous differences in history, language, and culture. But they also have much in common, including the basic problems of poverty, ignorance, disease, and civic inertia.

World-Wide Concern

A generation ago, many of the underdeveloped countries were under colonial rule. Their growing demand for freedom was accompanied by a widespread expectation that independence would bring rapid economic and social gains. However, as country after country became free, internal advances did not automatically follow. Indeed, general economic and social progress has been extremely elusive, especially in the rural areas. Many nations have achieved little if any net gain in the living standards of their peasant populations. Some are now convinced that among the problems confronting them, none is more serious--or more urgent--than improving the lot of their peasant people.

Their concern is shared. Since 1945, development in the emerging nations has become, as never before, a world-wide concern. The United Nations, its affiliated agencies, and governments of economically advanced countries have fostered wide, varied programs of economic and technical assistance. Private organizations of many kinds have entered the field. Significantly, some newly developing countries have themselves begun to share with others their experience and, in some cases, their technical personnel.

These diversified activities are rooted not only in humanitarian impulses, but also in a growing recognition of the interdependence of nations desiring to achieve peace and prosperity in a perilous, changing world.

Broadly speaking, the aid programs have the common objective of providing needed support to the emerging nations' own programs of investment and development. After more than twenty years of effort, broad advances have been made in some countries. But in most of the developing world, economic and social progress is painfully slow. The gap in per capita income between the rich nations and the poor nations is not narrowing, but widening. And there are, in the 1960's, more people suffering from hunger than ever before in human history.

Importance of the Rural People

What happens to the rural areas is of great consequence to each developing nation. It is here that the food is grown, that the widest poverty exists, and that most of the people live--seven-tenths of the combined population of Asia, Africa, and Latin America. They constitute each country's largest reservoir of strength--or of weakness.

FOOD AND POPULATION

The primary economic problem in most of the developing nations is how to produce enough food for their rapidly growing populations.

Food Deficiency

Food output per person, in Asia, Africa, and Latin America, dropped sharply during World War II, almost regained prewar levels during the early 1950's, then in the 1960's, disturbingly, began to show a downward trend.

During the last three decades, these regions have changed from food surplus to food deficit areas. Before the Second World War, they were exporting 11 million tons of grain per year to the developed countries. But after the war, the flow was reversed. In the late 1940's an average of 4 million tons of grain per year moved from the developed to the less developed world. In the late 1950's the average rose to 13 million tons, and in the early 1960's the less developed regions were importing an average of 23 million tons of grain per year. In simple terms, this means that a growing proportion of their people are being sustained not by increased production in their own countries, but by food shipments from the economically developed nations, principally the United States.

Land and People

Why is the less developed world losing the capacity to feed itself? There are two main reasons.

The first is shortage of land. Throughout history, until very recently, man has increased his food supply simply by expanding the area which he farmed. That recourse is no longer available to more than two-thirds of the people in the developing nations, because they now reside in "fixed-land" economies--that is, economies in which nearly all cultivable land has been brought into use.

The second reason is population growth. Asia, Africa, and Latin America now have more than 40 million _additional_ mouths to feed _every year_. In many countries, the number of people to be fed is growing more rapidly than the amount of food produced. That is why food output per capita, instead of rising, is declining.

Most authorities are now agreed that two broad developments are essential before this grim trend can be reversed. One is an acceleration of food production. The other is a slowing down in the rate of population growth.

Yield-Per-Hectare Takeoff

For an accelerating growth of food production, most developing countries must now look to rising yields per acre, or per hectare. They must generate a "yield per hectare takeoff"--that is, a sustained, continuing rise in yields per hectare. Up to now, the ability to generate a trend of steadily rising yields per hectare has been confined mainly to the more developed countries of North America and Western Europe, plus Japan, Australia, and, most recently, Taiwan. In North America, yield per hectare has risen 109 per cent since 1940. In the same period, it has climbed only 8 per cent in the less developed world. Generally speaking, the poorer the economy, the more difficult it is to increase agricultural production per hectare.

Against this somber picture, one encouraging fact stands out. Experience to date indicates clearly that once yield-per-hectare takeoffs are realized, yields tend to continue upwards, often at an accelerating rate. As one authority has said:

> Evidence indicates that yield takeoffs are not easily achieved, even in economically advanced countries. Once underway, however, yield takeoffs appear to be irreversible except in time of war or similar disaster. And thus far all have continued indefinitely--the rising yield trends have not leveled off or shown any tendency to level off.....The yield takeoff, as an agricultural phenomenon, appears to have the same definable characteristics whether it be in a semi-arid wheat-producing economy such as Australia, a high-rainfall, rice-producing economy such as Japan, or a highly diversified, grain-producing economy such as the United States.[1]

The big problem is how to generate the yield takeoff. What is needed? The answer is not simple, but the main factors, it is believed, are now generally understood.

Seven Factors

The first factor is the <u>education of farmers</u> to an acceptance of new ideas, practices, and techniques. For this, it is necessary to reach the farmer by approaches that command his confidence; to explain the newer techniques in terms that he can understand and apply; and to stimulate in him a desire to change his traditional practices and adopt scientific methods that will increase his yields.

It has been found in many countries that practical education of the farmers is greatly facilitated when literacy levels are high. One recent study shows that in a 25-year period, grain-producing countries with less than 50 per cent literacy raised their yields only 0.2 per cent per year, while countries with literacy levels between 50 and 80 per cent achieved an average gain per year of 1.1 per cent, and those with better than 80 per cent literacy increased their average yields by 1.4 per cent.

The second important factor is an <u>increase of capital inputs</u> such as fertilizers and pesticides. It is of course advantageous when these and other capital items the farmer needs can be produced economically within the country. This not only saves foreign exchange; it helps to assure more adequate supplies at prices farmers can afford.

A third broad factor consists of <u>services</u> to the agricultural community, such as credit, transportation, and research. To a very limited extent, farmers may be able to provide these services for themselves, but as the country develops, they inevitably have to rely more on the government and other parts of the economy.

For example, by maximizing their own meager savings and channeling them into well-managed credit unions, farmers may be able to meet, in part, their most urgent needs for credit. But through such small savings alone, they cannot pay for fertilizers and other capital inputs in the amounts needed to realize truly significant increases in yields per hectare. Once credit unions are well established, it is essential that they have access to banks or other sources of funds at economical interest rates.

Similarly, by combining their efforts, farmers may build short feeder roads. But the construction of the main road networks required in the rural areas must be financed by government.

Farmers cannot be expected to conduct serious agricultural research themselves, although they may cooperate in carrying out field tests and demonstrations. Both governmental and private agencies must conduct the research needed within the country.

The fourth important factor in generating a

yield-per-hectare takeoff is an <u>incentive</u> to increase production. Such an incentive exists when there is a strong link between a farmer's effort and the reward he receives.

This link is greatly affected by land tenure patterns and tax burdens. If, for example, the farmer is a tenant, and if he knows that any gains from a larger crop will go mainly to the landlord in the form of higher rent (in cash or in kind), he is not easily spurred to increase his exertions. Similarly, if he believes that a greater output will result in heavier taxes, leaving little to him as a net gain, he has little incentive to increase his output. Land tenure and tax reforms designed to assure to the farmer rewards commensurate with his efforts are a governmental responsibility.

The fifth factor in increasing yields is a <u>market orientation of agriculture</u>. This is not so essential when food production can be increased simply by expanding the area under cultivation. But when greater yields per hectare are imperative, farmers must be able to buy yield-raising inputs such as chemical fertilizers and pesticides. To get the necessary money, they must sell more of their produce, and they can do this only as agriculture becomes increasingly market-oriented. In the Philippines, the market orientation of agriculture is now considerably more advanced than in many emerging countries.

The sixth factor, which follows naturally, is <u>favorable prices for farm products</u>. The prices which the farmer receives for his crops must be advantageous in relation to the prices of the inputs he must acquire.

Such a relationship in prices is a proper objective of government policy, but it is not easy to bring about. The poorer the economy, the harder it is likely to be. Less developed economies usually have lower food prices and higher fertilizer costs than developed economies. For example, a pound of rice in Japan buys about three times as much ammonium sulphate as a pound of rice in India, and this is one reason why rice yield per hectare is so much higher in Japan than in India.

Seventh, as the above influences take effect, and there is the beginning of a sustained <u>rise in the</u>

average <u>level of income per person</u>, this itself accelerates a country's progress toward yield-per-hectare takeoff. With gradually increasing incomes, the people of the nation are better able to pay for farm products, and the farmers are more able to pay for fertilizers and other significant inputs.

All seven of these factors are needed to achieve a yield-per-hectare takeoff. That is one side of the picture.

The other is population growth which, if uncontrolled, may cancel out the effects of increased agricultural output. When the rate of population increase is more rapid than the increase of production of food and other necessities, there is not a rise but a decline in a country's living standards.

Population Control

The population problem, as we now know it, is of relatively recent origin. It has taken probably half a million years, or some 20,000 generations, for man to reach his present status. But it was only about a hundred years--or four generations--ago that certain technical advances were made that were to affect profoundly the rate of man's increase on the earth. Louis Pasteur of France developed the germ theory of disease. Joseph Lister of England carried out pioneering studies of infections and antiseptics. Robert Koch of Germany made early findings of specific agents causing diseases, which led in time to the production of immunizing substances. Many others participated in the early stages, and the expansion, of modern scientific medicine.

Subsequent developments have now spread around the world. They include better obstetrical and child care, the use of vaccines and antitoxins, and the discovery of insulin, sulfa drugs, penicillin, and other antibiotics. Increased specialization and the allocation of greater resources to research have made possible an acceleration of progress in the medical sciences. One area of inquiry and application has been that of public health, directed mainly toward the prevention of common diseases.

It is ironic that these beneficent developments have contributed to one of the greatest crises of human history. They have made possible such a reduction in death rates that the world's population, which was only 1.5 billion in 1900, has now more than doubled, and may pass the 6 billion mark before the year 2,000. The human family now faces a problem of enormous dimensions in finding enough food, clothing, and shelter for all the newcomers.

One among many illustrations that might be cited is that of Ceylon, where international public health programs have almost eradicated malaria and notably reduced deaths from other causes. Deaths per thousand of the population dropped from 20 in 1950 to 11 in 1955. Such a drastic decline in the death rate was achieved in Europe only over a period of centuries. With this sharp reduction in deaths, and with no corresponding decline in the birth rate, Ceylon's population increased in ten years from about 7 million to nearly 10 million. By 1980, it may reach 20 million.

Such swift population growth is out of all proportion to present and prospective rates of economic development. In many of the developing countries today, population growth is "eating up" hard-won gains in production; economic progress is thwarted. And the political and social problems of a country become more difficult to deal with when population is increasing at such an uncontrolled rate.

The "population explosion" has been called the world's number one problem today. Certainly it is one of the most serious problems that has ever confronted the human race. However, several recent developments give some ground for hope that it can be brought under control, gradually, through a widespread reduction in birth rates.

First, since about 1960, there has been a rapid increase of public awareness that a substantial lowering of birth rates, accompanied by rising economic productivity, can raise living standards in the more crowded regions of the earth.

Second, there has been a marked lessening of resistance, on cultural or religious grounds, to family planning through birth control, in order to have only children who are truly wanted, born at intervals that will protect the mother's health and make it more possible for each family to provide a healthy upbringing and a good start in life for each child.

Third, the tremendous progress made in reducing disease and infant mortality has largely eliminated the need of having, say, six children in the hope that three will survive to adulthood.

Fourth, recent research has led to the development of birth control methods that are dependable and, even more important, economically within reach of poorer families. It seems probable that continuing research will lead to the development of other methods acceptable to different religious and cultural groups.

Fifth, responsible national leadership in a growing number of countries is actively sponsoring programs of family limitation, through maternity health clinics and other agencies, with accompanying training for doctors, nurses, and other health personnel. The results now beginning to appear in several countries, notably South Korea and Taiwan, indicate that substantial reductions in birth rates may be attained in those countries within the foreseeable future.

Despite these first encouraging signs, however, the effort required to cope with the world's vast population problem has scarcely begun. In many countries, population continues to increase by about 3 per cent per year, while agricultural production and national income decline on a per capita basis.

EDUCATION

Only a decade ago, there was a general tendency for development programs to put much more emphasis on investment and technology than on education and training. But today there is a greater recognition of the extent to which human development is essential to healthy economic, social, and political development.

Human Resources

Fortunately, countries that are poor in material resources and production may be rich, potentially, in human abilities. It is the work of education to discover and develop these abilities. A beginning has been made, but only a beginning. Large and imaginative efforts are now needed to improve the content and quality of education, and to make it available on a vastly wider scale.

Only through such efforts can the emerging nations start tapping the great human resources that constitute their principal asset and hope for the future. Only then can the mass of the people begin to make effective use of applied science, which, as U.N. Secretary-General U Thant stated in 1963:

> ....can be the most powerful force in the world for raising living standards if action can be taken to harness it for that purpose-- if the Governments and peoples of the world can find the means and the will.[2]

Levels of Education--for Life

The challenge is a staggering one. About 700 million adults in the world today cannot read and write. And there is convincing evidence that growth in literacy in a majority of the less developed nations today is not even keeping up with population growth--which means that those nations are losing the battle against illiteracy. Nearly half the children in the developing nations do not go to school at all, and many who go for a short time leave without becoming literate. The rest do not usually get beyond the primary grades. Less than 10 per cent of the children between the ages of 14 and 18 are in secondary school, and only a small percentage of them have the opportunity to go on to a technical school or university.

Under these conditions, the education of teenagers and adults, by means other than formal schooling, assumes special importance. A country's economic and social advancement requires collective effort on all fronts. Development is seriously hampered unless the level of education of the working population enables them to participate not only in improved techniques and practices, but also in common understandings, attitudes, and aspirations. Such participation can be greatly hastened by well-conducted programs of youth and adult education, and these can have a strong impact on productivity. Moreover, the education of adults is the principal medium through which the home environments of children--so important in their development--can be favorably influenced.

Teen-age and adult education does not have to cover all the ground missed through a lack of formal schooling. What is needed, first, is literacy as a tool; then a supplanting of superstitious agricultural beliefs and low-yielding production methods; and, with these changes, the inculcation of broader outlooks, new attainable aspirations, and a greater sense of participation in--and responsibility to--the community.

By concentrating on such limited, essential aims, it is possible to develop enthusiasm in the rural community for adult education geared to the interests of different groups--such as the farmers' interest in better farming and the women's concern for the health and nutrition of their families.

Efforts along these lines do not diminish the urgent need for improving the education of the very young. But while that is being done, those who had little or no early opportunities for education can be brought into the mainstream of national development, and can make their important contribution to that development.

HEALTH

The early beginnings of a scientific attitude toward public health problems have been traced far back in history. In Babylonia, in the fifth century B.C., there was a recognition of the fly as a bearer of disease. More than a thousand years ago, Rhazes, known as the lute player of Baghdad, when ordered by the Caliph to build a hospital, first hung pieces of meat around the city, then built at the location where the meat putrefied least. But scientific medicine and public health have had their great development, as we have noted, in the last century and particularly during the last few decades.

Cure and Prevention

Refined methods of medical treatment have had a very limited effect on the masses of the people in the developing countries because of a shortage of doctors, dentists, and nurses, and of hospitals and clinical facilities. In the more developed nations, there is an average of one doctor for every 900 people. In the less developed regions, the average is one doctor for more than 6,000 people; furthermore, nearly all the doctors are in urban centers. This means that in most rural areas, the chances of obtaining modern medical treatment, however urgently needed, are often remote.

Preventive public health work through sanitation and immunization, however, has had a wide impact. While there is still a great deal to be done, significant strides have been made in reducing malaria, cholera, dysentery, diphtheria, smallpox, typhoid, typhus, yellow fever, and other killing and debilitating diseases.

The effectiveness of preventive measures depends partly on nutrition. People--especially children--who do not have a sufficient or well-balanced diet may be much more susceptible to many illnesses than people who are adequately fed.

Good nourishment, the prevention of diseases, and modern medical care are all basic factors in the robustness of a people, and therefore may affect greatly their rate of economic and social development.

Personnel Needs

The most acute needs in the health field, particularly in the rural areas, are for trained personnel and suitable organizations. It is essential that programs for training and mobilizing personnel should provide not only for doctors, dentists, and nurses, but also for several types of health workers including administrators, sanitarians, midwives, and supplementary personnel recruited from among the rural people.

A well-conceived system is required to make the most efficient use of limited numbers of doctors, dentists, nurses, midwives, sanitarians, and village health workers, and to encourage cooperation among them. Cooperation may be greatly facilitated, as a United Nations study emphasizes, if the principle of effective teamwork is reflected in all health training plans and programs.

CITIZENSHIP

Many developing countries are now engaged in evolving a democratic form of government. A profound process underlies this change in political forms. It is a transition into a society where the people exercise new freedoms, assume new responsibilities, take charge of their own affairs, and elect their own legislators and rulers.

A democratic society calls for citizens with much greater understanding and maturity than is required of those who simply follow the orders of an authoritarian regime. The people must be prepared for responsible citizenship before they can (a) participate constructively in local political activities and exert a strong, stabilizing influence on government at all levels; and (b) provide their developing democratic governments with the popular support they must have for difficult decisions and policies that are in the public interest.

There is a close interplay between the growth of responsible citizenship in the rural areas and the build-up of local self-government. As citizens become more enlightened, they are able to do a better job of selecting and supporting the members of their village councils. Conversely, an effective village council, answerable to the people, can do much to foster a community spirit and a sense of collective responsibility. It can also help to mobilize local manpower, womanpower, and youthpower for self-help programs in agriculture, education, and health. And it can represent the interests of the village people in dealing with higher levels of government.

Only when there is a responsible citizenry, and an expansion of effective local as well as national government, can there be a well-grounded hope that democracy in a nation will survive, and that government policies will reflect the best interests of the people as a whole.

Neglected Aspect of Development

Citizenship training and the promotion of effective government at the local level comprise, together, a crucial part of a nation's total development. Unfortunately, it is frequently the most neglected part--for a number of reasons.

In the schools, there may be a lack of capable instructors and suitable courses to provide the beginnings of citizenship training. In the colleges and universities, social science may still be largely an imported product, not yet adapted to realities within the country, and this may prevent the higher educational institutions from providing the intellectual leadership needed in political education. There may be little tradition, as yet, of responsible citizenship, and very few people's organizations through which ordinary men and women can acquire training and practice in civic activities.

Furthermore, those who are most concerned about improving conditions in the country are likely to be preoccupied with pressing needs in the fields of economic development, education, and health. These fields are the very ones in which foreign aid is most frequently requested. Citizenship training and the strengthening of local self-government fall into a sensitive political and administrative area where, it may be feared, external assistance, especially from another government, could be a step toward interference in the country's internal affairs.

But attention, within the country, to citizenship training and self-government is not easy either. Public and private organizations that might otherwise be concerned are apt to find that their experienced personnel are busy negotiating with numerous foreign aid agencies, as well as planning and conducting large numbers of individual projects. The very fact that government and foreign aid personnel are so engrossed in economic, educational, and health activities may contribute to an almost unconscious presumption that these are the only truly urgent facets of national development. Therefore, it is not wholly surprising that the political foundation work needed among the people, to build a vital democracy, seems to be a largely forgotten area in many developing countries.

Those who realize the importance of this foundation-building often find that local conditions tend to discourage effort in this field. In some nations, the political situation is chaotic following the break-up of previous regimes. In others, the social fabric has been weakened by regional or religious conflicts, by internecine warfare, or by revolution and inflation. Sometimes, governments are insecure due to a lack of experience or of broad popular support, and the political outlook is therefore uncertain. Under such circumstances, enlightened people in the country may feel that, until the general situation improves, it would be difficult to do anything very effective in fundamental citizenship training, or in the development of governmental institutions at the grass roots.

Tackling the Problem

But the problem will not go away. The longer it is ignored, the more serious it becomes. In the evolution of democratic government, as in other spheres, human development is the foundation for other development.

The cultivation of informed, responsible citizens and the fostering of self-government at the local level need to become prime objectives of development, taking their full place alongside economic and health and educational programs. Far from detracting from these other aspects of development, they can greatly stimulate and reinforce them.

Notes to Chapter 1

1. Lester R. Brown, <u>Increasing World Food Output</u>, U.S. Department of Agriculture, Foreign Agricultural Economic Report, No. 25 (Washington, D.C.: U.S. Department of Agriculture, 1965), pp. 27-28. See also Arthur T. Mosher, <u>Getting Agriculture Moving</u> (New York: Frederick A. Praeger, Publishers, 1966).

2. United Nations, <u>Science and Technology for Development</u>, Vol. I: <u>World of Opportunity</u>, A Report on the United Nations Conference on the Application of Science and Technology for the Benefit of the Less Developed Areas (New York: United Nations, 1963).

ORIENTATION

CHAPTER 2

INTERNATIONAL INSTITUTE OF RURAL RECONSTRUCTION AND PHILIPPINE RURAL RECONSTRUCTION MOVEMENT

by

Y.C. James Yen
President
International Institute of Rural Reconstruction

The International Institute of Rural Reconstruction is a direct outgrowth of our movement's forty years of experience in working with the peasant people, first in pre-Communist China[1] and later in the Philippines.

Throughout this period our central concern has been the development of human potentialities in village communities. This has been based on our conviction that the paramount need of the peasant people is not relief, but release--release of their own potential powers for individual growth, economic productivity, and social and political responsibility.

An emphasis on the development of human potentialities would have little effect if it were not embodied in a practical, workable program. Such a program does not come easily. In our case, it has involved many years of intensive study and extensive application. We had much to learn from our failures as well as our successes. But the heartening net result has been the evolution of a dynamic pattern of rural reconstruction. The purpose of the International Institute is to further improve this pattern and, using it, to help establish new rural reconstruction movements as pilot programs in other countries of Asia, Latin America, and Africa.

PHILIPPINE RURAL RECONSTRUCTION MOVEMENT

On learning about our China program in 1952, many of our Asian friends saw it as an answer to the basic needs of their peasant people. They recognized that our program had evolved on the soil of a less developed country and was especially adapted to the fundamental needs and conditions of the less developed peoples. They believed that it could offer their peasant people a basic start--without which modern agriculture and industry could not function effectively.

Friends and supporters of the movement in the United States were equally convinced that our China experience should prove valuable to other less developed countries with predominantly peasant populations.

On behalf of our Board of Directors in the United States, I made an exploratory trip to the leading countries of Asia to find out what government and private agencies were doing to help their peasant people, and whether any country would welcome our cooperation in starting a rural reconstruction program.

Each country I visited had many problems, and the Philippines was no exception. The government at that time was ineffectual, the national economy unstable, and there was unrest throughout the country. The situation was not unlike that prevailing in many countries of Asia, Latin America, and Africa today. What made us finally decide to select the Philippines was the presence of a small but influential group of public-spirited civic leaders who showed a profound concern for the sad plight of their peasant countrymen. They were eager to learn from our experience, in order to avoid the mistakes we had made and benefit by the successes we had achieved. They urged me to stay on to help them. As a result, the Philippine Rural Reconstruction Movement (PRRM) was organized, with a distinguished Board of Trustees under the chairmanship of Dean Conrado Benitez, the beloved educator and elder statesman of the Philippines.

Thus the Philippines became our first pilot country in rural reconstruction.

In cooperating with the PRRM, we had two important objectives. One was to assist our Filipino friends in launching a rural reconstruction program to raise the economic and social standard of their peasant people. The other was to help develop a national pattern of rural reconstruction, which, if successful, could be extended to other developing countries that would seek our assistance.

Mr. Ricardo Labez became the first Executive Director of the PRRM and helped lay the foundation for the young movement during its pioneering years. Mr. Cornelio Balmaceda, former Secretary of Commerce and Industry, served as the movement's first President, and under his leadership the PRRM became firmly established and gained national recognition. Mr. Gregorio Feliciano succeeded Mr. Balmaceda as PRRM President. In the last five years, he has broadened PRRM's base of support, strengthened its field operation, and made it a training center for public and private agencies engaged in rural work.

National Impact

From a handful of volunteer workers in 1952, the PRRM has developed into a potent force in the Philippines, working for the economic and social betterment of the peasant people. As a private movement, the PRRM does not aim at coverage but at excellence. Though it concentrates its studies and demonstrations in the pilot area of Nueva Ecija, a province in Central Luzon, its impact has been nationwide. Some of its wider effects may be cited below.

1. It has served as a catalyst in rural reconstruction and has stimulated the government to action. The late President Ramon Magsaysay of the Philippines was so impressed with the concrete results achieved in PRRM villages that he established a government agency called the Presidential Assistant for Community Development (PACD), for the uplift of the village people. PACD now has over 3,000 workers, covering more than 10,000 villages.

2. It has helped to generate a new sense of social values by bringing about a fundamental reorientation in the thinking and attitudes of an increasing number of civic leaders, scientists, and scholars. Throughout the country there is now a deepened sense of responsibility among the elite towards their less privileged countrymen, and an eagerness to have a meaningful part in the alleviation of their lot.

3. It has created a new vocation for educated youths as rural reconstruction workers. Restless, jobless, such educated youth could be a menace to the

nation; committed and trained, they become a dynamic force in village and national reconstruction.

4. It has been instrumental in bringing about a <u>fundamental political reform</u> at the village level. As a direct result of the studies and demonstrations PRRM made in village self-government, the Philippine Congress passed the Barrio Council Law in 1955, which provided that the village councillors should be elected, instead of appointed as from time immemorial. Thus democracy acquired a new dimension in the Philippines.

5. It has produced a <u>duplicable pattern</u> for healthy economic growth and social change in the rural areas.

In 1960, during the celebration of the fourteenth anniversary of Philippine independence, the President of the Philippines, Carlos Garcia, singled out the PRRM for his Presidential Award of Merit:

> For outstanding contribution to the country's economic and social development during the past eight years... through its significant pioneering work in rural reconstruction and community development....
>
> For having started a "silent but glorious revolution" among the rural people.... and
>
> For its sustaining leadership in rallying private efforts, national and international, to supplement and complement the Government's services in improving rural life in the Philippines....

NATIONAL PATTERN OF RURAL RECONSTRUCTION

The Philippine Movement has demonstrated that the basic philosophy, approaches, and techniques evolved in China were applicable, with adaptations, to another developing country with an utterly different historical and cultural background.

Thus a dynamic pattern of rural reconstruction came into being, bringing a new sense of self-respect to the people it touched, and demonstrating what the people of a country could do for themselves.

What are, one may ask, the salient features of this national pattern of rural reconstruction?

An Indigenous Movement

For a program of economic and social reconstruction to be effective and lasting in any country, its nationals must embrace it as their own. Although we had a part in bringing the PRRM into being and have continued to give it technical and financial assistance, the PRRM has been led and run by Filipinos themselves from the very outset. From the President to the village-level worker, the staff of the PRRM is 100 per cent Filipino. Outsiders can help, but insiders must do the job.

A Private Movement

The PRRM is a private movement. In developed countries such as the United States, many important enterprises are conducted by private organizations. But in Asia, Latin America, and Africa, the administration of sizable projects by private citizens is still rare. This is one important reason why it has been taken for granted that a program like rural development is exclusively a government affair, having little or nothing to do with the civic leaders of the community. But rural reconstruction is a gigantic task. To hasten progress, all resources--public and private--must be mobilized.

Moreover, a private movement has important advantages. For instance, it is free from political entanglements and political pressures. It is free to experiment and to innovate. It is in a better position than a government agency to stimulate the spirit of self-help and self-reliance; it is closer to the people and can more effectively identify itself with the people.

An Integrated Four-Fold Program

The basic problems of the peasant people--poverty, illiteracy, disease, and civic inertia--interlock. A sick peasant is a poor producer. An illiterate peasant makes a poor citizen. The solution of one problem depends on the solution of the others. Hence the PRRM's emphasis upon an integrated approach, as against a piecemeal approach. To put this approach into action, the PRRM conducts an integrated four-fold program of rural reconstruction, including (1) livelihood (agriculture, cooperative organizations, cottage industries), (2) education, (3) health, and (4) self-government, in order to make a concerted attack upon the four basic problems of the peasant people.

A Joint Leadership

The PRRM is led by a "coalition" of three key groups of the community.

The first group is made up of leading citizens of the country--businessmen, industrialists, bankers, and educators--who see the vital importance of a rural reconstruction program and have come forward to assume responsibility and give their full backing.

The second group consists of technical experts in the major fields of rural reconstruction. There exists a big gap today between modern science and technology, on the one hand, and the peasants, on the other. To bridge this gap, science must be "stepped down." For science, as it is taught in the colleges and universities, is beyond the comprehension of the peasants. For this we need creative, dedicated, and imaginative scientists and scholars, whom we call "science simplifiers." Their task is not to make new scientific discoveries but to apply the vast discoveries already made--in such fields as agricultural science, medical science, and social science--to the level of the peasants; that is, to simplify and translate the relevant scientific and technical knowledge into terms that the peasant can understand and apply. Serving in the PRRM is a fine nucleus of such dedicated and competent specialists, who have resigned from universities and government service to take on this difficult, challenging job.

The third group in the "coalition" is composed of the educated youths trained in the basic sciences, who are willing to live and work with the village people and to bring them the simplified scientific knowledge and down-to-earth skills that they need. They are what we call "science missionaries," young men and women with a sense of mission. About 150 young college graduates are working and living in PRRM-assisted villages, serving as a bridge between modern science and the peasant people.

Separately, what each group can accomplish is limited. But together, they form a "reconstruction coalition" that serves as a dynamic force within the nation working at the foundations for the economic and social betterment of their peasant countrymen.

Mobilization of the Peasant People

The PRRM worker does not deal with a few isolated individuals here and there in the villages. Instead, he aims to mobilize and train the three key segments of the village population--the men, women, and youth between the age of 15 and 45. The sad fact is that most of these men and women and youth have already passed school age and never had a chance for education. They are, in a sense, "educational outcasts." Yet, they are of immense importance to village development, because (a) they represent the great majority of the country's working population and (b) they are in the most productive period of their lives. It is, therefore, on this strategic group that the PRRM focuses its major attention.

In the PRRM-assisted villages, the men are organized into rural reconstruction men's associations, in which they learn about such subjects as plant production, animal production, fertilizers, insecticides, and cooperative organizations for credit, consumers, and marketing. The women are organized into rural reconstruction women's associations, in which they learn together about child care, hygiene, nutrition, family planning, health clinics, and vocational arts. And the youths of the village are organized into rural reconstruction youth associations, in which they are trained to serve as auxiliary health workers, auxiliary literacy teachers, and to undertake such projects as village plant nurseries, home-lot gardening, and cottage industries.

Thus the men, women, and youth of the village are mobilized and trained, each group to play the part it best can. As the village reconstruction progresses, one sees not only the emergence of a new village, but of new villagers, with new skills, new habits, a new outlook, and a new spirit. The village is important, but the villager is more important. Rural reconstruction is only the means, and human reconstruction the end.

A Rice-Roots Operation

Since our goal is to work with the peasant people, we must go where they are. Hence our worker does not merely visit the village; he lives in the village and works with the village people.

The motto of the PRRM states succinctly the principles underlying this rice-roots operation:

> Go to the people.
> Live among them.
> Learn from them.
> Serve them.
> Plan with them.
> Start with what they know.
> Build on what they have.

Each project to be undertaken must be simple so the people can understand it. It must be practical, meeting their felt needs, so they will want it. And it must be economical of time and cost so they can afford it. If a project is simple, practical, and economical, it will be duplicable--an important word in our lexicon!

Spirit of Dedication

Village work is tough work. It entails plenty of sweat and tears, setbacks and frustrations. Technical know-how is important, but technical know-how alone is never enough. Unless a worker is imbued with a crusading spirit, he may have the starting power, but he will not have the staying power.

INTERNATIONAL INSTITUTE OF RURAL RECONSTRUCTION

Heartened by the results to date, and challenged by the desperate needs of the peasant peoples around the world, we decided that the most effective way to help launch rural reconstruction movements similar to the PRRM in other countries was to establish an International Institute of Rural Reconstruction (IIRR).

The major functions of the International Institue are:

1. <u>International extension</u>. The Institute's primary task is to promote and help organize private,

indigenous rural reconstruction movements broadly patterned on the PRRM in countries that invite our cooperation.

2. <u>Leadership training</u>. The Institute conducts (a) "intensive training" for carefully chosen teams of specialists and educated youths from the cooperating national rural reconstruction movements, and (b) "extensive training," by special request, for workers connected with other agencies, public and private, concerned with rural development.

3. <u>Operational research</u>. Rural reconstruction in the less developed countries is a vast and urgent challenge. The fact that it has been so long neglected makes an effective approach all the more imperative now. This requires not only a deep study of what the problems are, but also practical demonstrations of what can be done about them, and how, with and by the rural peoples directly concerned.

It is for this reason that operational research is one of the most important functions of the Institute. It includes continuing, intensive field study and research into ways and means whereby (a) scientific and technical advances can be made available to the rural peoples most effectively in terms that they can comprehend and apply; (b) the villagers can best be helped to organize and run their own cooperative endeavors; and (c) different types of activity can best be coordinated so that they will reinforce each other in an integrated program affecting the total life of the individual and of the community. Operational research also includes the study of special problems that are characteristic of less developed rural societies, such as cooperative organization, land reform, family planning, relationships between agriculture and industry, and legislation affecting rural areas.

4. <u>Consultation and reflection</u>. The arts and techniques of rural reconstruction are not cut-and-dried. Well-conceived and creative experimentation followed by penetrating observation, analysis, and evaluation are needed. The Institute endeavors to provide opportunities for informal discussions, and for full interchange of ideas and experiences. Such cross-fertilization of ideas can be a constant source of fresh insights and better approaches.

5. *Conferences and publications*. Tentative plans have been made for periodic conferences at the Institute of rural reconstruction officers, specialists, and workers from cooperating and other interested countries, in which civic leaders and scholars will be invited to participate. These conferences will provide scope for lectures and reports on outstanding developments and progress in fields of vital interest, and for the dissemination of the findings of significant research.

Location of the International Institute

Although the International Institute is incorporated in the United States, it is based in the Philippines because of its strong historical ties and close working partnership with the PRRM. The training and research of the International Institute are conducted in cooperation with the PRRM, whose field operations in 200 villages serve as the Institute's social laboratory and training field.

More specifically, the principal reasons that the Philippines was chosen as the location for the IIRR are:

1. That there is in existence in the Philipines a strong, ongoing rural reconstruction program which can provide an adequate training field.

2. That there is now in the Philippines, as a result of more than ten years of grooming, a competent corps of experienced specialists who form the nucleus of the Institute's senior instructors--men who have been "through the mill" of rigorous field adaptation, discipline, and experience.

3. That there are in the Philippine Movement over 150 carefully selected college graduates who have not only mastered the techniques needed to become effective rural reconstruction workers, but also exemplify the dedication that is essential to the conduct of a vital, indigenous rural reconstruction movement. They serve as active, friendly "counterparts" to the youths brought in from other countries for training.

4. That the basic economic and social problems of the peasant people in the Philippines are similar to those in other developing countries. This ensures

a high degree of relevance in the practical aspects of the training program.

5. That the Philippines is relatively secure and stable politically, an important factor in considering a long-range program affecting many countries.

Criteria in Selecting a Cooperating Country

In selecting a country to be assisted in developing a national rural reconstruction movement, we are guided by the following criteria:

1. The presence in the country of a group of public-spirited and influential citizens, willing and able to take the lead in sponsoring a private, indigenous rural reconstruction movement.

2. The availability in the country of specialists in the major fields of rural reconstruction, willing to devote themselves to the cause of rural reconstruction, to play the role of "science simplifier," and to undergo intensive training in the application of their scientific knowledge to the needs and conditions of the peasant people.

3. The availability in the country of educated youths, young men and women willing to dedicate themselves to the service of their peasant countrymen, and to undergo rigorous training as rural reconstruction workers, live in the village to perform the function of "science missionary," and carry the major responsibility of inspiring, organizing, and training the villagers.

4. The willingness of the government (and of the Church, especially in Latin America) to welcome a private, indigenous rural reconstruction movement in the country.

New Pilot Countries in Latin America:
Guatemala and Colombia

In 1964 the International Institute launched its program of international extension. At the request of friends in Latin America to help them initiate private rural reconstruction movements patterned on the PRRM, we made exploratory visits to several leading Latin American countries. After careful consideration and full consultations with leaders in the countries we visited, we decided on Guatemala, representing Central America, and Colombia, representing South America, as the pilot countries in Latin America.

The Guatemalan Rural Reconstruction Movement and the Colombian Rural Reconstruction Movement, both privately supported and indigenously led, were inaugurated in 1964. Each movement is headed by a board of directors composed of leading citizens in education, law, medicine, business, banking, and industry.

Leadership Training at the International Institute

Two national rural reconstruction teams, from Guatemala and from Colombia, were carefully selected, in close collaboration with the International Institute, by their respective boards of directors, and were sent to the Philippines in January, 1965, for four months of intensive training. Each team was composed of an executive director, five senior specialists, and ten younger associates, who had three or more years of field experience with the peasant people.

Our central purpose in the training of these teams was to help prepare the key leadership needed to initiate effectively the field programs of the Guatemalan and Colombian Movements. The associates were given basic training in the interrelated fields of rural reconstruction--agricultural improvement, cooperative organizations, village industries, fundamental education, public health, and local self-government--so that upon their return, they could serve as effective multipurpose rural reconstruction workers, and later as instructors and supervisors of such workers in their own countries.

In the reorientation of the specialists, the purpose of the International Institute was not only to supplement their technical knowledge in areas where it might be needed. It was also to increase their awareness of the interdependence of the four major aspects of the rural reconstruction program, and of the importance of facets of rural reconstruction work outside their fields of specialization. It was, moreover, to give them the benefit of the movement's experience in translating the sciences into terms that the peasants can understand and apply. In addition, they were given counsel on planning and carrying out various types of rural projects in their respective fields, and on the coordination of their activities with those of other specialists and the multipurpose village workers.

Field observation and participation constituted an essential part of the training. Classroom instruction was directly related to actual field practice. Seminars were followed by visits to the field. The training culminated in each trainee's living in a village for a continuous period, working side by side with the movement's veteran rural reconstruction workers, in order to gain an intimate, day-to-day knowledge of village life and village problems.

A major part of the source material on which this Manual for Field Workers is based was used during their training, as reference and background information.

The Guatemalan and Colombian teams have since returned to their countries and started their programs in this field. While progress is necessarily gradual during the initial period, both movements have made a promising start.

In order to help the two movements build a firm foundation during their crucial years, the International Institute is cooperating closely with them, providing technical guidance and some financial assistance.

CENTERS OF EXCELLENCE IN RURAL RECONSTRUCTION

We have now been invited by leading citizens of South Korea and Thailand to assist them in organizing similar rural reconstruction movements in their countries. As in Guatemala and Colombia, we are collaborating with their boards of directors to recruit teams of specialists and associates to be sent to the International Institute for leadership training in 1967.

It is our aim to continue to assist responsible, public-spirited civic leaders, as we have done in the Philippines and are now doing in Guatemala and Colombia, to develop dynamic rural reconstruction movements in key countries of Asia, Latin America, and

Africa. They are to serve as "centers of excellence" in rural reconstruction--to demonstrate, on the one hand, what the people of a country can do for themselves, and on the other, to provide examples to their neighboring countries.

Note to Chapter 2

1. For an account of the program of the Mass Education and Rural Reconstruction Movement in China, see Pearl S. Buck, <u>Tell the People</u> (New York: International Mass Education Movement, 1959).

CHAPTER 3   PRRM ORGANIZATION, PLANNING, AND ADMINISTRATION

by

Gregorio M. Feliciano
President
Philippine Rural Reconstruction Movement

In the preceding chapter, Dr. Yen has presented a broad picture of the Philippine Rural Reconstruction Movement. He has discussed its pattern of leadership, organization, and operations, as well as its underlying philosophy and spirit. And he has described the way in which PRRM is now cooperating with IIRR in the latter's effort to help establish, in other developing countries, pilot programs, broadly patterned upon the PRRM, that will become "centers of excellence in rural reconstruction." While we are honored to be participating in this great task, we are also acutely conscious of limitations and imperfections, and of the necessity that PRRM's own search for excellence should be never-ending.

Nowhere is this continuing search more essential than in the areas of organization, planning, and administration. Any lowering of vision or energy in these areas would soon affect the entire movement.

ORGANIZATION

An effective organization does not just happen, especially in such a complex sphere of activity as rural reconstruction. It must have a clear sense of direction, and specific goals. It must be a product of experience, reflecting many insights and lessons cumulatively gained through trial and error. It must be soundly constructed and ably led. It must find, or help to create, suitable village institutions through which to work. It must be supported by good planning--at the center and in each barrio. It must strive constantly to strengthen both its staff and its program, to give to each participant a sense of belonging--with ample opportunity and incentive to make the best contribution of which he is capable.

To achieve positive results, moreover, an organization that is grappling with the tough and often lonely tasks of rural reconstruction must cultivate, internally, a strong and loyal spirit of teamwork; and it must foster, externally, harmonious, cooperative relations with other agencies. As a practical matter, it must also find the money needed to support its personnel and its operations.

This chapter discusses some of the ways in which PRRM strives to fulfill these diverse requirements of an effective organization. The discussion is fairly detailed, since it is our view that field workers should know thoroughly the organization in which they work, and the ways in which it strives to give them the backing they need. Let us begin by mentioning the main elements in the structure of the movement.

Board of Trustees, Council of Governors, and Committees

The governing body of PRRM, responsible for top appointments and for broad direction and management, is its Board of Trustees. This board is composed of eminent citizens of the country who share a deep concern for the rural people, and are willing to spend time and effort on their behalf.

In addition to administering the affairs of the movement, the trustees give significant help to PRRM in developing good relations with other organizations --public and private--and in raising the operating funds required each year. In these activities, the board is assisted by a Council of Governors and three special committees.

The Council of Governors, which has forty members, assists the board in obtaining support for PRRM and acts as an advisory body, without impairing the politically non-partisan character of the movement or its independent status as a private enterprise. The council is composed of some of the most distinguished government officials of the country and a few former members of the Board of Trustees. On the Council of Governors are the present and the past Vice-President of the Philippines, the Senate President, and the

PRRM ORGANIZATION, PLANNING, AND ADMINISTRATION 35

Speaker of the House. The President of the Philippines serves as Honorary President of PRRM.

There is a strong Finance Committee, composed of younger--but equally prominent--members. There is an active Health Committee, comprised of leaders in the medical profession and executives of drug companies, which assists PRRM health projects both financially and technically. And there is a Public Relations Committee, which enlists valuable backing for the entire PRRM program.

Staff

As the chief administrative officer, the President of PRRM is supported by a Senior Staff composed of specialists who serve as heads of technical departments, and field directors who are responsible for the organization and supervision of field operations.

The principal technical departments are those of plant production, animal production, education, health, self-government, cooperatives, vocational arts, and rural industries. Working in the field for each department are technical associates and technical assistants. Every technical department participates in the training of new rural reconstruction workers (RRWs), and each has its program in the barrios, planned and carried out in collaboration with the field directors and field staff. Each is also active in the planning and conduct of joint programs such as the Model Farm Family program and the Model Village program, which are discussed in later chapters.

Working with the field directors are team captains and, under their immediate supervision, RRWs who are assigned, individually, to live and work in the PRRM-aided barrios. Each team captain, equipped with a light motorcycle, supervises from eight to ten RRWs.

Distinctive Role of the RRW

One of the notable features of the PRRM organization is the distinctive role of the RRW. It would not be possible for PRRM (any more than for the government) to assign a whole group of technical assistants or extension workers--in, say, agriculture, education, health, self-government, and cooperatives --to every village receiving assistance. There are not enough technical personnel available, and, if there were, such large corps of specialized personnel would be too costly. Yet there is a real need to have in each aided barrio of 150 to 300 families a well-educated, well-trained, full-time worker, who becomes thoroughly acquainted with the people, gains their friendship and trust, and helps them to mobilize their own efforts in self-help programs. That is the role of the RRW. His day-to-day relations with the barrio men, women, and youth are of the greatest value in getting them actively involved in projects, in encouraging them to continue until the projects take firm root, and in nurturing among them the qualities of leadership, self-confidence, and self-reliance.

The RRW is, in effect, an extension worker for <u>all</u> the technical departments. As a multipurpose worker trained in the rudiments of each of the specialties, he is of incalculable help to the experts, technical associates, and technical assistants. He joins them in planning their activities in his barrio, gets them acquainted with the right people for their purposes, organizes meetings, assists in teaching, and does much of the follow-through work on individual projects. Much depends on his ability, his industriousness, and his skill in human relations. The RRW is an extremely busy person who is expected to be exceptionally intelligent, versatile, responsible, and dedicated. If he is not effective, other members of the staff are handicapped accordingly.

Barrio Institutions

As stated earlier, the PRRM staff endeavors to work with, rather than for, the barrio people. The way in which the people of the village organize to carry on their self-help programs is, therefore, fully as important as the organization of the PRRM staff.

Since, in most barrios, there has been very little experience in organizing community activities for economic and social development, one of PRRM's primary activities has been experimenting with different types of organization, and working with the people to develop those that best suit their own inclinations and the aims of the integrated development program.

PRRM ORGANIZATION, PLANNING, AND ADMINISTRATION

The principal organizations that have emerged to date are the barrio council; the three people's associations generally known as the Rural Reconstruction Men's Association (RRMA), the Rural Reconstruction Women's Association (RRWA), and the Rural Reconstruction Youth Association (RRYA); and organizations that are concerned with specialized activities, such as credit unions, farmers' classes and seminars, plant nursery committees, literacy classes, reading circles, mothers' classes, sewing classes, classes for auxiliary health workers, folk music and dancing groups, drama groups, sports and other recreational groups, and citizenship training classes. There are also important inter-barrio organizations such as the barrio leaders' training courses. All these local institutions are discussed in detail in succeeding chapters.

PLANNING

Within the PRRM organization, planning takes place mainly at two levels--at the center, and within the individual villages receiving assistance.

Central Planning

As intimated earlier, the focal point of central planning in PRRM is the Senior Staff, which meets weekly under the chairmanship of the President. Each meeting is attended, as a rule, by two RRWs, selected on a rotating basis, so that the viewpoint of staff members who spend their full time with the barrio people may be well represented in the consideration of all matters affecting the program.

Usually, a half-day is devoted to the weekly Senior Staff meeting. Reports are given on the progress of current projects. Operational and procedural problems are brought up for discussion. New ideas are explored. Assignments are made. Decisions are reached.

A fresh plan or proposal may be presented by any member for thorough review and discussion before action is taken to put it into effect, or modify it, or reject it. A new approach may be considered during successive staff meetings, and may undergo extensive revision before it takes final form. By then, disagreements have usually been ironed out, and the proposition has become a joint product, ready to be launched with the understanding and backing of the entire Senior Staff.

Once decisions are reached, they are conveyed to the rest of the PRRM organization. Actions which require explanation or discussion are usually conveyed by Senior Staff members to weekly departmental, district, or team meetings. Matters of special importance may be taken up during one of the semi-annual conferences of the entire PRRM staff.

However, technical associates and assistants, district directors, team captains, and RRWs are not only on the receiving end for instructions. They also have a vital part in central planning. They are urged to develop, and to present at their meetings, their own ideas for improvements or new departures. After careful consideration at a team, district, or departmental meeting, these ideas may then be transmitted to the Senior Staff for further consideration. Sometimes valuable new ideas are conveyed quite informally to visiting specialists or field directors by workers in the field, and are then introduced at Senior Staff meetings for consideration.

Another opportunity for younger members to participate in the central planning process comes during the semi-annual conferences of the entire PRRM staff. During the conference, suggestions for strengthening and improving all aspects of operations are encouraged.

One technique employed during the conference has been the presentation at panels of case studies based on field experience. Insights derived from these case studies have become increasingly important in refining plans and operations.

Central planning in PRRM is, then, a joint process in which RRWs and technical assistants, as well as the higher echelons, participate. While the main responsibility falls on the Senior Staff, the entire program is enriched by contributions from all parts of the organization.

Programming at the Village Level

Planning at the village level, jointly conducted by the RRW and the village leaders, constitutes one of PRRM's most interesting and distinctive activities. Technically, it is still in an early stage of evolution. But as a system it seems to be working, and to be capable of steady improvement and refinement.

As now conducted, this programming is essentially a process of target-setting, in relation to goals that have been established by PRRM for a "model village." (See Chapter 22.) The goals are quite detailed for all parts of the four-fold program.

The targets for a specific village are drawn up initially by the RRW, on the basis of his knowledge of the barrio's most urgent needs, the human and material resources that can be made available to meet them, and the interests and desires of the barrio people. The targets are drawn up in December for the following calendar year, after which they are broken down into targets for each successive quarter of the year. The procedure is described in Chapter 4, in the section on "Work Planning and Scheduling."

The next stage is a full discussion of the proposed targets with the village leaders most directly concerned, and then with the RRW's field and technical supervisors. The aim, without formal procedures or commitments, is to reach a consensus on what will constitute reasonable, specific development targets for the barrio during the four quarters of the ensuing year.

Thereafter, at the end of each quarter, the RRW prepares a detailed report in which actual progress is measured against the original targets. If the targets have been exceeded in any part of the program, the corresponding targets for the next quarter may be revised upward. If performance has fallen short, consideration is given to lowering them.

This practical approach to barrio programming has several distinct advantages. It gives to the RRW responsibility for initiative and leadership in the programming work. It brings the barrio leaders into the joint planning process at an early stage, thereby increasing their sense of responsibility and their capacity for future leadership in village planning. It deals with projects related to urgent needs--projects the people can understand. It is not concerned with allocation of money, which the barrio people do not have, but with the effective use of time and energy, which they do have. It gives opportunity for full discussions of projects before they are finally decided upon, and this lends to the proceedings a "folksy" character congenial to the psychology of the barrio people. And because it is geared to the fourfold program, it has a built-in bias in the direction of balanced, integrated development.

Programming at the village level might be characterized by professional economists as micro-programming (or programming on a small scale), as contrasted with macro-programming (or programming, by governments, on a large scale) to which economists are more accustomed. Village projects are small indeed compared with major government enterprises. The money that the barrio has to allocate for different purposes is infinitessimal compared to the financial resources at the command of the government, even in a poor country. At the village level, the tools of analysis are much less sophisticated, and the processes of decision-making are less complicated than at the national level. What is done in government programming may affect all the people in the country, whereas programming for a single village will directly affect, at most, a few hundred families.

But it would be a great mistake to assume that detailed programming at the village level is unimportant. For if a pattern is developed that can be widely applied, the ultimate consequences for the rural population may be great. Moreover, village programming may lead to some results that are, at present, unattainable through national programming, such as an effective mobilization of human resources, in the villages, for constructive activity through self-help programs.

ADMINISTRATION

In 1952, when the program was initiated, the rural workers consisted entirely of volunteers. They were enthusiastic, but continuity soon became a problem because they could not afford to donate their services for long periods of time.

In the second stage, the field workers were paid regular salaries, but technical personnel were secured on loan from government agencies. Since PRRM was short of funds, this was financially advantageous, but the arrangement did not make for reliable commitments and scheduling.

In the third stage, PRRM engaged its own technical experts and associates, and gave them, as members of the Senior Staff, the responsibility of coordinating the field work. Under this system, barrios under the supervision of one expert tended to develop good programs in the field of his special competence, but not necessarily in other fields. The four-fold concept was, therefore, affected. Experience showed, moreover, that a new field worker needs more help than the expert can readily provide, and that a competent field worker is ineffective if his personal problems in a village are not resolved first. It was found that giving necessary guidance and assistance in meeting these problems is not a task that should be loaded onto the technical staff; it becomes too great a diversion from the specialized work for which they are best qualified.

In the fourth stage, beginning in 1963, a special Department of Field Operations was created to take charge of field personnel and general operations in the PRRM barrios. A Field Director and a Deputy Field Director were appointed and given direct responsibility for the over-all management and supervision of the field staff. Under this arrangement, due attention is given to the individual problems of the workers as well as to the many-sided field operations. However, the technical aspects of projects in the barrios remain the responsibility of the department heads and their technical associates and assistants. This structural setup, which has worked well, has been subject to continuous streamlining during recent years. Some of the results are recorded in the next chapter.

Strengthening the Staff

A brilliant executive was once asked: "What is the most important principle for an administrator to bear in mind?" He thought a moment, then answered in three words: "Administration is men." PRRM fully shares the view that the most important element in any administration is the quality of its leaders. However, PRRM would have to expand the answer and say: "Administration is men and women." For in numbers, in quality, and in contributions to the program, the women of PRRM are equal to the men.

In PRRM, leadership is not restricted to the upper echelons of the organization. Every member of the professional staff--including every technical assistant and every RRW--is a leader in the barrios. This gives to each one a special significance, and underscores the need for every measure that can be taken to strengthen the staff.

Recruitment

From the beginning, PRRM has sought only high-quality personnel. Each year many more apply for training and work as RRWs than can be accepted, and this provides an opportunity for careful selection. As a prerequisite, a four-year college degree is required of all except midwifery graduates.

Each applicant is requested first to submit, in writing, information on his personal background, education, knowledge of languages and dialects, previous employment, vocational skills, hobbies, and organizational affiliations; and to furnish references as to his character and integrity. He is also asked to submit a health certificate, signed by a physician, which is subject to verification by the PRRM Health Staff.

The second step consists of a written intelligence test, which has been designed not only to check the general I.Q. of the applicant, but also his ability to meet unforeseen situations.

The third step consists of one or more unhurried interviews with members of the Senior Staff, during which the interviewers try to assess: (a) the applicant's genuine interest in rural reconstruction; (b) his willingness to live and work in the barrios; (c) whether his attitude toward the barrio people is one of love and respect, and a desire to understand and work with them; (d) his ability to learn new, practical skills quickly, and to apply them in the barrios; (e) his ability to cooperate with fellow workers, and to participate in group thinking and discussions; (f) his potentialities as a resourceful leader capable of stimulating self-help and a joint search for solutions to problems; (g) his abilities as a speaker; and (h) whether he possesses such personal qualities as common sense, a pleasant disposition, a sense of humor, and contagious enthusiasm.

Those who are still considered likely candidates after taking these tests are invited to take another, known as the "barrio test," in which each candidate lives with a village family for a whole month. This helps in evaluating the candidate's capacity to adjust to barrio conditions, and in discovering whether he really wants to. In short, it enables PRRM officers to ascertain with some assurance whether the applicant is a promising candidate.

Final selections are made each year by a committee which may include Senior Staff members, team captains, and technical associates.

Training

The training period for new personnel who are to work as RRWs or technical assistants lasts six months. Approximately one-third of this period is devoted to formal training through lectures, discussions, and reading, and two-thirds to practical work and observation in the barrios. The training course includes the history and philosophy of the Rural Reconstruction Movement, socio-economic conditions in Filipino barrios, basic principles of integrated rural development as they have evolved to date, and practical knowledge and skills in each part of the four-fold program of livelihood, education, health, and self-government. A modest allowance is given to each trainee to cover board, lodging, and incidentals at the training center and in the barrios.

After the formal training is completed, a month of apprenticeship under the guidance of a senior worker is necessary before graduation.

The graduation ceremony, coming at the end of this rigorous course, does not signify an end of training, but actually a commencement of deeper and more extensive learning. Effective rural reconstruction work demands an ever-widening range of practical knowledge and skills, especially on the part of the multipurpose workers who live--and lead--in the barrios.

After graduation, RRWs can keep adding to their skills and understanding in a number of ways. Every visit of technical personnel gives the RRW in a barrio an opportunity to learn more about the practical applications of technical knowledge and skills, and about enlisting the people's interest and participation in specific projects. PRRM also conducts fairly extensive in-service training--through refresher courses, special courses for the acquisition of new techniques, and the dissemination of information and instructions during weekly team meetings and periodic conferences. These activities are developed in a flexible way, often to meet a particular problem or training need that has become apparent during Senior Staff meetings.

Stimulus and Experience

PRRM's effort to strengthen its staff does not stop with rigorous recruitment and training. There is a third means: to make sure, as far as possible, that each staff member has experiences on the job that will help to bring out his latent capabilities.

Stimulus to personal growth may come to a staff member in many ways. It may stem from the ideals that permeate the Rural Reconstruction Movement, from a growing realization of the urgency of the barrio people's needs, and from a mounting confidence that these needs can be met through united effort. It may come from wise supervision, and others' expectations that one will do a good job; or from the strong sense of camaraderie and mutual support that exists within the PRRM organization; or from examples of extraordinary dedication among other staff members. It may grow out of interest in the work, plus the satisfaction of helping the barrio people and sensing their gratitude and trust. It may come from having a hard job to do, and putting one's best into it. "When the going gets tough, the tough get going."

Among these, none has proved more decisive than the last mentioned. External stimuli and support may contribute a great deal to one's development. But the crucial test of capacity for personal development is how the staff member responds when things are not easy. Recognizing this, PRRM seeks to give each worker responsibilities that are fully commensurate with his capabilities. The RRW or the technical assistant, for example, has an important, complex job to do that calls for his finest talents and efforts. As he strives, under experienced supervision, to meet each tough situation to the best of his ability, there is a steady growth in his skills, resiliency, and competence as a leader.

Standard Administrative Procedures

PRRM's administrative procedures have gone through a considerable evolution. These are described in circulars which are distributed to all personnel; as changes are made, new circulars are issued. The procedures currently in force are too detailed for inclusion in this manual, but a few of their general features may be mentioned.

Appointments   A trainee who completes the requirements for graduation as a rural reconstruction worker is eligible for appointment to a vacant position upon favorable recommendation of the training committee and Field Operations Department. Appointments are approved by the Senior Staff, subject to the concurrence of the Board of Trustees. After an induction procedure, in which provision is made for the maintenance of systematic personnel records, the worker is assigned to a barrio, and introduced there in the manner described in the following chapter.

Remuneration   It is essential to good morale that all members of the organization feel that their remuneration is fairly determined. The range of pay for each category of field and technical personnel is standardized, therefore, on a published scale in which gradations are determined by the responsibility of the work performed. All new appointments and promotions are in accordance with this scale.

Promotions   There are two types of promotions: those made within a grade, and those made by reclassification into another grade. In either case, the promotions are normally made upon the recommendation of immediate supervisors and the determination of the Field Director's office or technical department heads, subject to approval of the Senior Staff and the President.

Transfers and Reassignments   Upon the approval of the Field Operations Department, the Senior Staff, and the President, transfers and reassignments are made to meet the changing requirements of the program, or to bring about better relationships between individuals and their jobs or environments. Some misfits are inevitable, and when other remedial measures fail, well-considered transfers or reassignments are effected.

Separations Personnel may be separated from PRRM service either by voluntary resignation or by discharge. Resignations become effective upon acceptance by appropriate officers, including the President, and are officially completed only after appropriate clearances by the property officer, library, staff members' credit union, finance officer, and supervisory personnel. Employees may be dismissed by the President, in consultation with the supervisory officers concerned; approval by the Senior Staff finalizes the action. Grounds for dismissal are: inefficiency, dishonesty, insubordination, immorality, indifference to work, unreasonable absences, physical unfitness, fomenting discord among the staff, destructive negligence, wastefulness, and violation of PRRM regulations.

Working Hours and Work Week These are defined with due regard to the varying requirements of the work to be done by field, technical, and office personnel.

Leaves of Absence Full-time employees are entitled to the privileges afforded under existing regulations which provide for vacation, sick, maternity, or military leaves, and leave without pay.

Marriage A female RRW who gets married is encouraged to remain in the organization if her husband raises no objection. During her first pregnancy, an RRW is allowed to stay on provided her efficiency is not impaired. During a second pregnancy, the situation is reassessed, since the continuation of full-time service in a barrio by a young mother may affect adversely the best interests of her family. In such cases, voluntary resignation is accepted, with a full understanding that she may apply for a return to PRRM service when her children are grown.

Medical Care Sick leave with pay is allowed, up to fifteen days per year. When medical care is needed, PRRM health personnel should be notified, if possible; otherwise, the nearest doctor should be consulted. When a field worker is ill, a co-worker who is a good friend and of the same sex is automatically excused from his (or her) own post to stay with the sick person as long as he (or she) definitely needs such care; in such cases, the attending worker must keep supervisors notified regarding his (or her) whereabouts. Consultation with PRRM medical personnel is free; staff members may have complete checkups at a standardized minimal cost to them. From time to time, emergency medicines for common ailments are issued to field personnel without cost.

<u>Use of Vehicles</u>   PRRM's limited supply of vehicles makes it necessary to use them with maximum efficiency. First priority is given to use for field visitations and technical assistance. Scheduling is done each Saturday for the following week, and the schedules are posted for the information of all staff members. Use of any vehicle by outsiders, except as passengers on a scheduled ride, is strictly governed by regulations. Detailed regulations are also in force governing payments for gasoline and systematic maintenance of the vehicles.

Strengthening the Program

PRRM's continuous efforts to strengthen the program have not been derived from any rule book. They owe their origin to alert staff members who have developed practical, constructive ideas, and to the spirit of teamwork that prevails within the movement. Many examples are cited in other parts of the manual. It may be useful to mention here a few developments at the center, which followed naturally, one upon another, during an approximate two-year period.

<u>Evaluations</u>

In late 1963, a need was felt to evaluate the program, especially in barrios where PRRM had completed periods of assistance ranging from two to eight years. To what extent was the momentum of the four-fold program being sustained by the village people themselves since the transfer of PRRM personnel to other barrios? To find the answer, a research project was started for 44 barrios which PRRM had left two to five years earlier. The results of this survey, which took two years, were especially helpful in identifying strong and weak points in the current barrio programs.

At about the same time, another method of evaluation was started. All field workers were asked, during a general December conference, to make detailed case studies of successful, unsuccessful, and partially successful approaches that they had made in connection with programs for which they were responsible in the barrios. From this exercise, PRRM gleaned a wealth of information and ideas for improvements in the program.

One fact that stood out, as a result of both types of evaluation, was that gains in livelihood had not been as rapid as hoped for, and that this was due in many cases to insufficiency of capital. This led naturally to an increased emphasis on the promotion of credit unions, with a target set of twenty-five new unions during the following year. (The target was exceeded.)

Balanced Targets and Records

Another fact which became apparent was that PRRM's system of records covering the various parts of the four-fold program in each barrio was neither uniform nor accurate. After discussion of this problem at a Senior Staff meeting, one of the members broached the concept of criteria for "model barrios," and the regular recording of progress in each barrio in relation to these criteria. (The "Model Village" program, which has since become a central feature of the PRRM operation, is described in Chapter 22.)

It was soon apparent that specific targets were highly desirable not only for the barrios, but for every individual member of the PRRM staff, from the President to the RRW. The RRWs' targets would naturally be closely tied to those of the barrios in which they worked.

A parallel system was started under which all PRRM field and technical personnel would set up annual program targets for themselves, against which progress could be measured once every quarter. This exercise had four purposes:

1. To establish a base from which the individual could project his targets for the coming year. This required the recording of fundamental data which would accurately reflect the current situation.

2. To improve and systematize the methods of recording data, in order to ensure an objective measurement of results every three months.

3. To initiate a system of individual and collective evaluation of results, so that everyone would know how he or his team or department was doing.

PRRM ORGANIZATION, PLANNING, AND ADMINISTRATION 49

4. To force all members of the staff to plan ahead, and to maintain a full, steady pace of work.

PRRM has found that this technique induces each staff member to become his own supervisor to some degree, and to maintain a higher level of efficiency. It also contributes greatly to more balanced progress in all parts of the program.

Staff Initiative in the Villages

Many public and private agencies concerned with community development around the world lay great stress on the people's "felt needs," and hesitate to initiate projects of any kind until there is convincing evidence that they are strongly desired by the people. There are, of course, good reasons for this. It is usually quite futile to launch projects in which the people have no real interest, and it would be presumptuous to tell them what they want. The risks in being so pushing may be sensed, especially, and rightly so, by administrators of foreign aid programs. Even the nationals of a country may feel that generally they should follow rather than lead the rural people in the choice of projects to be undertaken.

PRRM experience suggests that better results may be achieved if such reticence is not overemphasized. Of course, every project launched should be of real potential value to the people, and capable of enlisting their wholehearted participation. But it is not necessary, especially in the early stages of a program, to wait for them to take the lead. On the contrary, several considerations weigh in favor of considerable initiative on the part of the staff--working always in close consultation and cooperation with leaders, or potential leaders, in each barrio.

First, rural development is a race against time. In many countries, the expansion of agricultural and other types of production until their rate of growth is higher than that of the population is a life and death matter.

Second, there is usually a limited awareness among the rural people of the practical possibilities from which they can choose, and of their own abilities to learn to do new things. They frequently have little experience in working together.

Third, the farmers' hopes and aspirations have often been blunted by past discouragements, deprivations, and injustices.

Finally, it is PRRM's experience that the rural people welcome leadership from others whom they have come to know and trust, if it is given in a friendly way--with respect, not condescension; if proposed projects are thoroughly explained and discussed; and if they, the people, have the final say as to what they will do about any course of action that is recommended to them.

In short, PRRM has found that skillful leadership, especially in the earlier stages of a village program, helps to overcome local feelings of helplessness and enlists cooperative action that is beneficial to the rural people; and that they welcome such leadership. As the people gain experience, they are able to take more and more initiative themselves.

Full Participation of the Barrio People

Every facet of the program is designed to enlist, at an early stage, the hearty support of the village people themselves, expressed through the various barrio institutions mentioned above. This applies to all parts of the four-fold program, each of which constitutes a system of field activities closely interrelated with the other systems.

Literacy, for example, is not seen as an end in itself, but as a window to further learning, and as part of a rudimentary but fundamental educational system. So it is linked with the preparation and production of an interesting literature--simple, informative, up-to-date--dealing not only with traditional education themes, but also, in a practical way, with the other aspects of the four-fold program: livelihood, health, and self-government. This simple educational system is of basic importance to the realization of PRRM's objectives as a whole.

Similarly, there is a health extension system that includes public education and group activities relating to environmental sanitation, immunization, pure water supply, maternal and child care, family planning, and simple clinical services--some conducted in cooperation with national and local health authorities, and some carried on independently.

The livelihood system involves activities relating to plant and animal production, marketing, credit unions, village industries and vocational arts--all designed (a) to help afford greater economic opportunity to men, women, and youth in each barrio, according to their interests and talents, and (b) to lead to a general rise in income levels--which is so essential to advances in other areas, such as education and health.

In the villages where its aid has been requested, PRRM seeks to help build local self-government into a vital system. At the top, in each village, is the barrio council, which is now elected by the people and has definite functions, established by law. Barrio lieutenants and other members of the barrio councils are invited, from time to time, to participate in the barrio leaders' training courses, where they may acquire a dynamic view of their functions and opportunities as leaders in their communities. Each council has councillors for agriculture, education, and health. They, and other members, are urged to take a leading role in promoting the three people's associations--of men, women, and youth--as well as the cooperative societies and other village institutions; the more familiar they are with the activities of all these groups, the more wisely they are able to use the 10 per cent of the barrio's land taxes over which they have jurisdiction. They are also invited to assist in promoting citizenship training classes. In these and other ways, the barrio government can give status to, and strengthen, all parts of the four-fold program.

Guidelines derived from PRRM's experience in conducting these interrelated field programs are set forth, in some detail, in later chapters of this manual.

Mobilization of Human Resources

It is now widely agreed that the most valuable--and the most neglected--of all resources for economic and social development are human resources. Those of an agrarian economy are not fixed; they are not determined simply by numbers of people. Human resources for economic and social development can be greatly improved by the acquisition of new skills. They can be greatly expanded by the more efficient use of human energies. Their productivity can be multiplied by the appropriate employment of non-human sources of energy. And they can be made more effective by better organization.

As indicated in subsequent chapters, PRRM aims to help increase the skills of the rural populace on a wide front, through farmers' classes, seminars, and demonstrations; through training in the organization and management of cooperative unions; through the cultivation of new skills in local industrial and vocational arts; through a wide dissemination of the tools of reading, writing, and simple arithmetic among those who have passed the school age but are still illiterate; through the training of sanitarians and auxiliary health workers among the people; and in many other ways.

PRRM programming at the village level also lays much stress upon the fuller and more efficient use of human energies. This is an area in which PRRM's lack of financial and material resources, though a handicap, has also been an advantage. These lacks have made it necessary to concentrate on ways and means of (a) stimulating more efficient production, for which the producer will get a better financial return; and (b) promoting many forms of voluntary activity for self-improvement, and for the benefit of the family and community. Through these efforts, as will be seen in later chapters, PRRM has begun to tap a vast reservoir of human resources heretofore largely neglected. And while doing so, PRRM has learned that many incentives besides economic gain can be brought into play--the desire for self-respect, pride of workmanship, the need for participation in group activities, the enjoyment of competition, and the satisfaction of filling a useful role in the community.

The other barrio institutions mentioned earlier have provided PRRM's principal means for the better organization of human resources at the village level. Without them, the best-laid plans would have had little lasting effect.

Developing Good Relations with Other Agencies

Each member of the Board of Trustees, and of its supporting committees and the Council of Governors, has useful contacts in governmental, business, educational, and professional circles, and is therefore in a position to help in promoting cooperation between

PRRM and other national organizations.

Relations with other agencies are also important at the municipal and barrio levels. Year by year, PRRM has found more and more channels of fruitful cooperation with governmental organs, national and local, in the fields of agriculture, education, health, and cooperatives; and with many private agencies working in the same broad fields of interest.

Winning Financial Support

In its early years, PRRM was supported largely by contributions from the International Mass Education Movement, a sponsoring private organization with headquarters in New York. (The IMEM's Board of Directors consisted of distinguished Americans who strongly backed Dr. Yen and the Rural Reconstruction Movement of which he is the founder and leader.)

From the outset, however, it was intended that PRRM should gradually become increasingly self-supporting. As PRRM became better established, the proportion of its operating costs raised within the Philippines, by PRRM, increased greatly. At this writing, it has reached a level of more than half a million pesos a year, in cash and in materials.

In soliciting contributions, PRRM makes use of six main methods: (1) sending out solicitation letters, signed by appropriate members of the Board or by the President; (2) distributing literature and pledge forms during meetings, or by mail; (3) arranging talks by Board or staff members before clubs and other private organizations; (4) setting up special luncheons, usually given by Board members for their friends and associates, at which briefings are given on the work of PRRM; (5) conducting a year-round publicity program which facilitates fund-raising work; and (6) arranging for possible prospective donors to visit PRRM's field headquarters in Nieves, and its operations in the barrios. The last-mentioned has been the most effective of all the methods used.

For various reasons, some supporters prefer to make their contributions in materials rather than in money. It has been found useful to have ready a list of supplies that can be used advantageously in the program, such as construction materials, office equipment, gasoline, certified seeds, fertilizers, drugs and medicines, and books.

From time to time, specific project grants may be obtained from foundations, trade or civic organizations, and, occasionally, government agencies. If PRRM has an urgent project for which support is desired, it aims, first, to locate a group that would have a natural interest in supporting it, and, second, to prepare a presentation and a project analysis in the form preferred. Significant grants have been obtained in this way from the National Science Development Board, the Drug Association of the Philippines, Catholic Relief Services, the Asia Foundation, and CARE.

Another important category of support consists of contributions under PRRM's barrio sponsorship scheme. An individual or organization can "sponsor" PRRM assistance in a barrio by paying a specified amount each year for at least three years. The present amount, subject to change in the future, is ₱3,800, or $1,000, a year. All of the PRRM-aided barrios outside Nueva Ecija province are now "sponsored." Every effort is made to involve the sponsor in the barrio development activities, and to keep him well informed on their progress. Recently, PRRM has been experimenting with similar sponsorship by municipal governments, to determine whether this can be arranged without excessive red tape, and without interfering with PRRM's freedom of action in municipality-sponsored barrios.

PRRM has also been exploring the possibilities of some assistance from the government in ways that would not compromise the movement's independence or make it subject to political influences. Such assistance is occasionally available through land grants which the government allots to civic and charitable institutions, and through shares in the proceeds of the Philippine Charity Sweepstakes, which are managed by the government. In both cases, outright grants are made to private bodies on the merits of their work, with no political or administrative strings attached.

Members of the Board and the staff believe in their program and its goals. They have confidence in the rural people. Their enthusiasm has been contagious. And their friends have not let them down.

PRRM ORGANIZATION, PLANNING, AND ADMINISTRATION

Looking Ahead

As in any dynamic organization, those who work in the PRRM are more concerned about the future than the past.

Self-Criticism

One of the healthiest features of the Philippine Movement, we believe, is its habit of self-criticism. At weekly meetings of the Senior Staff, and of captains with their teams of RRWs, analysis of current operations to detect weaknesses and failures, and to determine their causes, is an unending process. The field directors and specialists are also constantly at work evaluating projects, and thinking about practical means of improving them. And during the semi-annual conferences of the entire PRRM staff, all programs are subject to joint, critical review.

There are, as a result, constant reminders of areas in which individual work, and PRRM operations as a whole, need strengthening. How can the rural reconstruction worker stay "on top" of his many-sided, demanding, and often frustrating work? How can the team captains, the technical associates and assistants, the field directors and the specialists carry out their responsibilities more efficiently, and with greater imagination and resourcefulness? How can the staff, at all levels, work more effectively with the barrio people, ever nurturing _their_ initiative and _their_ capacity to take responsibility? Which programs are most in need of enrichment? Among new projects suggested, which should be launched? How can field operations be improved?

These are but a few of the many questions that arise, again and again, as PRRM continues its search for greater efficiency and better results in the field of rural reconstruction.

Duplicability

PRRM recognizes that an acid test of a rural program's probable significance for the future is the extent of its duplicability. (I am not speaking here of research and experimentation, but of practical field work.) A project or program that cannot, in essence, be reproduced again and again is not likely to have an appreciable impact on the rural development of a district or a nation. PRRM consciously applies the duplicability test, therefore, to individual projects, to rounded village programs, and to its general pattern of organization and operation.

Developing a duplicable project--in the sphere of livelihood, or education, or health, or self-government--is quite different from developing one that is a "showcase." Almost any project can be made glamorous if enough money and time are put into it. But if the investment is high, and if a comparable outlay is needed each time the project is repeated, it has very restricted applicability and is of limited value to the people. Glamour is a poor criterion in a development program. PRRM has found that if other criteria are used--that if each project is scrutinized, before launching, to make certain that it is simple, practical, and economical--then there is a high degree of probability that it will also be duplicable.

PRRM has also sought a larger duplicability. It has discovered that if flexibility is maintained, the use of the movement's still-evolving pattern of village reconstruction makes for well-balanced development, and greatly facilitates the transfer to new communities of lessons from previous experience. One key feature of the pattern now in use is the integrated four-fold program. Another is the central emphasis on human development, with resultant efforts to find and train leaders among the people for all parts of the program. A third is the promotion of types of barrio institutions that have now been well tested. A fourth is the key role, in each village program, of the well-trained rural reconstruction worker. A fifth is the guidance given to all the village programs by seasoned technical and field operational personnel.

The Philippine Rural Reconstruction Movement as a whole has provided a still broader test of duplicability. It was started as a pilot program designed primarily to help the village people in the Philippines. But it also had a complementary aim, which was to determine whether the principal features of the earlier dynamic rural reconstruction movement in pre-Communist China could be reproduced, with discriminating adaptations, in the very different historical and cultural setting of the Philippines. The degree of success of this test, to date, has convinced the leadership of IIRR and PRRM that the main features of the present PRRM pattern can be duplicated, with suitable adaptations, in other developing countries. This confidence has been strengthened by the reactions to PRRM of discerning visitors from many newly developing countries. The outstanding features of the PRRM pattern that are believed to be applicable in other countries are the indigenous character of the movement, its effective mobilization of pioneering leadership in the private sector, its integrated four-fold program, the many ways in which the staff members help the barrio people to mobilize their own efforts, and a strong spirit of dedication throughout the organization. It is PRRM's experience that when these features are all developed simultaneously within a single movement, they can powerfully reinforce one another.

OPERATIONS

CHAPTER **4** FIELD OPERATIONS

The strength of PRRM lies in effective teamwork at all levels. A crucial part of this teamwork consists of close, daily cooperation between the field operations staff and the technical departments. Even more crucial is the cooperation developed between PRRM personnel and the barrio people.

The field operations staff is composed mainly of "generalists" or "multipurpose" personnel. Under the Field Director and the Deputy Field Director are one senior field assistant, three district field assistants, a group of team captains, and a corps of about 150 rural reconstruction workers (RRWs) individually stationed in the barrios for full-time work in intimate contact with the rural people.

The technical departments are also deeply and directly involved in work in the barrios through their activities in technical training, and the conduct and supervision of specialized programs and operational research. These departments consist of experts, technical associates, and technical assistants in the fields of plant and animal production, cooperatives, rural industries and vocational arts, education, health, and village self-government.

This chapter deals with the field operations staff members and their jobs, the personal qualities they need, their relations with technical personnel, and some of the practical guidelines that experience has shown to be important--for the RRWs and for the field operations administration personnel as they pursue their common objective of helping the people to help themselves.

FIELD WORKERS AND THEIR JOBS

Job descriptions covering the duties and responsibilities of field operations personnel may be summarized briefly.

The Rural Reconstruction Worker (RRW)

After completing his training, the RRW is assigned to the barrio in which he will reside. There he establishes friendly relationships with the leaders and people of the barrio, and seeks to stimulate their interest in developing self-help projects within the scope of the integrated four-fold program for livelihood, education, health, and self-government.

With the advice of his team captain, the RRW draws up a plan for his own work, and prepares a systematic scheduling of his activities. Periodically, in the light of experience gained, he revises his work plans and sets up a new schedule for the ensuing period.

Soon after his arrival in the barrio, he conducts a socio-economic survey in order to ascertain the actual condition and needs of the people in the village, and to facilitate an adaptation of the program to these realities.

He assists the people in establishing their own institutions, through which they can cooperate effectively in the pursuit of common goals. Key institutions usually organized in each barrio at an early stage are a Rural Reconstruction Men's Association (RRMA), a Rural Reconstruction Women's Association (RRWA), and a Rural Reconstruction Youth Association (RRYA).

Working through these and other channels, the RRW stimulates and helps the people to initiate projects that will increase their self-reliance and contribute to the well-being of their families and community.

The RRW gives full cooperation and support to PRRM technical personnel in the development of specialized projects. In concert with them, with his team captain, and with the barrio people, he exerts every effort to advance the PRRM program as projected.

He keeps monthly records of actual accomplishments in the barrio, in each part of the four-fold program. Once every quarter, he prepares a report on the progress made toward the level of a "model village." (See Chapter 22.) In addition, before the

FIELD OPERATIONS 63

beginning of each year, he prepares, with the advice of the technical departments, a projection of goals for the entire year. At three-month intervals, thereafter, this projection is compared with the quarterly achievement reports to give a picture of how the year's work is progressing.

The RRW observes carefully the people's response to all parts of the program, and the extent and enthusiasm of their participation. From time to time, he makes full reports to his team captain on the attitudes of the leaders and the people in his barrio, and on the principal problems he has encountered in the course of his work.

He takes an active part in team meetings called by his captain. At these meetings, he learns from the experiences of other RRWs in the area, and gives them the benefit of lessons gained from his own successes and failures.

The Team Captain

The team captain is the leader of the eight to ten RRWs assigned to his team. He advises and assists them and supervises their work.

He resides, usually on a monthly rotating basis, in the PRRM-aided barrios under his supervision.

He serves as a liaison between the barrio people and the municipal government or other agencies that can render useful services to the barrios.

In all the barrios to which he is assigned, he coordinates his work with that of the PRRM technical experts, on matters pertaining to the programs with which they are directly concerned.

He presents regularly, to the Field Operations Office, reports on the regularity, work performance, and special problems of the RRWs on his team, and on any extraordinary needs of the RRWs or of the barrios in which they are working.

He does all in his power to improve the work in his barrios, and makes requests to all PRRM personnel concerned for assistance or cooperation as needed.

The District Field Assistant

The district field assistant is directly responsible to the Field Director for work in the district to which he is assigned.

Within that district, he provides field leadership among the technical assistants, as well as the team captains and RRWs, generally supervising and coordinating their work.

He recommends promotions, transfers, suspensions, or dismissals of personnel under his supervision.

He cooperates closely with all PRRM technical personnel, to enable them to provide adequate guidance and services in his district.

He facilitates the implementation of the fourfold program in the barrios in his district by directing all his efforts to meeting their problems. He reports fully on his activities to the Field Operations Office.

He serves as liaison between the PRRM and government agencies or civic organizations in his district, in order to promote cordial, cooperative relationships.

He renders special reports that may be requested by the President, by the Field Operations Office, or by the technical experts through the Field Director.

The Senior Field Assistant

The senior field assistant assists in the performance of the duties of the Deputy Field Director and the Field Director. He acts in their absence. All decisions, however, must be reported to them. Consultation and referral to the President and the Senior Staff are required whenever major problems and policies are involved.

He performs such other duties as may be assigned by the President, the Field Director, the Deputy Field Director, and the Senior Staff.

FIELD OPERATIONS   65

The Deputy Field Director

The Deputy Field Director assists in the performance of the duties of the Field Director. He acts in his absence, and reports all decisions to him. On major problems of policy, he consults the President and the Senior Staff before acting, or refers matters to them for decision.

He performs such other tasks as may be assigned to him by the President, the Field Director, and the Senior Staff.

The Field Director

The Field Director is directly responsible to the President for all field operations personnel and activities. He assists the President in the administration of the field program, and directs the field operations personnel in the performance of their duties. He devises ways and means of improving the skill and efficiency of the field workers.

He conducts special studies in cooperation with the technical experts, with a view to achiving continuous improvement in field operations.

He inspects the field activities, prepares progress reports, and attends to the problems and needs of the field personnel.

He presides over the weekly meetings of the field operations staff. He coordinates programming and field operations with the activities of the technical experts and technical staff, in order to facilitate implementation of the four-fold program in all areas where PRRM is operating. On major problems or questions of policy, he consults the President and the Senior Staff, or refers matters to them for decision.

He renders reports on all phases of the field work, and performs other tasks that may be assigned to him, from time to time, by the President or the Board of Trustees.

Personal Qualities Needed

The PRRM devotes a great deal of attention to the caliber of the personnel chosen for its ranks.

This is so because an unusual combination of qualities is needed for effective participation in the difficult but exciting task of rural reconstruction. It is especially important that those who are engaged in field work shall possess these qualities. The fundamental attributes which, without sacrifice of individuality, are considered most important are these:

1. <u>Devotion to the welfare of the people and the interest of the nation</u>. For every member of PRRM, rural reconstruction work is a career of his own choice, involving a pledge of dedicated service to the people and the nation. One who has made this choice can never forget that he has entered upon a creative career to which the standards of a routine "job" do not apply. There should be no wasted motions, no bureaucratic red tape, no self-pampering spirit, and no "mañana" system. The field worker shares, in a large measure, the life of the rural people he serves, with little thought about his own comforts and conveniences, and little concern about praise. His mind and spirit are absorbed in his work with the people. He finds his greatest satisfaction in a job well done, and in the responsiveness of the people to his efforts to help them help themselves.

2. <u>Eagerness to learn</u>. A person embodying such a spirit is eager to acquire all kinds of knowledge relating to rural reconstruction, and to absorb the philosophy and meaning of the PRRM. He welcomes the challenge to study at firsthand the problems of the barrio people, and to think hard about how to tackle them. He seizes each opportunity to gain new insights and skills from experienced persons who have command of techniques he will need to employ. With the humility of a true scientific attitude, he listens gladly to different viewpoints, including those contrary to his own, and is not reluctant to set aside his own opinions when he finds them unsound. He is able and willing to recognize his mistakes, and to improve his methods and attitudes.

3. <u>Ability to work as a team member</u>. The field worker soon discovers the tremendous value of group thinking and group action. He finds that the results achieved by distilling and applying the wisdom of the group can be far superior to those attained by individual efforts alone. He recognizes an obligation of loyalty to plans and procedures that have been

FIELD OPERATIONS   67

collectively worked out. In response to the warm
backing he receives from his associates, he gives his
own warm support to the group and all its members.

    4. Respect for, and faith in, the people. The
rural reconstruction field worker strives always to
understand the people's problems and to work with
them toward solutions. But he never assumes an attitude of pity or condescension toward the people he
serves. On the contrary, he is keenly alert to their
potentialities. He therefore does all he can to help
them stand on their own feet, and encourages them to
cope with their problems through their own efforts.
He has faith that the people, with such help and encouragement, have the power to become self-reliant
citizens and to accomplish great things together.

    5. Desire to become a citizen of the barrio.
These attitudes engender in the rural worker a desire
to live in the barrio because he realizes that only in
this way can he truly identify himself with the
people and work effectively with them. His aim is
not to form a separate entity, but to become an integral part of the community. He does not wish to be
an outsider or an intruder, but a true friend and
neighbor who deserves the people's trust. He never
makes a promise that he cannot keep. He is careful
not to offer a "solution" to a problem he does not
quite understand. He tries not to urge actions for
which the people are not mentally prepared. And he
gives foremost attention to problems which the people
themselves consider most urgent.

    6. Skill in enlisting help when needed. A
practical experience may be cited. In Marikina,
Rizal, the most urgent need of a group of farmers was
for irrigation. On 236 hectares of land, no second
crop was planted due to lack of water. One day,
three workers conferred with one of the farmers.
Though illiterate, he was experienced and intelligent. He told them about a mountain spring nearby
from which water could be routed through a short canal to some of the barrio fields. The next day, a
PRRM agriculturist and a senior field worker went to
see the place. Two days later, a PRRM Board member
was asked to help secure the services of engineers
from the Irrigation Service Unit of the government's
Bureau of Public Works. Five days after that, an en-
gineering team arrived to make an initial survey. A
week later, another engineer from the same unit de-

termined the proposed alignment for the new canal and its length: 268 meters. On the same day, 16 farmers, 8 young people from the barrio, 1 landowner, and 5 PRRM workers started the digging. In another seven days, the canal was completed, and water flowed through it to 25 hectares of rice land, assuring 13 families a second crop each year. This small project is one of thousands that illustrate the importance of cooperative relations with civic leaders and government agencies. Skill in developing and utilizing such relationships for the benefit of the people is often essential to the success of a program.

7. <u>Statesmanlike leadership</u>. Rural reconstruction within a barrio affects every aspect of the people's lives. At the municipal and provincial levels, it affects the life of the nation and impinges on major questions of policy and legislation. Those responsible for planning and promoting rural reconstruction programs at all levels must therefore develop as fully as they can the qualities of statesmanlike leadership.

In the context of the PRRM program, a statesmanlike leader is one who looks at questions from the broad viewpoint of the best interests of all the people. He is objective, and receptive to new ideas. Brushing aside gossip and propaganda, he seeks the unvarnished truth. He is well trained in seeking useful knowledge and putting it to work for the people's benefit. Through reading and thinking, he keeps growing mentally and spiritually. He is not swept away by his emotions, but remains calm and flexible. He knows that deep-seated habits and outlooks will not change overnight.

Not only does he carry out his own work well; he also inspires others to work, think, change, grow, and develop. Because he is warm-hearted, others feel at ease with him. He knows how to get people organized in a democratic way, so that each member of a group has something definite, suitable, and useful to do, without losing the freedom to exercise personal initiative. He personifies the spirit, philosophy, purposes, and skills of the Rural Reconstruction Movement.

In the barrio, just as in the nation, such statesmanlike leadership is urgently needed--and warmly welcomed.

FIELD OPERATIONS 69

Relations Between Operational and Technical Personnel

One problem that is almost universal in both public and privately sponsored development programs around the world is that of relationships between "technical" and "operational" personnel. Competition and friction between these groups is often a source of inefficiency and frustration.

With the freedom that a private agency enjoys to experiment and innovate, PRRM has attempted, by trial and error, to develop close, effective teamwork between the two types of personnel. A pattern of relationships has emerged gradually, which is now in force within the PRRM.

Coordination at the top level is achieved mainly through weekly meetings of the Senior Staff, held under the chairmanship of the President. Participants include all heads of the technical departments, and the Director and Deputy Director of Field Operations. At these meetings, plans, problems, questions of policy, and matters of general concern are fully discussed before decisions are reached. This provides an opportunity to anticipate, or identify at an early stage, any problems of relationship between different parts of the staff, and to deal with them before difficulties develop. On the basis of decisions made at the Senior Staff meetings, the scheduling of both technical and field operations can be conducted in a coordinated manner. As a result, visits of technical personnel to all PRRM-aided barrios are scheduled far in advance on a systematic, rotating, sector-by-sector basis. This greatly facilitates orderly planning and preparation by the RRWs and other members of the Field Operations Staff.

At the village level, the person primarily responsible for effective coordination is the multi-purpose rural reconstruction worker (RRW), working within the framework of over-all plans, directives, and schedules issued by the Office of Field Operations. On the one hand, the RRW works under the direct supervision of his team captain and the senior personnel of the field operations staff. On the other, he gives all-out cooperation and support to each departmental project, in any technical field, within his barrio. The RRW has received instruction, guidance, and help in innumerable ways from the technical departments during his initial training, and this continues during his years of residence and work in the barrios. In return, the RRW gives crucial assistance to technical personnel by stimulating interest among the people in specific projects, or by bringing together appropriate groups to meet with the technicians when they come to the barrio. He also does extensive follow-up work on each of the programs in the barrio.

At the intermediate level, between the top staff and the RRWs, a somewhat different pattern of cooperation is followed. Technical associates and assistants work in close collaboration with the district field assistants and team captains, as well as with the RRWs. They and the heads of the technical departments frequently attend the meetings of team captains with the RRWs under their supervision, in order to discuss field projects in which all the groups are involved. Technical and field operational personnel also come together in many other conferences or seminars for purposes of training, program planning, or evaluation. Through these frequent associations, camaraderie is maintained and all are made to feel that they are members of a single team with united purposes and goals.

GUIDELINES FOR RURAL RECONSTRUCTION WORKERS (RRWS)

The RRW normally lives as a paying boarder with one of the families in the barrio. The selection of the home is important for his health, security, peace of mind, and working efficiency. For this reason, field officers frequently assist the RRW in choosing the home where he will board, and in making arrangements with the landlord.

Criteria in Selecting a Home for the RRW

In selecting the RRW's first home in the barrio, these criteria are borne in mind, to be applied flexibly according to conditions in the barrio:

1. That the landlord be an influential and respected member of the community, and that his family be of sound health and good moral character.

2. That the economic and social status of the family be at least equal to the average in the bar-

rio.

3. That the landlord and his wife be willing to accept the RRW as a "member of the family," to watch over his (or her) health and security, and to accept reasonable payment, on a businesslike basis, for food and lodging.

4. That the house have no more than six occupants. If the RRW is a woman, the occupants should not include a marriageable bachelor.

5. That there be a separate room for the RRW, assuring privacy, and at least minimal health facilities such as toilet, bathroom, and safe drinking water.

6. That the house be conveniently located within the community, with a surrounding area large enough for a homelot vegetable and flower garden.

Steps in Selecting the RRW's Barrio Home

On the basis of past experience, these steps are recommended to the RRW:

1. Seek the advice and active help of your team captain and senior personnel of the field operations staff.

2. Discuss with the barrio captain and other leading citizens of the community the criteria cited above, and solicit their counsel and help in finding a suitable home.

3. Visit the houses suggested, and select the one that is most suitable according to the criteria.

4. Reach a definite understanding with the landlady concerning living arrangements and the amount to be paid for board and room.

Transferring from One Boarding House to Another

It has been PRRM's experience that it is preferable for the RRW not to change his boarding house if it is fairly suitable and relationships are reasonably satisfactory. This reduces the need for new adjustments. However, if problems arise, a change of residence may be desirable. When a transfer is contemplated, and a suitable home is known to be available, these steps are recommended:

1. Make the landlady understand that it is a common practice of the PRRM to have RRWs change their residences in the barrio from time to time, and explain the reasons for this.

2. In making arrangements for the transfer, obtain the help of your team captain or a PRRM senior staff member.

3. It is generally advisable to have a letter with the PRRM letterhead sent from the Field Operations Office to the homeowner, giving reasons for the transfer. It is also advisable to send copies of the letter to the barrio captain and other key persons in the barrio. This ensures that the transfer does not reflect on the original homeowner, or make him lose face in the barrio.

Recurring Problems

Selecting a suitable home in the barrio and making a successful adjustment to that home is not always easy. It has given rise to several problems in the past, which must be fully and frankly recognized. Here follows a brief summary of the principal problems that have come up, and the responses to those problems that, to date, have proven most effective.

1) No adequate housing available in the barrio. It has often been found that none of the housing in the barrio meets all the criteria mentioned above, especially that of adequate health facilities and that of a room that can be turned over to the RRW for his (or her) private use.

   Response: Try to convince the family that is chosen to provide the necessary facilities if it possibly can, and offer to pay part of the cost. If the first family selected cannot do this, make a similar effort with the second choice.

2) Family apprehension. The family may fear that it cannot measure up to the expectations of PRRM and the RRW, or meet his needs, because of lack of time, or lack of help in the home.

   Response: Explain that the RRW is a boarder, and

should not be regarded as a guest or helper, but as a member of the family; that he can adjust, having been trained to live and work in the barrios; and that he will share the expense by regular payment of a reasonable amount.

3) Unwillingness to accept pay. The landlady in the selected home may not wish to charge for the RRW's board or keep, on the grounds that he is there to serve the community and no payment should be necessary.

Response: If she cannot be persuaded to accept a reasonable remuneration, arrange to pay indirectly by making gifts to the family on special occasions, and by sharing unobtrusively in the costs of family marketing. The RRW should keep a record of what he spends in these ways, and make sure that the total amount is at least equal to what is usually paid as a boarding fee.

As a general rule, it is best to work out, after a few months, a flat rate for regular payment. Explain that it is not a lodging fee but a nominal amount to help defray some of the household expenses. Acceptance by the landlady is easier if other people of the barrio are not present when the payment is made.

Getting Along in the New Home

To establish and maintain harmonious relations with all members of the new household may not be easy. Some RRWs have been fortunate in finding an especially congenial home at the outset, and in developing rather quickly a good, friendly relationship with the family. But many RRWs have learned, through sad and even bitter experience, that achieving such a relationship may require exceptional sensitivity, adaptability, and effort. They have found, too, that the experiences of other RRWs may be of great use to them.

Methods and Procedures

Among many methods and procedures tried out by the RRWs to date, these have been among the more successful:

1. Try to understand every member of the family

as an individual. Learn each one's likes and dislikes, and find ways to adjust to them. Try to establish a good rapport with everyone in the family.

    2. Learn the language, customs, and traditions of the family.

    3. Never be superior or "offish" in manner. Show respect to the elderly members of the household by greeting and answering them in the established manner. Toward the head of the home and his wife, act as though you were a son or daughter, or a younger brother or sister. Be friendly with the younger members of the household, but do not court or fall in love with a son or daughter in the home.

    4. Avoid unnecessary arguments, and refrain from thoughtless remarks or actions that might lead to criticism or resentment.

    5. From time to time, bring home gifts such as bread, candies, fish, fruit, or something special for the children. In these ways, and by birthday and Christmas remembrances, show real concern for your adopted family.

    6. If it is feasible, invite members of the family to your own home, and welcome them there as friends.

    7. Pay regularly and promptly for your room and board. If the landlady has declined to accept such payment, do not forget to compensate her with an equivalent value in goods.

Recurring Problems

    The problems that have come up most frequently after the RRW has begun to live with his adopted family, and the best ways to deal with them, according to experience gained so far, are as follows:

1) A jealous landlady or landlord. Sometimes the RRW is misunderstood because of his, or her, friendliness with the wife or husband in the home, and jealousy develops.

    Response: If such jealousy is apparent, discuss the matter openly and quietly with the landlady and landlord, treating them with dignity and

FIELD OPERATIONS

respect. Or seek the assistance of your team captain, or other field operations personnel. Or request guidance from experienced visiting technical personnel.

2) "Borrowing" of personal belongings. Sometimes a member of the household may use the RRW's personal belongings without asking. This may simply be a matter of free and easy sharing, as practiced within the family.

Response: It is better not to let this become a habit. Discuss the matter tactfully with the person concerned. Lock up personal belongings before leaving the house.

3) Requests for monetary loans. The landlady may ask to borrow money.

Response: Try to forestall this by never mentioning any extra money you may have. Do not tell how much you receive in salary; though modest, it might seem like a great deal to the landlady. If you anticipate the possibility of a request for a loan, you might mention to the landlady, casually, obligations that you must meet each month, such as helping to pay for the education of brothers and sisters.

4) Demands on the RRW's time. At times, an RRW may be requested to baby-sit or to spend hours helping with family chores.

Response: Keep busy with official duties and personal chores. Show willingness to be helpful in the home, as a "member of the family," when time permits. But make it clear, in a tactful way, that your responsibility is to the barrio, and that it requires most of your time. Show appreciation that the arrangements you have both agreed on for your room and board enable you to give your energies to the barrio as a whole.

5) Indifference of the landlady, for unknown reasons. A landlady who was at first cordial and helpful may, for no apparent reason, begin to show an indifferent attitude.

Response: If this happens, it is possible that you have offended her unintentionally, or that your presence in the home is felt to be a burden. Try to understand what may have happened to cause this change in her attitude, and avoid actions that may affect her disagreeably, remembering her special dislikes and sensitivities. And go out of your way to help her in any way you can.

6) Courtship of women RRWs. A son or close relative of the landlady may develop a romantic interest in an RRW.

Response: Avoid indecorous behavior that could be misunderstood by the young man. If he persists, explain in a nice way that it is contrary to PRRM policy to permit such romances among its personnel in the field. Be tactful and forceful with your "no." If he does not accept it, transfer to another boarding house, or request transfer to another barrio.

7) Separate food and eating place for the RRW. This may be provided because the landlady thinks the RRW will be more comfortable with such an arrangement, or for some other reason.

Response: Try to find out the reason for this special treatment. Then speak to the family respectfully, considering the feelings they may have about it. Explain your spirit of oneness with them, and your desire not to be treated as a special guest.

8) An unbalanced diet. The range of foods provided may be very restricted, with the result that all members of the household, including the RRW, have an unbalanced diet.

Response: Explain to the landlady, in a friendly and tactful way, the meaning and importance of a balanced diet. Invite her to attend cooking and nutrition classes being organized in the barrio. When possible, invite her and other members of the family to your own home or that of a close relative and serve a good, balanced meal.

9) Unsanitary conditions. The home and its surroundings may be unsanitary and hazardous to health.

Response: Conduct a seminar in the barrio on

FIELD OPERATIONS   77

health and environmental sanitation, and invite
the landlady or the landlord to attend. Then assist them in planning and developing sanitary
conditions in and around their home. If there is
illness in the home, try to help arrange for medical attention, and explain the importance of
keeping separate cups, spoons, and plates for the
sick person. If the illness is contagious, protect yourself and your work by transferring to
another boarding house.

10) Lack of privacy for the RRW. Members of the family may invade the RRW's privacy to such an extent that he has little time to think and plan,
or to attend to personal matters.

Response: Try, in a friendly way, to explain the
necessity of having some time alone to draw up
plans and reports and to get personal things
done. If necessary, request the assistance of
your field captain or of visiting technical personnel in tactfully explaining this to members of
the family.

11) Gambling or excessive drinking in the home. The
RRW may discover, after taking up residence, that
the house is a gambling den, or that the landlord
drinks excessively and presses the RRW and others
to drink with him.

Response: After developing a friendly relationship with the landlord, try to persuade him that
his money would bring much greater benefit to him
and his family if he used it for productive investment and education for his children rather
than gambling. Respectfully decline to drink,
for reasons of health. If you can do so without
giving offense, describe the frequently harmful
effects of alcohol. If either gambling or drinking in the home becomes a handicap to you in your
work, or in your relations with other families in
the barrio, transfer to another boarding house.

12) Religious differences. The RRW may find that his
adopted family has different religious affiliations or practices from his own.

Response: Keep busy outside of the home when the
family is having religious observances. However,
if you find it would be welcomed, attend once in

a while as a sign of friendliness and courtesy.

Conducting a Socio-Economic Survey

One of the first responsibilities of an RRW starting in a new barrio is to conduct a socio-economic survey. The main purpose of the survey is to obtain an objective picture of social and economic conditions in the barrio, and of the human and material resources which could be mobilized in each sector of the PRRM program. A secondary purpose is to give the RRW an opportunity to get acquainted with all the families in the barrio.

In conducting the survey, the RRW uses questionnaire forms provided by the PRRM. The results he obtains are of great help in determining the principal needs of the barrio, and the types of projects that should be undertaken during the first months.

Procedures

1. Explain to members of the barrio council the reasons for the survey, and the use that will be made of the information gained. Ask for their moral support.

2. If the barrio is divided, as is customary, into sections or "puroks," proceed with the survey in one purok at a time. Try to obtain the active backing of the purok leader at the outset. Arrange, if possible, with his help, a meeting of all residents of the purok, in order to explain to them the purpose and importance of the survey, and to invite their cooperation in answering the questions. This will reduce greatly the need for detailed explanations in each household as the survey is conducted.

3. Invite one of the purok officials to accompany you as you make the rounds of individual households. If he is willing, this will speed up your introductions and make you appear less an outsider.

4. In each household, try to establish at the beginning a rapport with someone capable of answering the questions fully and reliably, preferably the father or mother, otherwise an elder son or daughter.

5. While conducting the survey, be friendly, tactful, and patient. Do not use terms that the peo-

FIELD OPERATIONS

ple will not understand. If it seems desirable, reword the questions in very simple language. At the end of each interview, be sure to express appreciation of the cooperation given.

6. Some family-scale projects can be started in the homes as you conduct the survey. This may give practical meaning to the questions you are asking, and help to stimulate the interest of family members.

Recurring Problems

1) **Lack of official assistance.** The barrio or purok official requested may not be able to accompany the RRW during the survey.

   Response: Try to secure the help of another village leader, or a son or daughter of one of the barrio or purok officials.

2) **Erroneous information.** One member of the family may give information with which others disagree, or which seems to be inaccurate.

   Response: Make a note of the answer and try later to verify or correct the information, with a neighbor's help.

3) **Unwillingness to be interviewed.** Occasionally, due to timidity or some other reason, the members of a household will be unwilling to answer questions.

   Response: Try to obtain the requisite information from a friendly neighbor.

4) **Fear of the tax collector.** The RRW may encounter reluctance in answering questions due to suspicion that he is an agent of the Bureau of Internal Revenue.

   Response: Ask for the help of your team captain or of visiting technical personnel in explaining to the people that the information obtained is not for tax purposes but for reference in planning development programs.

Getting to Know More People in the Barrio

The vitality of the PRRM program in each barrio

depends on the involvement and active participation of all segments of the population. One of the most important tasks of the RRW, therefore, is to get well acquainted with the people in his barrio--men, women, and youth. It is not enough merely to recognize people and know their names. One needs to learn about their individual interests and abilities in order to gain some appreciation of their potential contributions. Getting to know the people of the barrio, in this deeper sense, requires persistent effort.

Approaches

These are the approaches that RRW have found most helpful, to date, in extending their acquaintanceship in the barrios:

1. During your conduct of the economic survey, take time to make friends with one or more members of each household and learn something about their interests.

2. Get well acquainted with local school teachers. Take an interest in their work and problems. Tell them about the PRRM program and aims. If they seem to be good observers, learn from them all you can about the people they know.

3. Find any of your own kin, or people from your own province who may live in the barrio, and get information from them about other people in the community.

4. Visit the homes of key people in the barrio. Establish a friendly relationship with them. Make sure they understand the true purpose of PRRM in making your services available. And seek their counsel on how best to get further acquainted with others.

5. Accept invitations that may lead to good opportunities to extend your friendships in a natural and easy way. With the same purpose, attend gatherings for baptisms, weddings, birthdays, and funerals.

6. To forestall possible difficulties, establish a friendly relationship with those regarded as "tough guys," or "filosofos," or "canto" boys (children out of school).

7. Each day, try to make two or more home or

FIELD OPERATIONS

farm visits, to extend and deepen your friendships.

Recurring Problems

The RRWs have encountered many problems in their efforts to become well acquainted with all segments of the barrio people. These are some of the more common problems, and effective ways of dealing with them:

1) Language barrier. In spite of the fact that it is PRRM practice to assign RRWs to barrios in which dialects known to them are spoken, some of the people in a barrio may speak a dialect with which the RRW is not familiar.

   Response: At first, try to obtain the help of someone who can interpret for you. Then, by alert listening and practice, learn gradually to understand and use the dialect.

2) Reticence on the part of the RRW. While still new in the community, the RRW may be shyly reluctant to approach, without assistance, the more influential people in the barrio.

   Response: Such reserve must be overcome if the RRW is to be a truly effective worker. However, it may be helpful at the beginning to seek the assistance of third parties known to be friendly with leading citizens. But do not become dependent on such "crutches." Develop greater self-confidence through practice.

3) Pressures to refrain. Sometimes the RRW's parents or sweethearts urge them to refrain from joining the barrio people's parties or excursions. This may be due to apprehension growing out of ignorance of the people and their ways.

   Response: Explain how necessary it is to become acquainted with the people of the barrio, and that attending such functions is one of the best ways to achieve this goal. Ask your parents or sweetheart to come to the barrio so they can meet some of your new friends.

4) Shyness of some villagers. Many RRWs have found that some of the people in their barrios, especially those who are illiterate or unusually

poor, tend to be shy and rather unapproachable.

Response: Approach them in a casual and friendly manner. Tell some jokes. Visit their homes. In almost all cases, you will find that they gradually respond to such warmth and friendliness.

5) Possessive attitudes. Occasionally, some persons with possessive attitudes toward their families will oppose their becoming friendly with the RRW.

Response: Make it a point to befriend the one who has these possessive feelings. If his good will is won, he will not be so likely to stand in the way of others. If this is not successful, seek the assistance of a third party well known to all concerned.

6) Unfortunate previous experience. The RRW may find among some of the people considerable reserve and caution due to unfortunate experiences with a previous village worker, perhaps from another agency.

Response: Work hard with the people that you have come to know. Show sincerity of purpose. And, as you have opportunity to do so, tell about your own aims and hopes in coming to the barrio.

7) Political, religious, and family barriers. The RRW may discover that political or religious differences are an initial handicap, or that his close association with some families may impede his relations with others.

Response: Explain that PRRM is non-political and non-sectarian. Do not get involved in political controversies. Develop harmonious relations with people of different religious sects. It may be helpful to attend services of different sects. Try, through casual talks and personal calls, to expand your friendships among many families in all parts of the barrio. Do not gossip. Avoid identification with any clique. If it is needed, to "break the ice" with some families, seek the help of a mutual friend.

Conducting Home Visits

Among all the approaches employed by PRRM field

workers in promoting and carrying forward the program, home visiting is the most common and the most popular. Through home visits, workers and the barrio people come to know and understand each other, and the RRWs gain new insights into the people's attitudes, needs, and problems. Much of the discussion necessary to persuade individuals to take an active part in new programs takes place in the easy atmosphere of a home visit. And the real value of projects already under way is often best tested by frank questions and answers during such visits.

Thus a home visit, by an RRW, is more than a social call. It is a principal means of forwarding the four-fold program, and the RRW learns to use it with increasing skill.

Techniques

1. Plan the home visit before you go. Think about its purpose, the emphasis you wish to make, and approximately how long you will stay. Dress suitably. And remember to observe the social customs of the community.

2. Time each visit well, normally at an hour when all or most of the occupants will be at home. When you are calling for the first time, request the help of the head of the home or his wife in introducing you to the others, so that you will be properly identified.

3. Establish an easy rapport by asking friendly questions about the family, the sitio or barrio, the composition and size of crops, and other subjects of mutual interest. Be courteous and respectful throughout. If, during some of the home visits, you can learn about any previous experiences the people may have had with development programs, this may give you valuable clues regarding what the people like, and also pitfalls that should be avoided.

4. Discuss problems in which interest is shown. If you are informed about tested means of dealing with the problems, mention them, but not in an officious or "knowing" way. One approach is to cite the successful experience of farmers in another barrio, or the recommendations of a good technical institution, or some other source of your information. Do not pose as an authority. A patronizing attitude

creates a negative impression. And remember that harm may be done by encouraging the people to expect too much with too little effort.

5. Learn all you can from the farmer and his family. It will enrich your knowledge and make your own contributions more effective.

6. If you can get a barrio leader to join you during an important home visit, do so. This is especially valuable if you wish to discuss a particular project, and can bring a leader connected with that project.

7. On your second or third visit, observe changes in the home or the homelot. Comment on the good practices you observe, and express your interest and enthusiasm over accomplishments of the family or any of its members. If you have previously discussed particular projects with the family, review progress on those projects.

8. Try to distribute your visits equitably among the homes and sections of the barrio. In some cases, this can best be done by scheduling your visits systematically, on a rotating basis. This helps to ensure an even distribution of your home visits, and forestalls any suspicion of favoritism.

Recurring Problems

These are some of the problems most frequently encountered in making home visits, and the responses that have proven most effective.

1) Loose dogs on the premises. Many RRWs have been attacked by dogs, and even bitten in some cases, when entering yards.

    Response: A systematic program of anti-rabies vaccination of dogs in the barrio helps to protect all of the people against rabies. It is wise to carry a stick to ward away and drive off aggressive dogs when entering a strange yard. Call out to the homeowner in approaching the fence entrance, as recognition from the master makes the dog go away.

2) Jealousy of husband. This problem is rather common when repeated home visits are made by male

FIELD OPERATIONS

RRWs when the husband is away.

Response: Visits should be well distributed among the barrio homes. It is always good to have company on visits so that a third person is present. If one does make the visit alone, it is best to conduct the conversation in the yard and not in the house, to avoid gossip.

Building Village Institutions

After the RRW gets well acquainted in a barrio, his central task, for a time, may be to help the people form their own organizations, through which they can learn to work together on many projects in the fields of livelihood, education, health, and local self-government.

Three main organizations are established in each PRRM-aided barrio: a Rural Reconstruction Men's Association (RRMA), a Rural Reconstruction Women's Association (RRWA), and a Rural Reconstruction Youth Association (RRYA). The RRW has a crucial role in promoting each of these organizations.

He also takes an active part in the formation and encouragement of other organizations in the barrio, such as farmers' classes and seminars; cooperative unions; literacy classes and reading circles; dramatic, musical or folk dancing clubs; classes for mothers, and for the training of auxiliary health workers; and training seminars for barrio leaders.

The techniques and problems involved in all these activities are discussed in subsequent chapters.

Work Planning and Scheduling

The work of the RRW is so many-sided that he cannot possibly stay "on top of his job" or keep his activities in proper balance without realistic planning and scheduling.

Building on past experience, PRRM has developed a basic planning and scheduling system for carrying forward the four-fold program in the barrios. Efforts are constantly being made to improve the system.

PRRM also seeks to assist the RRWs in understanding and fulfilling their planning and scheduling responsibilities. This is done through training, and through the provision of guidelines, encouragement, and supervision. All this is highly important, for the successful functioning of the PRRM depends to a large extent on the RRWs' effectiveness in both planning and execution.

The system which PRRM has devised and now uses involves yearly, quarterly, monthly, and weekly planning. Before the beginning of each year, all RRWs take time to project, in a preliminary way, their program goals and targets for the coming year, broken down on a quarterly basis. The goals envisage a balanced development of the four-fold program in every PRRM-assisted barrio. As explained in detail in Chapter 22, quantitative targets are established in relation to specific phases of plant production, animal production, cooperatives, supplemental income projects, public works, health, education, self-government, and general objectives such as cleanliness of streets and side canals, maintenance and efficient utilization of the barrio plaza, and a steady increase in the number of "model farm families." (See Chapter 21.)

The establishment of reasonable annual and quarterly targets for a barrio requires hard thinking and hard work. Drawing on his knowledge of the people in the barrio--their developing interests and desires, their present and potential leadership and capabilities--the RRW must first make his own preliminary estimates of suitable targets for the next four quarters. He must then discuss and thresh them out, in turn, with the barrio leaders, the PRRM technical departments concerned, and the field operations supervisors.

Once the goals are agreed on, all efforts are directed toward their realization. This means the efforts of the people, of the RRW, and of PRRM technical and field supervisory personnel.

At the end of each quarter, an assessment is made, using the "model village" criteria described in Chapter 22. In this way, progress is measured not only against the detailed barrio targets established for the quarter, but also against the criteria set up for the achievement of a model village rating.

General planning may have little effect if it is not followed up by realistic scheduling and action. Before the beginning of every month, each RRW prepares a detailed schedule in which he specifies the activities in which he expects to be engaged during each day of the month. A duplicate copy is prepared for the team captain. In making this schedule, the RRW needs to keep in mind not only the on-going activities of the various barrio organizations, and the progress and needs of each project, but also the desirability of making continuous advances in all sectors of the program as projected in the quarterly targets. When the RRWs' schedules have all been completed, they are reviewed by the PRRM field operations supervisors, then consolidated and distributed to all supervisory and technical personnel. This is of great value in enabling supervisors and technicians to plan their own schedules in such a way as to keep in close touch with specific barrio activities with which they are concerned.

At the beginning of each week, the RRW refers to his monthly plan and prepares an hourly schedule of his activities for the next seven days. He must, of course, allow enough time for each activity, and there must be room for necessary adjustments as the week progresses. This scheduling of each day's activities has proven to be of immense help to the RRW. It gives structure to his daily life and work. It gives him assurance that, while his attention is focused on one activity, other responsibilities will not be neglected. And it enables him to keep clearly in mind the relationship between his day-to-day work and the monthly and quarterly goals toward which he and the barrio people are striving.

Promoting Projects

Specific projects fitting into the various segments of the four-fold program are taken up in later chapters. But there are certain basic considerations to be borne in mind in connection with all projects.

The needs of a barrio are so great that there may be a natural desire to launch several projects at once. But the human and material resources available for carrying out new projects are limited, and each project undertaken requires careful planning and execution. It is therefore essential that choices be made and priorities established. Every project must be considered carefully before it is actually launched. Questions pertaining to each project under consideration, which the RRW should be prepared to study and discuss with the PRRM technical personnel concerned, and with interested people in the barrio, may be listed for convenient reference.

1. Is there a problem or situation in the barrio which justifies the launching of such a project? Among all the projects under consideration, is it one of the more urgent?

2. Does the project meet the basic PRRM criteria for all projects: Is it simple? Is it economical? Is it practical? Is it duplicable?

3. If the project is undertaken, what will be its effects? How many people and how large an area will benefit? How much do the people want it?

4. Who will be responsible for conducting the project? How many people will take part in it, and who are they? Will they require any special training? If so, who will do the training, and when?

5. How long will it take to complete the project? Will it then need to be continued and maintained? If so, who will take over that responsibility?

6. What are the financial and material requirements of the project? Who will provide the money? How will the materials be obtained?

7. How will the project be supervised? When it is completed, who will be responsible for checking the work and evaluating its quality and over-all contribution?

Not all these questions are applicable to every project. But they may serve as a checklist to ensure that important aspects are not overlooked when the project is in the planning stage.

Making the Visits of the Technical Personnel Effective

Intelligent collaboration between members of the technical departments and the RRWs is at the very heart of the PRRM operation. This collaboration de-

FIELD OPERATIONS

velops mainly during regularly scheduled, rotating visits of technical personnel to the barrios.

The main purpose of the visits is to bring to bear the special knowledge and skills of the technician as projects are prepared, launched, and carried forward to completion. It is a universal opinion among RRWs and technical personnel alike that the more frequently these visits are made, the better the chances are for the success of projects in all parts of the four-fold program.

To the RRW, they mean an assurance of requisite knowledge and backing at important stages of the projects for which he is responsible. He learns much from the visiting technician, thereby increasing his abilities and self-confidence. Each visit, as a rule, also gives a boost to his morale.

To the technician, the visits provide the opportunities he needs for continuous contacts with the barrio people--contacts which are much closer and more productive because of the groundwork already done by the RRW. Through their active relations with the village people, the technical personnel acquire a much more realistic grasp of conditions in the barrios than they could in any other way. As a result, they plan their work more intelligently, set up the projects in a more practical manner, and give more pertinent counsel to the RRWs and the barrio people as problems arise.

Directive to RRWs

1. Make plans for the technical visitor well in advance. If it is needed, set up a meeting of participants, or prospective participants, in the project with which the visitor is especially concerned. Plan his itinerary for the time he is scheduled to spend in the barrio. Allow time, also, for a personal talk.

2. Always leave information about your whereabouts at the barrio hall or at your boarding house, so that the technical visitor will not have to waste time looking for you after he arrives.

3. Brief the technical visitor on latest developments in the barrio, and particularly on the progress of projects with which he is directly concerned.

4. Display enthusiasm in showing the accomplishments of the barrio people to the visitor, and make sure he meets the leading people in the barrio who are interested in his area of operations.

5. Collaborate closely with the specialist as he works with the people. Use the opportunity to raise questions which you or the barrio participants may have about the project. Cultivate a sense of active involvement among the barrio people. This will strengthen their feelings of responsibility as they work with the specialist.

6. If there is time, take advantage of his presence by inviting him to meetings where his interest and encouragement might give a boost to the program, or by enlisting his help in stimulating interest among any villagers who have remained indifferent to the PRRM program.

7. After the technical visitor leaves, follow up immediately on the recommendations he has made.

If the RRW is facing any problem, either technical or personal, on which he feels the need of counsel, he should feel free to seek the PRRM visitor's advice. Such friendly consultation has often proved to be of great value.

Directive to Visiting Technical Personnel

1. Prepare well in advance for every visit, and allocate ample time to each barrio. Preparatory work includes detailed planning for specific projects, arrangements for transportation, and assembling of visual aids and other materials.

2. Time your arrival well. Look for the RRW as soon as you reach a barrio. This will not only contribute to the effectiveness of your work; it will also enhance the worker's prestige in the eyes of the people.

3. After you have worked on any project with the RRW and the barrio participants, and have answered their questions to the best of your ability, make clear your specific recommendations regarding next steps. As a rule, your comments and suggestions should be written down while you are still in the barrio. This will ensure better understanding of

FIELD OPERATIONS 91

them, and increase the probability of prompt implementation.

4. Use the occasion of your visit to enlarge the circle of your friends and acquaintances among the barrio people. Take a genuine interest in their accomplishments, as well as in their problems.

5. In each barrio you visit, do not forget to give all the help and encouragement you can to the RRWs as they carry on their indispensable, difficult front-line work.

Avoiding Political Entanglements

Exceptional skill and tact on the part of RRWs and other field personnel are sometimes needed in order to avoid political entanglements. For there are many ways in which political rivalries in a barrio may impinge upon, and do harm to, PRRM-sponsored programs.

Difficulties Created by Political Rivalries

A few examples of situations actually encountered by PRRM field workers indicate the types of difficulties that may arise.

In one community, a fund to which the barrio council was legally entitled was withheld by the mayor of the municipality because the officials of the barrio council belonged to a different political party. As a result, the construction of a multipurpose barrio hall which PRRM had promoted, and which the barrio leaders wanted to construct, was held up indefinitely.

In another community, funds raised by the barrio council, through collection of a small percentage of the farmers' payments for the use of a rice thresher, became the source of a controversy between two rival groups. The barrio council itself wished to use the funds to construct a barrio hall. But officers of the parent-teacher association wanted to employ the funds to build additional schoolrooms. The deadlock continued for some time.

After an election, in a third community, the incoming barrio captain refused to carry forward a worthwhile project which had been started by his predecessor, who belonged to a rival political party.

An RRW, in a fourth community, found herself in difficulty because she had developed a good cooperative working relationship with a barrio captain who was defeated in a later election. The incoming barrio captain thought she was in favor of his predecessor, and for this reason refused to support any project with which she was associated.

In a fifth community, an RRW suffered a serious loss of prestige, as an impartial teacher and leader, when he allowed himself to become directly embroiled in a local political dispute.

Such examples could be multiplied. Some RRWs have found it more difficult to work effectively because the real leaders in their barrios, not wanting to be associated with the party in power, refused to accept any official responsibilities. And many RRWs have been confronted by rival political groups whose members refused to work together on community programs.

PRRM Policy

Political rivalries are a fact of life, and PRRM fully recognizes the importance of political struggle on behalf of good leaders and causes. PRRM is aware, too, of the duty and right of citizens in a democracy to vote for the candidates of their choice. But PRRM does not permit its personnel to take a partisan role in any political controversies in the barrios, for the simple reason that to do so would be to court failure in the program.

The PRRM field worker is expected to be an impartial friend to all the leaders and all the people in a barrio, and to do his best to win their cooperation in developing and carrying forward projects that will benefit the whole community. If the barrio leaders with whom he is associating belong to one political party, he should extend his friendly relations to members of rival parties as well, making it clear that PRRM is non-political and non-sectarian. If he is invited to participate in a political meeting, or asked to summon a partisan political speaker to a PRRM-sponsored meeting, he should politely decline, explaining the PRRM policy of non-involvement in political matters.

FIELD OPERATIONS

Recent experience has proven the advisability of the RRWs leaving their barrio assignments for a few days (not to exceed a total of one week) before and after national and local elections. One worker was branded as a partisan of a political party simply because he walked with the candidate of that party on election day. The brief absence affords the RRW the chance to go home and vote and, at the same time, helps him to avoid political entanglements in his barrio.

Receiving Visitors

In recent years, PRRM has had an increasing number of visitors, from the Philippines and from other countries. Most have heard or read about the PRRM, and are anxious to see for themselves just what the program is and how it works.

Instead of regarding these visits as a burden, PRRM tries to make them interesting and fruitful. If visitors are given a good opportunity to observe some aspects of rural reconstruction work in the barrios, they may gain insights that will be useful to them in their support of rural programs elsewhere, or they may be a source of great encouragement to the barrio people. For these reasons, the visitors should be given general briefings on the PRRM program before they go to the barrios. Their visits should be planned to give them opportunities to see in action the facets of the program in which they are most interested.

Much depends on the reception and handling of the visitors within the barrios, and here the responsibility is likely to fall mainly on the RRWs and other field personnel.

Techniques

For an announced visit, the following techniques, adapted to the composition and size of the visiting group, have been found useful:

1. Prepare to extend a warm Filipino welcome, by putting up welcoming signs, or obtaining leis. The expected arrival of distinguished visitors may provide a good occasion to suggest a general clean-up of the barrio.

2. If it seems warranted, invite the barrio captain and some of the village leaders to be on hand to welcome the visitors.

3. When the visitors arrive, they should be introduced individually to the RRW, the barrio captain, and the other barrio leaders present.

4. Give the visitors a short, informative briefing on activities in the barrio, then show them some of the principal projects under way. While conducting the visitors around, be responsive to their special interests.

5. Sometimes visits are timed to coincide with a scheduled program that they would enjoy attending. There may be other times when a special program is desirable, consisting of brief talks by some of the barrio leaders or PRRM personnel, and perhaps by one or two of the visitors, interspersed with musical or dancing numbers. Try to prevent these programs from becoming over-long.

It can be a source of keen disappointment to the barrio leaders if anticipated visitors fail to arrive until long after the scheduled hour; it is much worse if they fail to show up at all. Those planning and conducting visits must prevent these disappointments if humanly possible. If a visit is seriously delayed or must be cancelled, the RRWs concerned should be notified immediately.

In case of an unscheduled or unannounced visit, it is still possible to give the visitors a warm sense of welcome, to introduce them to the RRW and village leaders available, to give them an impromptu briefing, and to show them projects in which they express interest. Before the visitors leave, it is sometimes appropriate to ask for any suggestions they may have for improving the program.

Leaving a Barrio

No RRW can stay forever in one barrio. The concept of self-help demands that people develop their own powers of leadership and that they cope, to an increasing extent, with their own problems. The time eventually comes when the worker must leave the barrio, and this must be prepared for, since it is not easy. You arrived as a stranger, and you leave as a

FIELD OPERATIONS

close friend, perhaps as an adopted son or daughter of the barrio.

If you are transferring to another barrio or another job, and someone is coming to take your place, it is important to ensure a graceful and orderly turnover. The reasons for the transfer should be explained to members of the barrio council and to leaders of the people's associations. If circumstances permit, introduce your successor personally to the village people, and help him to get off to a good start. Plan to make a return visit to the barrio whenever you can.

If there will be no successor after your departure, then the leave-taking is more difficult. After making sure that the leaders understand fully the reasons for your going, your main concern should be to leave all projects in a healthy state, with the leaders in the barrio determined to carry them forward. These specific steps are recommended:

1. Give to the barrio council, and the leaders of the people's associations, a proper explanation for the decision to terminate your work in the barrio. If possible, have with you at these meetings a member of the Senior Staff or your team captain, or both. Discuss with the barrio leaders the ongoing projects, and express, as far as you can, your sincere conviction that they will carry on the projects with undiminished enthusiasm.

2. Prepare and conduct an orderly turnover of your responsibilities to the barrio leaders who will carry them on. Make sure that all accounts are paid up before you leave, and that all records are in good order. In spite of any past disappointments, do not say anything against anybody.

3. Make personal calls on your many friends in the barrio, and try to infuse them with confidence that they can carry on, with continuing progress, after your departure.

GUIDELINES FOR FIELD OPERATIONS
ADMINISTRATIVE PERSONNEL

Responsibility for the direction of PRRM field operations is mainly that of the field operations administrative personnel: team captains, district field assistants, senior field assistants, and the Deputy Director and Director of Field Operations. This responsibility covers not only the general planning and administration of field operations, and the handling of relationships in the field with governmental and other agencies; it also includes a large part of the day-to-day supervision and support of the RRWs. Administrative supervision is the responsibility of the field operations administrative staff; technical supervision is the responsibility of the technical departments.

However, a private organization with good interdepartmental understanding and collaboration does not need to be rigid about such distinctions. For example, technical personnel with wide field experience are frequently able to assist in dealing, on the spot, with some types of administrative or public relations problems. In the same way, experienced field operations personnel can often lend a helping hand on technical matters with which they have become familiar.

The guidelines which follow, relating to specific tasks, are intended primarily for field operations administrative personnel.

Selecting a Barrio for Assistance

The barrios receiving PRRM assistance fall into two categories. The larger category is that of barrios selected by PRRM after consultations with leading citizens of the barrio. The smaller, but growing, category is that of "sponsored" barrios, in each of which PRRM assistance is provided at the request of a sponsor who agrees to pay a stated amount per year to cover the basic operating cost if PRRM will agree to undertake a rural reconstruction program. In respect to the second category, PRRM is of course free to accept or decline the request for assistance, but it is not quite so free in applying its own criteria for the selection of the barrio.

Criteria in Making the Selection

The criteria which follow have been evolved over a considerable period of time. It is not expected that any barrio will meet all these criteria. An effort is made, however, to select in most cases barrios which meet 70 per cent or more of the criteria now being employed.

General criteria include genuine receptivity among the barrio officials and leaders, and the concurrence or "blessing" of the municipal officials. The barrio chosen should be accessible; that is, within reasonable walking distance from the nearest passable road. The barrio should be predominantly rural. It should have sufficient space for a plant nursery and for homelot gardens, also for a modest barrio hall and a health center. There must be a minimal supply of water, as well as land and other resources that can be used for development. An important criterion is evidence of latent capacities for leadership among the people of the barrio. There should be a real need for PRRM assistance, in the sense that no other agency is engaged in an intensive all-round development program in the barrio. And, generally speaking, only barrios that have at least 100 homes or a population of 500 or more are chosen.

More specifically, with respect to the potential for a fruitful livelihood program, it is preferred that at least 60 per cent of the people shall be engaged in farming; usually the percentage is considerably higher. Irrigation facilities are desirable but, of course, not insisted upon. However, there should be enough water for homelot gardening. The availability of local materials for animal shelters, and local feeds to supplement commercial feeds, is desirable. Skilled craftsmen and availability of local raw materials like bamboo, curi, and coconut midrib are also assets, as are people who are willing to learn to become auxiliary vocational or craft teachers, or to offer the use of their houses or equipment for classes. Receptivity of the barrio people to starting a cooperative society is considered a further advantage.

Conditions favorable to the development of a health program are considered, such as the availability of local materials for the construction and installation of sanitary toilets, and the availability of fencing materials for sanitary purposes.

The chances of enlisting PRRM assistance are further enhanced if the barrio council and other leaders are prepared to cooperate in a literacy campaign in the barrio, to set up a reading center, and to help promote cultural activities such as folk drama, folk singing, and folk dancing.

From the standpoint of the self-government program, it is desirable that the barrio should be registered, with its boundaries defined by the municipal provincial council; and that it should have in office a barrio council duly elected and constituted in accordance with the law. It is further desirable that the barrio council prepare a petition formally requesting PRRM assistance.

Steps in Opening a Barrio

What is done in the initial stage of work in a barrio may have a decisive effect on the rate of progress thereafter. It is therefore important that the steps which have proven most helpful in opening a barrio should be kept in mind, not to be applied automatically but flexibly, with appropriate adjustment to the situation in each barrio. The principal steps are as follows:

1. Make a preliminary survey, which may require several visits, to determine how well the barrio meets the criteria outlined above.

2. If practicable, obtain from the barrio council a resolution or formal petition requesting PRRM assistance. This may not be feasible in the case of sponsored barrios, where the initiative is taken by a sponsor.

3. Select a boarding house for the RRW in the manner described earlier in this chapter.

4. Make a courtesy call on municipal officials to acquaint them with PRRM activities in their area, to win their good will, and to lay the basis for future contacts.

5. Have a meeting with the barrio council, to inform them in further detail of the ways in which PRRM is prepared to work with them. Arrange at this session for a mass meeting of the barrio people.

6. At the mass meeting, have several persons present who can help present to the people an interesting picture of the ways in which the PRRM is prepared to cooperate with them in promoting self-help

programs. Do not arouse exaggerated expectations. The barrio captain and members of the barrio council should have a prominent role in conducting this meeting. At the meeting, the RRW appointed to live and work in the barrio should be formally introduced and given a good "send-off."

7. See that the RRW makes a prompt beginning on house-to-house calls for the dual purpose of (a) getting acquainted with the people, and (b) conducting the preliminary socio-economic survey for the acquisition of basic data.

8. Assist the RRW, as needed, in the early phases of action programming with the people, on the basis of the problems found in the barrio.

9. Give careful supervisory attention and assistance, as needed, in connection with the organization of the three people's associations.

Dealing with a Barrio Sponsor

A substantial part of the income raised by the PRRM comes from barrio sponsorship fees. It has been the aim of PRRM not only to attract sponsorships, but to make the sponsors thoroughly familiar with the PRRM program and to get them actively involved in the work in the barrios they sponsor. This is good for the program, and it increases the probability of the sponsor's continuing support. A sensitive and selective use of the following approaches is recommended in dealing with a sponsor.

1. Invite him to attend barrio meetings and to visit individual projects in the barrio.

2. Once each quarter give him a summary report on the progress of activities in the barrio. Send him clippings or other items of interest bearing on the work. He should also be given promptly copies of any PRRM Board actions relating to the sponsored barrios.

3. The team captain, with the RRW, should call on the sponsor from time to time and discuss the program, its progress and its problems. Use these visits as occasions for requesting any special cooperation that would be helpful.

4. After some real progress has been made in the barrio, suggest, if it seems appropriate, a resolution of appreciation from the barrio council to the sponsor for making PRRM assistance possible. Or, alternatively, arrange for some special recognition of the sponsor when he can be present at a general meeting of the people.

Backing up the RRWs

PRRM's rural reconstruction workers neither want nor need to be pampered. But they do need to feel that they are recognized in the barrios, and that they can depend on the understanding and loyal support of their team captains and other co-workers in the PRRM. The following paragraphs summarize a few of the ways in which the field operations administrative staff can effectively back up the RRWs.

1. Make certain that each RRW has both a suitable place to live and some space where he can do essential office work.

2. At an early stage, take the RRW personally to call on some of the leading people of the village.

3. Whenever you visit the barrio, look up the RRW first. Show by your manner that he has the confidence of the PRRM administration. Be generous in recognizing good work. Do not fail to exercise necessary discipline, but never reprimand the RRW in front of other people.

4. Act as a helpful liaison between the RRW and the PRRM departments, and in relations between the RRW and local governmental or other personnel. Transmit promptly communications between the RRW and the technical or other departments of PRRM.

5. Help the RRW to forward his personal development, through wise counseling, by providing well-chosen reading materials, and by holding occasional team seminars on professional growth.

6. Keep watch on the RRW's health. Help him in case of an emergency need for funds. And try, through occasional team outings or socials, to help meet his social needs.

7. Make your own experience useful to the RRW.

FIELD OPERATIONS

Anticipate problems that may confront him, so precautionary measures may be taken. Find time to listen thoughtfully to his questions or problems, and assist when you can in meeting them.

Holding Team Meetings

Regular meetings of RRWs with their team captains serve a number of important purposes. They give the RRWs opportunity to present their problems and seek solutions, and to enjoy a free exchange of ideas and experiences. They also provide suitable occasions for transmitting to the RRWs new policies, memoranda, circulars, or bulletins from the administration. Technical personnel often visit these meetings and discuss developing programs or answer questions asked by the RRWs. The team meetings also promote understanding and harmony among the workers, and give the team captains opportunities to receive regular reports from the RRWs and to further evaluate their development on the job.

Make certain that the time and place of all team meetings are known to each RRW well in advance. Meetings often coincide with payday, which makes it simple to distribute pay envelopes to the workers. The site of the meeting should be rotated among the different barrios of the team if it is not held at the PRRM Center. When a meeting is held in a barrio, new projects should be visited. When it is held at the Center, the RRWs' meals and transportation are paid for by PRRM.

Evaluating Personnel

A democratic system for evaluating personnel, and for acquainting them with the results of these evaluations, is a part of PRRM's standard procedures. RRWs are evaluated by team captains, and by technical assistants, associates, and experts. However, only those who have visited the barrios and seen the actual performance of the RRWs are allowed to participate in the evaluations. Team captains and technical assistants and associates are evaluated not only by their administrative and technical equals and superiors, but also by the RRWs under their supervision.

The following items are considered in each quarterly rating of the RRWs: (a) technical know-how, as shown in their performance; (b) social know-how, as demonstrated in their relationships with the barrio people, and with their fellow workers; (c) dedication; and (d) progress in the barrio, taking into account the length of the RRW's service there and the receptivity of the people.

The following items are considered in semi-annual ratings of team captains, technical assistants, and technical associates: (a) technical know-how; (b) social know-how; (c) dedication; and (d) supervisory and administrative abilities and performance.

The timing of the evaluations, and the procedures to be followed, are announced by the Field Operations Office. The results of the evaluations are made known only to the individuals concerned and to responsible senior personnel. They are used in making decisions respecting salary advances, promotions, and special awards. But their principal value is in helping the staff members themselves to learn where their strengths and weaknesses lie, and to work more intelligently for their own steady improvement on the job.

FOUR-FOLD PROGRAM IN ACTION

　　　　I.　LIVELIHOOD

CHAPTER 5 AIMS AND SCOPE OF THE LIVELIHOOD PROGRAM

We turn now to one of the four main parts of the PRRM program: livelihood, which includes activities in the fields of plant production, animal production, cooperatives, village industries, and vocational arts.

In 1952, when this program began, the agrarian economy of the Philippines was comparable to that of almost every other developing nation. Agricultural technology was almost static. Education of the farmers in modern methods of cultivation had scarcely begun. Capital inputs into agriculture were extremely small. Only rarely did a farmer have access to the services that are especially needed by agricultural communities--such as transport and credit and research.

A large proportion of the farmers were sharecroppers who had little incentive to increase their output. What they produced was mainly for subsistence. Only a fraction of it ever reached local, regional, national, or international markets. The prices of farm products, generally depressed, were subject to severe fluctuations. As might be expected under these circumstances, the average income of rural families was only a little above a subsistence level. In short, the factors required to bring about agricultural modernization and a "yield-per-acre takeoff" (see Chapter 1) were almost wholly lacking.

While there have been improvements in some localities, these conditions persist throughout a large part of the Philippines--as they do in most of the developing nations. This is evidence of the truth that it is exceedingly difficult for a populous newly developing country to bring about fundamental economic gains among the masses of its rural people, especially during the earlier stages of economic growth.

GENERAL FEATURES

Under such conditions, what should a private organization like the PRRM undertake in the field of livelihood? What can it hope to accomplish? Should the scope of its efforts be restricted, and if so, how? What should be its main areas of emphasis? How can its pilot program best complement the government's efforts, and be of most value to the rural people and to the country?

PRRM's approach to these questions has been more practical than theoretical. Its general objective in the sphere of livelihood has been to help the barrio people increase their production and income, and thereby enlarge their opportunities for all-round development and a good life. Within the scope of this broad objective, PRRM's selection of activities has been determined by the interests and desires of the people, and by considerations of economy, practicality, learnability, and the anticipated value and duplicability of selected projects.

Specific aims of the PRRM livelihood program, as actually developed, have been: (a) to increase the quantity, quality, and efficiency of agricultural production in all PRRM-aided barrios; (b) to develop the knowledge, skills, incentives, and cooperative efforts of the producers; (c) to evolve, within the PRRM pilot program, an effective pattern of extension work; (d) to promote the development of credit facilities, and of local responsibility in their management and use; and (e) to facilitate a growth of supplementary employment through village industries and vocational arts.

Agricultural Productivity

The quantity and quality of agricultural production are, of course, the chief determinants of the living standards of farm families.

In this area, PRRM's first interest was in helping the farmers to increase their rice yields, by methods discussed in the following chapter.

Then came an interest in diversification in each family's production, in order to provide a better balanced diet for them, and to increase the items that could be sold for cash to augment the family in-

AIMS AND SCOPE OF THE LIVELIHOOD PROGRAM

come. Diversification has taken three main forms: the introduction of secondary crops, the development of homelot gardening, and the promotion of hog and chicken raising. In each case, PRRM's concern has been for quality as well as quantity of production.

A complementary interest has been in the greater --and better--employment of available resources. The use of idle land for homelot gardening has been mentioned. Decomposed vegetable matter from compost pits has provided good plant food, supplementing or taking the place of chemical fertilizers. Even meat scraps, fish gills and intestines, chicken entrails, fresh water mollusks and tadpoles, as pointed out in Chapter 7, have been found effective as protein-rich substitutes for commercial feeds.

Knowledge and Skills

A major reason for poverty in the rural areas is the inadequate knowledge and skills of the cultivators. Many farmers do not realize that they can acquire valuable new knowledge and skills, or that this is necessary to improving their economic situation.

PRRM seeks to teach the farmers to pinpoint their own problems. It seeks to help them acquire the new knowledge and skills they most need, and to inspire them to action. But it does not try to force anything on them, believing that whatever action they take should be their own action, developing out of their own knowledge and skills and convictions.

Incentives

PRRM does aim to help develop and nurture the farmers' incentives to learn about new ways of doing things, and to adopt techniques that will enhance their production and income. It is not easy for the barrio people to change their outlooks, or to modify practices that have come down through generations, or to assume the risk of serious losses if new methods should not work out. Agricultural extension programs may produce meager results if no way is found to overcome a lack of interest in new and better methods of production.

This problem is sometimes evaded with the allegation that it cannot really be dealt with until the producer gets a fairer return on his labor, through basic reforms in land tenure or taxation or marketing. Such reforms may indeed have a great effect on the farmers' will to produce, and their consequent readiness to learn about new techniques. But PRRM has found that it is not necessary to wait idly until basic agrarian reforms are carried out by government. Farmers can be shown that new methods can bring them better yields and better incomes, even though the increased benefits to them are not as large as they would be under a more equitable social system.

PRRM has tried out, with varying success, many ways of enlisting participation in agricultural improvement programs--such as visits to the farmers in their homes, to explain a new method of cultivation and its benefits; study groups, to go into problems together; organized meetings, where informative talks are given, followed by full discussion of all questions raised; well-planned demonstrations that help to instill confidence in a new technology while proving that it is not too difficult to master; and visits to neighboring barrios where new techniques are already being successfully applied. These and other approaches are referred to frequently in the chapters that follow. One of the most effective means yet developed by PRRM for increasing incentives to better production is the MAC Project, described in Chapter 10. This project sets up specific targets for increased family income, by specific means, with detailed records and the added zest of competition.

Extension System

One of PRRM's primary aims has been to develop an effective, duplicable system of agricultural extension work--for the dissemination of scientific information and practical know-how. What has evolved so far is not yet a fully matured approach. But it has vitality. It enlists lively interest and cooperation among the farmers. And it has produced a valuable accumulation of practical experience. Four elements in the pattern that has developed, to date, are especially noteworthy.

The first is close cooperation between the specialists and the multipurpose--or "generalist"-- rural reconstruction workers (RRWs) in the PRRM staff. The specialists are not of the ivory-tower variety. In addition to competence in their own fields, they have a social vision and a practical

AIMS AND SCOPE OF THE LIVELIHOOD PROGRAM

bent, a feeling for the barrio people and a strong desire to help them. They give technical guidance to the RRWs, who live full-time in the barrios and command the people's respect and trust. Teamwork between the specialists and the RRWs is a hallmark of the PRRM extension system.

Second, PRRM's organizational approach to agricultural extension work fits into a broader institutional approach relating to all parts of the fourfold program. Normally, the first organization formed by the men in a PRRM-aided barrio is not a farmers' seminar but a Rural Reconstruction Men's Association (RRMA), which has an interest in all the major lines of development. Committees are formed to take active responsibility for different parts of the program. After that comes an enlistment of the RRMA members who are most interested, for the first general meetings on specific agricultural subjects, and then for the first farmers' classes and seminars. These activities provide opportunities not only for valuable educational work, but also for better personal knowledge of the farmers, and an assessment of their individual interests and capabilities.

Third, major emphasis is then given to effective demonstrations, conducted with the cooperation of carefully chosen demonstration farmers, in the types of plant and animal production in which there appear possibilities of developing promising projects.

Fourth, attention is then directed to a vigorous promotion of individual projects, utilizing the experience and results achieved by the demonstration farmers; and to the joint, cooperative development of appropriate group projects. A good example of the latter is the barrio plant nursery, where grain and vegetable seeds of good quality can be produced in sufficient quantity to meet the needs of the barrio farmers, and can then be properly stored in "seed banks" until they are needed. This has proven to be a valuable supplement to the government's certified seed programs and those of private concerns, which are not yet able to supply to the nation's farmers, at low cost, all the varieties and quantities of certified seed they need. The barrio plant nurseries have also been highly useful as centers for demonstration and training in methods of cultivation. And they have proven to be valuable local versions, on a smaller scale, of the extension farms operated by municipal governments, which are often too distant to be of much practical help to farmers out in the barrios.

The order in which these four steps occur may vary somewhat from barrio to barrio, according to local circumstances. The foregoing description reflects a sequence that is typical in most PRRM-aided barrios.

One technique that PRRM has introduced and found especially useful in its extension work is that of discussing with the farmers, during classes or seminars, the question of how they can make the best use of their time.

The basic facts employed in starting such a discussion are surprising to the farmers themselves. A survey conducted a few years ago by the Philippine Council for U.S. Aid and the U.S. Operations Mission indicated that, out of an assumed 300 working days of 8 hours each, the average Filipino farmer devotes only the equivalent of 102 full days to productive activity that contributes directly to his livelihood. The remaining 198 days are spent in miscellaneous other activities or inactivity.

The questions raised for discussion, in which the farmers participate in a lively fashion, are: (a) Would it be wise to plan systematically for the efficient use of one's time? (b) How can the best use be made of the 8 working hours, and the 8 other waking hours, of each day? (c) How can one plan for the effective use of 365 days each year, taking into account the farmer's and his family's needs not only for greater production and income, but also for barrio activities and the broadening of knowledge, as well as for rest, recreation, and social functions?

These discussions, further described in Chapter 10, have had a salutary effect in bringing to many a farmer the realization that he might accomplish much more than he is presently accomplishing. He might start growing a secondary crop to sell for cash. He might develop a homelot garden. He might raise chickens, or start a little piggery. Or he might engage in other remunerative work during times of the year when he would otherwise be relatively idle.

AIMS AND SCOPE OF THE LIVELIHOOD PROGRAM 111

Savings and Credit

There is a perennial shortage of credit in the barrios. Most of the people, living close to a subsistence level, have never acquired the habit of saving money, even in small amounts. When their cash is exhausted and they must borrow, their only recourse, usually, is to local moneylenders who charge exorbitant interest rates. Neither the government nor private business and banking interests have yet found the means of making available an adequate supply of low-interest credit to farmers throughout the country.

PRRM did not wait for ideal conditions to develop. It addressed itself to the question of what could be done by a private agency, under conditions as they were. In the field of credit, PRRM's emphasis to date has been mainly on (a) encouraging habits of regular saving, even in very small amounts; (b) the promotion of local credit unions, in the PRRM-aided barrios, through which savings could be mobilized and made a source of credit for its members, for productive and other urgent purposes; (c) the conduct of intensive training for all participants in the credit unions, as a means of assuring full responsibility in handling funds, and in making deposits and repayments as they fall due; (d) cooperating with government authorities in the development and maintenance of adequate supervision for the credit unions; and (e) preparing for the time when, it is hoped, much more adequate credit will be available to agricultural producers throughout the nation.

Supplemental Employment

PRRM has endeavored to promote, experimentally, village industries and vocational arts that might be sources of additional earnings or savings for barrio families.

The work with village industries began with experimentation in the use of locally available raw materials for making various handicraft products. The principal materials used have been bamboo, abaca or Manila hemp, buri--a fiber gathered from unopened leafstalks of the talipot palm--and various kinds of wood. From these materials, as indicated in Chapter 9, a number of attractive and useful handicraft products have been developed, most of them suitable for

local markets, and a few for export. Much remains to
be done, however, through market studies, promotion,
training, the standardization of products, and the
development of suitable distribution channels, before
these industries can become a major source of additional income to the people living in PRRM-aided barrios.

   Vocational arts--especially dressmaking, tailoring, and embroidering--have had a longer development
in the PRRM program, and have become economically important in many homes. Their value is not primarily
as a source of cash income, but as a means of reducing the strains on family budgets. Many sewing
classes have been conducted in the PRRM-aided barrios. The women and girls who have graduated from
them are able to make much of the clothing needed by
their families, in quality at least equal to that of
purchased garments, and at a much lower cost.

CHANGE AND GROWTH

   All parts of the PRRM program, including livelihood, are in a never-ceasing process of change and
growth. Many changes of the past started as experimental innovations. While future changes are unpre-
dictable, they may be foretokened by present hopes
and plans.

Innovations

   Within the livelihood program, PRRM has introduced, tested, and promoted for the first time in
many barrios: (1) a simplified yet comprehensive
method of teaching farmers how to grow bigger and
better rice crops; (2) experimentation with, and development of, significant secondary crops; (3) homelot gardening; (4) plant nurseries and seed banks;
(5) scientific composting; (6) continuous farmers'
classes, seminars, and study groups; (7) the hatching
of purebred New Hampshire eggs; (8) the caponization
of cockerels; (9) hog-breeding; (10) a range of experimental village industries; (11) wide training in
selected vocational arts; and (12) intensive preparation and training prior to the initiation of credit
unions.

   These innovations have been carried forward,
along with less novel aspects of the program, as part

AIMS AND SCOPE OF THE LIVELIHOOD PROGRAM

of PRRM's integrated four-fold approach. This is in itself an innovation. As mentioned earlier, agricultural improvement and extension activities are conducted as integral parts of the work of the Rural Reconstruction Men's Associations. The diversified efforts to increase production and income are frequently implemented within the context of coordinated Minimum-Additional-Income or Model-Farm-Family projects. (See Chapters 10 and 21.) Farmers, in short, are dealt with not merely as producers or consumers, but as human beings with various needs and interests and capabilities.

A Look Ahead

PRRM has many ideas and plans for further activities in the livelihood sphere. A few might be mentioned.

There will be an intensification of educational efforts among the farmers, and more critical evaluation of the effectiveness and duplicability of the extension methods now being employed. The aim will be to perfect a flexible pattern of agricultural extension work that embodies the essential values of the PRRM approach, and is capable of wide application under governmental as well as private auspices.

In collaboration with the IIRR, there will be steadily growing emphasis on operational research in all parts of the program.

There may be an expansion of cooperation with government agencies, without detriment to PRRM's independent status as a private agency, especially in areas where PRRM may be in a position to conduct experiments or special training of value to the government in programs affecting the rural people. There will also be an increase in active cooperation with academic and research organizations, such as the University of the Philippines College of Agriculture, Central Luzon University's Agricultural College, and the International Rice Research Institute.

There will be an expanding promotion of village industries. This will involve further studies of available raw materials and their properties, of existing skills among the barrio people, of potential markets, quality controls, and new industries that might be developed, including the preserving and processing of various foods.

There will be an effort to expand the membership of credit unions in PRRM-aided barrios, and to assist them in gaining access to new and larger financial resources that can be drawn on for productive purposes.

CHAPTER 6   PLANT PRODUCTION

The Philippines is predominantly an agricultural country; food production is the leading occupation of the people. Yet the amount produced is insufficient. It is necessary, year after year, to use precious foreign exchange reserves to purchase rice and other foodstuffs. Even then the supply is often inadequate. During times of relative shortage, especially before the main crops come in, food prices may rise steeply.

The result for many thousands of families is economic uncertainty, with recurring periods of malnutrition and distress. For the nation as a whole, there is a retarded rate of economic growth, and social unrest in districts where the most acute shortages occur. Because the population of the Philippines is growing rapidly, the food problem is becoming ever more serious.

But there is a more encouraging side to this picture. The country has considerable stretches of unused, arable land. More important, land already under cultivation can be made, by modern scientific methods, to produce far more than it is now producing. Most important, there is at present a great underutilization of human resources. If these potentials can be developed well enough and rapidly enough, the Philippines can become a food surplus country with rising internal prosperity.

One of PRRM's main objectives is the discovery of increasingly practical ways to help farm families to increase their production of foodstuffs, in order to meet their own needs and those of the nation. Many technical and social approaches have been tried out by PRRM's Plant Production Department. There has been a gradual selection through trial and error of those which, so far, have proven most effective and best adapted to rural conditions in the Philippines.

EMPHASES IN PLANT PRODUCTION PROGRAM

The principal emphases in the PRRM plant production program, now, are on (1) improving the culture of rice in order to achieve bigger and better yields; (2) expanding the production of secondary crops; (3) stimulating homelot gardening; (4) developing extension farms in the municipalities (counties) where PRRM is at work, and associated plant nurseries in all PRRM-aided barrios; (5) developing a seed bank in each barrio; (6) promoting the practice of composting by modern methods; and (7) organizing and conducting farmers' classes, seminars, and study groups.

Although additional approaches are being tested, this chapter concentrates upon these seven.

IMPROVING RICE CULTURE

Experiments under way in the Philippines are adding significantly to the world's store of scientific knowledge about rice production. When the newer techniques now being developed at the International Rice Research Institute at Los Banos are generally applied, important increases in output will result; the Philippines will become a rice surplus instead of a rice deficit area.

Since rice is the country's staple food, these increases will be of broad benefit to the national economy. Farmers' incomes will rise; their families will be better fed. Urban centers will be assured of an adequate supply of rice throughout the year, at relatively stable prices. The country's dependence on external sources of foodstuffs will be greatly diminished. And by exporting rice not needed at home, the Philippines will acquire foreign exchange critically required for new investments in agriculture and industry.

Before these great gains can be realized, however, the nation's farmers must learn well how to apply improved methods of rice production. The best technology can have only limited results until it is put to use across the land. The _acquisition_ of new knowledge by a few must be followed by widespread, practical _application_ by many. PRRM workers are deeply involved in this process of practical application.

PLANT PRODUCTION

Masagana System: 12 Steps

Diverse methods of rice culture employed in various countries, and many combinations of these methods, have been tried out in the Philippines. The methods found most adaptable have been gathered together to form what we now call the "Masagana system." This system does not represent a single new method of rice culture. It is, rather, a general combination of methods and techniques which, so far, have proven most successful.

The Masagana system involves 12 steps. Each of them utilizes, in simplified and easily understood form, the results of extensive research. Each is subject to continuing improvement and refinement as new knowledge is gained. What follows is an extremely brief summary of the 12 steps with which each RRW should be thoroughly familiar. For a detailed discussion, see PRRM's "Training Materials on Plant Production," pp. 1-19.

Step 1. <u>Use certified or selected seeds</u>. The Philippine Rice Seed Board issues, from time to time, lists of the varieties of rice seeds that have been certified for lowland and upland culture. Each RRW is expected to keep these lists available for ready reference, together with standard tables showing, for each certified variety, regional adaptability, seasonal features, and growth characteristics including number of days between planting and heading; also plant height, lodging character, tillering capacity, and yield capacity (cavans per hectare).

A few weeks before the planting season begins, the RRW makes sure that the farmers in his barrio know how to obtain the certified rice seeds most appropriate for their use.

In many districts, the farmers are accustomed to collecting and saving their own seeds for the next planting season. When this is the case, the RRW should be prepared to show how it can be done in the most efficient manner, especially when there may be difficulty in obtaining suitable certified seeds. The most important rules are:

a) Select your seeds at harvest time from a field planted with certified seeds. Do not gather seeds from plants near the dikes or irrigation ditches. They tend to be less resistant to drought, pests, and diseases.

b) Select seeds from vigorous plants, of more or less the same height, that are free from pests and diseases.

c) Choose the big, sound panicles with plenty of healthy, well-ripened grains.

d) Collect 15 gantas of palay for every hectare of land to be planted.

e) Spread and dry the seeds thoroughly under the sun.

f) Treat the seeds, put them in clean jute bags, and store them in a dry, well-ventilated place until needed. This is necessary to keep them free from seedborne diseases and to protect them from weevils.

Step 2. Prepare the seedbed. The essential steps are as follows:

a) Immediately after harvest, select for the next seedbed the most fertile area of a field that is exposed to sunlight and near the water supply. Plow this area at once to aerate the soil.

b) When sowing time comes, plow the selected area again, harrow it, and remove all weeds.

c) Make raised seedbeds of convenient sizes (e.g. 1 x 40 meters). Allow 1 cavan of seed for each 1,000 square meters of land.

d) For each 40 square meters, add to the soil 100 kilos of compost or animal manure, and 2 to 3 kilos of complete fertilizer.

e) Mix the compost and complete fertilizer thoroughly with the soil on the seedbed, and level the top of the bed before sowing the seeds.

Step 3. Plant the seeds in the seedbed. Before sowing, it is important to put the seeds through a salt solution in order to eradicate seedborne diseases. This will also remove defective and empty seeds which tend to germinate but do not produce

PLANT PRODUCTION

healthy plants.

a) Make a salt solution, using two small evaporated milk cans of common table salt for each kerosene tin of clean water.

b) Transfer the solution to a large container and pour the seeds slowly into the solution, stirring to allow the defective and empty seeds to float. Remove them, and plant only the seeds that have settled to the bottom.

c) After separating out the good seeds, wash them two or three times with clean fresh water until the salt is removed.

d) Place the good seeds in a sack, allowing space for swelling. Soak the sack in fresh water for 12 hours, drain it for 12 hours, then airdry the seeds.

e) Finally, sow the seeds uniformly on the seedbeds at a rate of 1 ganta per bed of 1 x 40 meters. Cover the seeds on the beds with a thin layer of light humus soil, and keep the soil moist.

Step 4. Care for the seedlings. Close care is necessary to ensure the growth of healthy seedlings.

a) Keep the seedbeds free from weeds and moth eggs from the time of sowing to the time of transplanting. While weeding, search for and destroy any moth eggs you may find on the underside of the leaves of the seedlings.

b) Spray the seedlings with a recommended insecticide and/or fungicide for prevention or control of pests and diseases. One week before transplanting, spray again to exterminate all pests.

c) Maintain constant moisture in the seedbeds of the growing plants.

Step 5. Prepare the main field for transplanting. The essential steps are:

a) Immediately after harvest, plow the field to expose the soil to sun and air.

b) After the first rain in May, apply 5 to 10 tons

of manure or compost per hectare, depending on the fertility of the soil. Then plow the field a second time.

c) Repair dikes, making sure all holes and cracks are filled as the paddies are flooded.

d) One week after the second plowing, harrow the flooded paddies to destroy growing weeds and to mix grass with the soil to decay.

e) When the seedlings are ready, paddle the soil thoroughly, removing all weeds or burying them deep in the mud.

f) After paddling, level the paddies and apply 1/3 of the recommended amount of inorganic fertilizer per hectare to hasten the growth of the seedlings after transplanting. The field is now ready.

Step 6. Transplant the seedlings. The best age for transplanting the seedlings depends on their variety and the fertility of the soil; it is usually at 3 to 5 weeks after sowing.

a) Prepare the field for straight-row planting, as directed in "Training Materials on Plant Production," p. 5.

b) Before pulling the rice seedlings, see to it that the soil of the seedbed is well watered. While pulling, take care to avoid breaking or bruising the stems and roots. Wash off the soil with water and remove any weeds found with the seedlings.

c) Plant 3 or 4 seedlings to a hill. The distance between hills depends on the variety being planted and the fertility of the soil. Plant the seedlings erect and in straight lines. Protect the roots while planting. The roots must not be pushed ahead of the fingers; the fingers must dig holes for the roots.

Step 7. Conserve and manage the water supply. Repair all leaks in the dikes, to prevent water from flowing out of the paddy.

a) After transplanting, gradually increase the depth of the water as the crop grows; this will virtu-

PLANT PRODUCTION   121

ally eliminate the growth of weeds if the land has been properly prepared. Yields are usually higher when irrigation water is maintained at a depth of about 15 cm. during the 3-month vegetative period of the crop.

b) Drain off and replenish the water twice before heading time, once before making split application of nitrogen fertilizer. This will ensure most effective use of the fertilizer, and the drainings will also prevent stagnant water which favors stem rot.

c) For uniform grain maturity, and minimum loss from shattering, drain the field again 2 weeks after heading time.

Step 8. Weed the field. Weeding begins 2 weeks after transplanting. If the first weeding is thorough, other weedings will be easy.

a) Remove all weeds, not just most of them, by rotary weeding, handpicking, or chemicals, as described in the training materials. Weeds should be pulled out before they develop extensive roots that will intertwine with the roots of the rice plants.

b) The pulled weeds should be trampled into the mud and buried deep so that, instead of stealing the food of the rice plants, they will become food for the rice. "Volunteers" (plants of a different variety) that would only contaminate the purity of the crop should be treated as weeds.

Step 9. Apply fertilizers correctly. Before suitable recommendations can be made regarding the type of fertilizer to be used, and the intensity of application, it is important to make a composite soil sampling from the field where the fertilizer is to be employed, and have it analyzed. Detailed instructions for this are contained in the training materials.

a) Pull weeds before applying the recommended fertilizer. Drain paddies to about 1 inch of water before broadcasting the fertilizer, to ensure even distribution. Close the dikes so the fertilizer will be retained. Apply the fertilizer in the late afternoon, preferably on a calm and sunny day to minimize leaf burning.

b) If the soil has not been analyzed, proceed with specified standard fertilizers. Follow instructions contained in the training materials.

Step 10. Control pests. Farmers should be helped, if they need it, to identify the common rice plant pests, especially stem borers, rice bugs, army worms, cutworms, leaf rollers, leaf folders, case worms, and migrating locusts. They can also learn about latest methods of pest control at PRRM-sponsored farmers' seminars, and by consulting nearby government or private agriculturalists. Here are a few general pointers:

a) Two weeks after transplanting, spray the rice plants with recommended chemicals to prevent infestation by stem borers and other pests. Repeat this periodically as a preventative measure. When spraying, include the dikes and irrigation canal banks.

b) The grasses on the dikes and canal banks should be uprooted or cut close to the ground to do away with weeds where pests might lay their eggs during the rice plants' early stage of growth.

c) Light traps may be set to catch adult insects that destroy rice plants.

d) Early attacks of pests should be brought under control at once to prevent serious infestation.

e) If other pests, including rats, mice, and several species of birds such as the "mayang pula" become a menace to the rice crop, or to the stored grain after harvest, bring a specialist into the area to discuss with the farmers effective methods of pest control.

Step 11. Control the rice plant diseases. Farmers should have training in identifying the most common diseases of rice, including blast rotten neck, cercospora leaf spot, helminthosporium (brown spot), seedling blight, false or green smut, dwarf or stunt disease, and stem or calm rot. The more effective general methods of disease control are:

a) Rotate crops.

PLANT PRODUCTION   123

b) Use certified seeds, selecting disease-resistant varieties.

c) While the rice is growing, rogue (remove) infected plants and burn them.

d) Keep irrigation water from becoming stagnant.

e) Treat seeds collected with semesan or arasan or other tested chemicals.

Step 12. <u>Harvest when ripe</u>. The principal rules to remember are:

a) Plan the harvesting in a way that will reduce to a minimum the essential processes of handling and transfer. This will help to prevent losses through large amounts of grain dropping to the ground.

b) Harvest the palay when it is fully matured, making sure that panicles are not left in the field uncollected.

Persuading Farmers to Adopt the Masagana System

A farmer who learns and applies the above methods systematically should be able to increase his rice yield by at least ten cavans per hectare per year; under favorable conditions, the increase may be much greater. But before these results can be hoped for, it is necessary to convince farmers to change and modify techniques which they and their forefathers may have used for generations. This is not easy.

PRRM technicians and workers have tried out many approaches; these have been most successful to date:

1. Organize a class for demonstration farmers, to be jointly conducted by RRWs and PRRM technical personnel. Start with farmers you have chosen for their intelligence and willingness to try out new techniques. Carry out the training with a combination of lectures, audio-visual aids, discussions, and practical demonstrations of each step of the Masagana system. The new knowledge and skills which the farmers acquire in this way, and the greater yields they achieve, should enable them to become convincing demonstration farmers in their own right, from whom other rice growers in their villages will gladly

learn.

2. Give the main responsibility for the organization and conduct of the demonstration farmers' class to the rural reconstruction worker (RRW) in each village. He, more than anyone else, knows the farmers in the barrio personally and has won their friendship and confidence through daily association. This personal relationship, in PRRM's experience, is vital to the development of wholehearted cooperation in each barrio.

3. Plan and administer with great care the technical advice, supervision, and support given to each RRW by members of PRRM's Plant Production Department. A carefully scheduled program of field visitations and group conferences enables the technical personnel to keep in constant touch with the RRWs and to give them the technical help they need--through individual consultations and frequent participation in the farmers' classes, demonstration programs, and other activities. The Plant Production Department can also work with the RRWs to help farmers obtain certified seeds, or, if they cannot afford them, to select the best available seeds out of their own crops for use the following year.

4. In barrios where a substantial percentage of the farmers are tenants, seek the cooperation of the landowners. This makes it much easier for the tenants to adopt new practices.

5. Make use, as far as practicable, of additional techniques which RRWs have frequently employed in the past with good results. (a) Organize field trips, for interested farmers, to government seed farms or to nearby barrios where the Masagana system of rice culture is being successfully applied. (b) Organize rice-planting classes among the members of the three people's associations. Women and youth, as well as men, play an important part in the strenuous work of transplanting the seedlings. (c) Conduct planting festivals in the barrios, demonstrating the Masagana techniques. This serves to arouse mass interest in the adoption of better planting practices. (d) Pay frequent visits to the demonstration farmers to make sure they are adhering to the Masagana system.

Recurring Problems

1) <u>Resistance to change</u>. The farmers are often reluctant to embark upon new methods. This makes it difficult for an RRW to organize a meeting to explain the advantages and techniques of the Masagana system.

    <u>Response</u>: To cope with this basic problem, RRWs have used all the approaches outlined above. In addition, they have often found it useful at the outset to invite in a well-known "resource person"--from government service or from public life--whom the farmers would wish to hear, and who can explain in a general way the benefits of the Masagana system. A meeting held for this purpose should be followed up promptly by organizing a farmers' class, seminar, or study group. In the preliminary meeting, as well as follow-up sessions, make full use of the audio-visual aids provided by PRRM.

2) <u>Youthfulness of the RRW</u>. The RRWs frequently find that their youthfulness is a handicap, especially when they are just beginning their work in a barrio. The farmers may not take their advice seriously, and may even treat it as a joke, believing that the young person advising them has not had the experience they themselves have had.

    <u>Response</u>: The RRW must realize with good humor that this reaction is natural, and that the farmers' respect for him will surely grow after a period of deeper acquaintanceship and testing. Since this takes time, it may be necessary in the early stages to rely more heavily on assistance from senior PRRM personnel, and also on other "resource persons" of the type mentioned above. The fact that the RRW is instrumental in bringing in such respected persons gives him an advantage in promoting follow-up activities.

3) <u>Difficulties and cost of the Masagana system</u>. Farmers may hesitate because the Masagana system consumes more time and labor than traditional methods, and is therefore more costly.

    <u>Response</u>: Organize a trip to one or more demonstration farms where the Masagana system is being used, where the farmers can see for themselves

how much yields can be increased by using the newer techniques. This may be followed by a detailed explanation, showing how the increased production more than compensates for the extra time and labor expended.

4) <u>Fear of failure</u>. In many cases the livelihood of the farmers' family depends on his rice crop. He cannot afford to take chances by adopting new-fangled methods that may not succeed.

    <u>Response</u>: Explain quietly that risks under the old system are the same as under the new, and that each of the changes recommended has been thoroughly tested. Failure will come only if the cultivator does not understand the new system. If the new techniques are used correctly, then, barring some natural calamity, the crop will not fail, but will be better than before.

5) <u>The part-time farmer</u>. Some farmers work only part-time at their farming, and engage on the side in some unrelated pursuits. This is usually due to the insufficient income derived from their low rice yields.

    <u>Response</u>: Show the farmer how he can increase his rice production--and his income--by using the Masagana system. If this is not an adequate answer to his problem, and if he needs additional supplementary income, encourage him to engage in swine or poultry raising, or put him in touch with PRRM personnel who can teach him a profitable handicraft such as mat or basket weaving.

6) <u>Need for skilled workers</u>. Landowners using hired labor may hesitate because the Masagana system requires skilled planters who demand high rates of pay.

    <u>Response</u>: Train members of the youth associations who, in turn, can train other farmers and family members in the newer techniques. This will tend to reduce the exorbitant rates that may prevail when only a few know the better methods, and increase the incomes of those who use the new methods, on their own land or that of others. Smaller landowners can often reduce their cash outlays by participating in <u>bayanihan</u>, or cooperative labor on each other's land.

7) <u>Lack of water</u>. Many farmers have no irrigation facilities and therefore produce rice only in the rainy season.

   <u>Response</u>: Advise them to cultivate only varieties that mature early, so they can be planted at the start of the rainy season and harvested before the drought begins. When this is done, there is nothing to prevent use of the Masagana system.

8) <u>Lack of capital</u>. A farmer may lack the capital required for certified seeds, fertilizers, and skilled labor.

   <u>Response</u>: Encourage him to engage in the production of secondary cash crops, as well as poultry and swine. Explain that this will increase his earnings and produce capital which he can apply to improving his rice production. Encourage him to engage in green manuring and the use of composts as a means of reducing the chemical fertilizers required. And urge him to join the local credit union, if there is one, as a means toward meeting his future needs for investment capital.

EXPANDING THE PRODUCTION OF SECONDARY CROPS

A farmer benefits in many ways from the production of secondary crops. He reduces his dependence on a single crop. He is able to increase his income and to have it distributed more evenly through the year. His land is better utilized. His family is better fed. The fertility of his soil is not only maintained; it can be improved, especially if he uses a legume as a secondary crop. The new harvest may provide one or more useful by-products such as animal feeds, fuels, and fencing materials. If the farmer hires extra help in producing the new crop, underemployment in the barrio is reduced.

PRRM experience indicates that once a farmer has successfully produced a well-chosen secondary crop, he will almost certainly continue to do so from year to year.

Cropping Patterns

A wise selection of secondary crops takes into

account soil, climate, and market demands. Each item grown should be part of a total cropping pattern that, even as it uses an area of land more fully, also provides for a replenishment of nutrients in the soil.

Many patterns have been tried out under the PRRM program, with varying degrees of success. One that has worked well on irrigated lowlands, where rice is the main crop, calls for onions in December and January, legumes for green manure as well as food in the spring months, an early variety of rice that is transplanted in July, and sitao or mungo among the dikes in September and October.

A pattern well-adapted to ricefield land that is only rain-fed includes tomatoes, eggplants, melons, or tobacco in the winter months; corn in February; mungo in the spring; and sitao or mungo again, along the dikes, in September and October.

An upland pattern that has proven satisfactory calls for tomatoes, eggplants, beans (any of several varieties), cassava or tobacco in the winter; corn in February; squash in March; peanuts, mungo, or soybean bush sitao in April, May, and June; and, instead of rice, corn and soybeans, intercropped, beginning in July.

A special pattern, tried out successfully on sandy tumanal land or bakood, includes pechay, cauliflower, cabbage, or radishes, with frequent cultivation, watering and fertilizing, and diligent pest control, in November and December; tomatoes in February; legumes for marketing or green manure in the spring; and, beginning in July, sugar cane, corn, gabi, eggplants, or tomatoes.

These are merely illustrative patterns. Secondary crops that have been tried out successfully, within suitable year-round crop patterns, include several types of peas and beans, and a number of vine crops such as ampalaya, cucumbers, squash, patola, and upo.

A special secondary crop is the mushroom, produced by techniques developed in The Agricultural College of the University of the Philippines and Central Luzon State University. It has turned out to be an exceptionally satisfactory crop, for several rea-

PLANT PRODUCTION   129

sons. It is grown in layers of straw beds, utilizing local waste materials and requiring little capital and small space. It can be grown month after month without having to be fitted into a year-round crop pattern. Spawns in sufficient quantity are readily available. Production techniques are fairly easily learned. And, entering into export as well as local markets, the crop normally yields a good profit. Detailed instructions for cultivating mushrooms and other leading secondary crops are contained in the PRRM training materials on plant production.

Before trying to advise farmers on the selection and planning of their crop patterns, or on the cultivation of specific secondary crops, the RRW should review carefully the relevant sections of training materials and seek, when needed, the counsel of technical personnel in the Plant Production Department.

Basic and Special Practices

Basic practices applicable to the production of virtually all secondary crops should be constantly borne in mind. (a) Select and use high-yielding seeds of good quality. (b) Prepare the land thoroughly, with 2 to 3 plowings and harrowings. (c) Carry out proper cultivation and weeding. (d) Use fertilizers correctly. (e) Be diligent in controlling pests and diseases.

In addition, special practices cited in the training materials must be mastered and followed in connection with crop rotation, green manuring, planting off-season crops, intercropping, and converting barren to productive land.

How to Introduce a New Secondary Crop

Experience of the RRWs has shown that these procedures are usually effective in introducing new secondary crops:

1. Conduct experiments in the barrio plant nursery before discussing new crops in detail with the farmers. Select crops for which there is a known demand. After verifying the adaptability of a given crop to the climate and soil of the locality, start arousing the farmers' interest in it.

2. With the assistance of technical personnel

from the Plant Production Department, set up and conduct a farmers' seminar, class, or study group to learn about the new crop and how it is produced, and to discuss its advantages in terms of food, supplementary income, and the restoring and maintaining of soil fertility.

3. Select a few of the most interested farmers and ask if they will undertake, with technical help, the cultivation of the new secondary crop. This will prepare them to serve as demonstrators to other farmers of how the crop is produced, and the benefits to be derived from its production.

4. Distribute to the farmers reading materials about the new crop, in the vernacular if possible.

5. During home and farm visits, explain further to the farmers and their families the advantages of the new crop.

6. Once the idea is accepted, and the crop has been started on a number of farms, provide technical advice as well as assistance in the field, to help ensure good results.

Recurring Problems

Among many problems the RRWs have encountered in connection with secondary crops, these are the most common:

1) No irrigation system in many barrios. This makes it difficult to introduce a new secondary crop, especially during the dry season.

Response: (a) Advise and assist the farmers in digging open wells or, if they can afford them, pump wells, and in using this new source to water their secondary crops. (b) Alternatively, if there is a creek, brook, swamp, or lake nearby, suggest that they obtain water from that source. (c) If there is an irrigation system in the vicinity, encourage the barrio council to request the assistance of the appropriate government agency in obtaining an extension of the system to their barrio. The RRW may be able to assist in preparing or presenting such a request. (d) If the water supply cannot be increased by these means, consult PRRM plant production personnel

PLANT PRODUCTION   131

>   about the feasibility of introducing secondary
>   crops requiring a minimum of moisture.

2)   Lack of technical knowledge. Sometimes neither
     the RRW nor the farmer has sufficient technical
     know-how.

   Response: Seize the first opportunity to participate in special in-service training in the production of major secondary crops, given periodically by PRRM. Afterwards, conduct a special farmers' seminar or study group, with the assistance of PRRM technical personnel, in order to discuss with the cultivators the kinds of secondary crops they could grow, when and how they could be grown, and the economic advantages that would follow. During the seminar, make full use of available audio-visual aids, and distribute available reading materials on the crops that have been discussed.

   Then select a few members of the seminar, preferably from among those who are already demonstration farmers. Persuade them to plant the selected secondary crops, and to show their results to other farmers. Special incentives are frequently introduced with good results by awarding prizes to the farmers who produce the best secondary crops, and to those who show exceptional leadership in promoting their production.

3)   Lack of interest. The farmers of a barrio may
     not be particularly interested in producing a
     secondary crop. This may be due to customary idleness during certain seasons, or to unawareness of the benefits to be gained, or to innate conservatism and fear of failure.

   Response: Visit the farmers at their homes and talk casually with them and their families about one or more well-tested crops, emphasizing without exaggeration the benefits they can bring. Then organize a visit to another barrio where farmers from your barrio can see the new crop being grown successfully. If the response is favorable, then, as suggested above, set up a special study group or seminar to learn all about the production and advantages of the new crop.

4) <u>Inability to invest</u>. Some farmers lack the small amount of seeds or other capital needed to start producing the new crop.

   <u>Response</u>: Urge those who are interested to join the local credit union, or to organize one with PRRM assistance. These unions are becoming an increasingly important source of small capital loans. Also, encourage the farmers to raise pigs or poultry from which they can derive additional income and capital. If the necessary seeds are lacking, seek the help of the Bureau of Plant Industry, provincial nurseries or seed farms, or private agencies. Seeds from these sources may be bought or obtained by donation, then made available to the farmers at cost, or free.

5) <u>Plant pests and diseases</u>, which are frequently a menace to the new crop.

   <u>Response</u>: With the assistance of PRRM's Plant Production Department, seek the help of the government's Bureau of Plant Industry in eradicating or controlling the threatening pests or diseases. Demonstrate to the farmers the use of insecticides or pesticides that will help to protect their secondary crops, consulting PRRM specialists if necessary on the selection of chemicals to be used.

6) <u>Flooding</u>. Much of the cultivable land around low-lying barrios is subject to periodic flooding.

   <u>Response</u>: Select the available areas of higher elevation, and encourage the production of the new secondary crops in these areas.

7) <u>Theft</u>. Law and order may not be adequately maintained in the barrio, and crops and animals may be stolen. This tends to discourage the production of secondary crops.

   <u>Response</u>: Meet with the members of the barrio council and urge them to provide, if they can, the means of restoring law and order in the barrio. If they cannot cope with the situation, advise them to make representations to their municipal council and, if necessary, to provincial officials, requesting their help. These authori-

ties may assign extra police, or pass an ordinance requiring curfew hours until stability is restored.

STIMULATING HOMELOT GARDENING

Many farm families suffer from malnutrition and poor health because they do not understand the importance of a balanced diet, or do not realize it is within their power to produce such a diet for themselves. They can often do so by utilizing the traditionally wasted land around their own homes for the production of nourishing, vitamin-rich vegetables and fruits for table use. At the same time, they can grow flowers that will beautify their home surroundings and enhance their families' self-respect and enjoyment of life.

Most of the farm families in the Philippines have around their houses sufficient land for at least a small, well-developed homelot garden to meet these needs. The encouragement of homelot gardening was one of the first means tried out by the PRRM to improve the well-being of farm families. It has proved widely beneficial to health, and to the cleanliness and beauty of village life. It has also provided a welcome source of additional income for many poor families, who can sell the vegetables and fruits they grow in excess of their own pressing needs.

General Pointers

1. Before starting a homelot garden, plan suitable locations for the various types of vegetables, fruits, and ornamental plants to be grown. Locate the vegetable garden near the house for convenience in tending, and to make it easy to gather vegetables, as needed, for cooking.

2. As far as possible, plant crops that will utilize the land the year around, using a rotation that will maintain soil fertility. As a rule, group together vegetables which are planted at about the same time, and mature at the same time. Detailed information and instructions pertaining to the planting and cultivation of numerous types of vegetables, fruits, and flowers are contained in the PRRM training materials on plant production. When in doubt on any question, consult PRRM specialists or nearby gov-

ernment technical personnel.

3. Always have a compost pit, conveniently located, to ensure a good supply of compost ready for use as needed.

Some Good Practices

1. Fence in the homelot garden, to keep it clean and protect it from roving livestock. Living plants like kaukauati, ipil-ipil, katuray, and malungay are economical and readily available, and they make good fencing. Katuray and malungay may also be sources of nutrition and income for the family, and these living plants may be helpful as windbreaks. When it is more convenient, use bamboo or other materials for fencing.

2. Composting is a "must." Instructions are given later in this chapter on how to pile garden and animal waste into a pit and let it decompose. The resultant compost, when used, adds fertility to the soil. It is especially high in nitrogen, which is widely recommended for vegetable gardens.

3. Encourage frequent weeding, to protect the growing plants from the pests and diseases that harbor in weeds, and to safeguard the soil nutrients needed by the growing crops.

4. Encourage frequent cultivation as well. This is important, since the loosening of earth near the base of the plants permits needed aeration of the soil.

5. Stress the importance of controlling pests and diseases by the standard methods described in the training materials.

Selection of Plants

Farm families now have a wide choice of well-tested varieties of plants suitable for homelot gardening. When asked for advice on types of vegetables and fruits to be grown, suggest only varieties that are of proven adaptability and hardiness in the locality, and types that are not too difficult to cultivate. Bear in mind also probable returns in food value, and perhaps in cash income. Recommend for consideration flowers or other ornamental plants that

PLANT PRODUCTION   135

are not only attractive to the senses, but also resistant to drought, pests, and diseases.

DEVELOPING EXTENSION FARMS AND PLANT NURSERIES

One of PRRM's principal aims is to help farmers "reforest" their land with improved plants, and to produce those plants in a scientific manner. How is this being done?

The government has provincial plant nurseries located, usually, in or near the provincial capitals. A farmer in need of improved seeds or seedlings may not have the time or money to go to these centers, which are likely to be far from his home. Even if he does go, he may not be able to learn all he needs to know about the scientific production of the new or improved crop he is planning to grow, or whether it is a suitable choice for his locality.

Therefore, if the barrios aided by PRRM are to be "reforested" with improved plants, and the farmers are to be exposed to scientific methods of agriculture, plant nurseries must be located where they are most needed--right in the barrios.

To meet this problem, PRRM has evolved and is developing a modest network of extension farms and plant nurseries. The extension farm is usually located in a central barrio of a municipality. Linked with the extension farm, PRRM aims to have an efficiently run, up-to-date plant nursery in every barrio it is helping.

The Extension Farm

Each extension farm is operated by farmers of the barrio in which it is located, with the active guidance and assistance of PRRM personnel. Its purposes are: (a) as an experiment station, to test _locally_ the applicability of scientific findings of research and technical institutions; (b) as a plant nursery, to make available to surrounding nurseries, as well as to farm families in the barrio, high-quality seeds and other planting materials for vegetables, fruit trees, ornamental plants, and, to some extent, field crops (if other good sources are not readily available); (c) as a demonstration station, to show how new or improved crops should be grown;

and (d) as a training station, to serve new PRRM workers, local farmers, and other interested parties.

The resident rural reconstruction worker assists the barrio council in obtaining land for the extension farm. If possible, it is acquired from one or a group of larger landowners on a rent-free basis. Otherwise it is rented for a period of five years, renewable for another five years. If the land is rented, responsibility for payment is normally assumed by the barrio council or the Rural Reconstruction Men's Association (RRMA).

Criteria now observed as far as possible in selecting sites for extension farms are: (a) It shall be centrally located. (b) It shall have an area of at least 1,000 square meters. (c) The terrain shall be reasonably level. (d) The soil shall be fertile and well drained. (e) The water supply shall be steady and sufficient.

General management of the extension farm is normally the responsibility of the committee on livelihood of the barrio council. The councilman on livelihood serves as chairman, and the chairmen on livelihood of the three peoples' associations as members. The actual establishment and operation of the extension farm is undertaken by the resident RRW and interested farmers, with technical support from the Plant Production Department of PRRM.

The Plant Nursery

A barrio plant nursery is like an extension farm except that is is smaller and has more limited objectives. Each plant nursery aims (a) to produce throughout the year a sufficient supply of high-quality planting materials for all homelots in the barrio and, to some extent, for farmlots as well; (b) to maintain a seed bank (discussed below) for quality seeds to be stored, propagated, and distributed to the homelots and farmlots as needed; and (c) to be a demonstration and training center for the people of the barrio. Criteria followed in selecting a site for a barrio plant nursery are similar to those descibed above for an extension farm, except that the nursery can be considerably smaller, with a minimum area of 200 square meters.

PLANT PRODUCTION 137

Promotional Methods and Procedures

The involvement of the barrio people in the development of a good plant nursery requires a great deal of attention and effort on the part of the RRW. The following approaches, evolved through a long period of trial and error, have produced positive results:

   1. At the start, present to a responsible group in the village the idea of developing a plant nursery to serve the needs of their barrio. An appropriate group is the committee on livelihood of the barrio council, together with selected representatives of the three people's associations (RRMA, RRWA, and RRYA). Explain fully what a plant nursery is and how it can be established. Then ask for questions and a full discussion. If the presentation is made clearly and questions are answered satisfactorily, there is likely to be an agreement, at the end of one or two meetings, to establish a plant nursery.

   2. Seek the help of the barrio council as a whole, and of teachers and other influential leaders, in winning understanding and support for the project. This is necessary in order to ensure wide participation in the work and benefits of the nursery.

   3. Work with the barrio leaders concerned in acquiring the use of a plot of land for the nursery--either rent-free, if one or more larger landowners can be persuaded to make it available on that basis, or at a reasonable rental for a five-year period, subject to renewal. Note that the amount of land needed (200 square meters or more) is not large. A definite understanding must be reached as to what group will assume responsibility for rental payments.

   4. After this preliminary work is accomplished, join the interested village leaders in summoning members of the three people's associations to special meetings in order to acquaint them fully with the project. Enlist their cooperation in developing and observing and using the new nursery. When it is clear that some of the officers and members of each association have become genuinely interested, ask them to take responsibility for specific aspects of the development and maintenance of the nursery. It is important that leadership acceptable to the group should be assigned for each task. The RRW should

then work closely with the leaders, especially in the early stages, to make sure that each task is well understood and fully performed.

5. To promote widening participation, organize at an appropriate time a general meeting of the people of the barrio. Discuss there the need for the plant nursery, the advantages it will bring, and the desirability of wide cooperation in developing, using, and maintaining it. In promoting and conducting the meeting, enlist the cooperation of the barrio captain, the barrio council, and the officers and members of the three people's associations.

6. After the nursery is well started, make sure that it continues to meet the real needs of the people. This means it must provide seeds and other planting materials, as well as information and demonstrations relating to the cultivation of new garden and other crops. Demonstrations of familiar crops, with the use of improved seeds and cultivating practices, may be especially effective if the demonstration plots are located beside plots on which the same types of crops are grown by traditional methods. When practicable, it is also desirable for demonstration plots to be near a road or a frequented path where people can see them as they pass by.

7. In due course, take advantage of general meetings in the barrio to sustain interest in the plant nursery. See that information is well presented on the progress of the nursery and the ways in which it is being used by members of the community.

If these steps are taken, there is every likelihood that the plant nursery will become one of the most valued projects undertaken in the barrio.

Recurring Problems

1) Reluctance to accept responsibility for the promotion or management of the nursery.

   Response: Talk individually with a few of the natural leaders in the barrio. Be sure they understand the project and what it could mean to future production and living standards. Then try to persuade them that the nursery can only be a success if they will assume a share of responsibility for it, and encourage others to do the same. Assure them that PRRM will give them both moral and technical backing. Then, at general meetings, encourage the people to support those who are assuming responsibility for the nursery.

2) **Lack of time**. People may say they do not have time to take up such a new activity. This is most frequently heard during the busier farm seasons.

   Response: Promote the establishment of the nursery during periods when the people are not so busy with their farm operations.

3) **Indifference**, even after the promotional efforts cited above.

   Response: Organize one or more field trips to other barrios where progressive plant nurseries are already in operation. When the less interested farmers see for themselves the benefits derived by the people in these barrios from the planting materials, demonstrations, and training provided through their plant nurseries, their indifference tends gradually to disappear. Follow up these visits by talks with the farmers in their own homes, to encourage their new interest.

4) **Social cleavages**. Families belonging to different political or religious organizations may not like to work together, particularly in community projects.

   Response: In individual homes of leaders in the barrio, explain the importance of village-wide cooperation in the development of the four-fold program, in which the plant nursery is one key project. Many village leaders are fully capable of understanding that such cooperation is essential to enable the barrio to move forward into the modern world. Explain also that PRRM, in its effort to assist the barrio, is a purely civic organization, favoring no political party or religious organization or racial group; its only aim is to help all the people. Emphasize the fact that without everyone's cooperation, community improvement projects like the plant nursery will be seriously handicapped.

5) <u>Insufficient water supply</u>, which may make it difficult to establish a plant nursery.

<u>Response</u>: At first, select for the nursery plants known to be drought-resistant or to require only limited amounts of water. Then suggest to the barrio captain and the members of the barrio council that they seek the assistance of government officials in securing, if possible, an extension to their barrio of canals connecting with an existing irrigation system. If this is not feasible, it may be possible to increase the supply by digging or drilling wells, with the technical help of PRRM engineers.

6) <u>Desire for pay</u>. Some of the people may expect monetary rewards for services rendered to the community.

<u>Response</u>: Explain to them that the project will redound to their own benefit, and that the only way in which it can be developed is through the active, voluntary cooperation of the people. It is they who must see that the nursery is properly maintained, and that its services are diffused throughout the barrio. Make it clear that PRRM has only very limited resources and can be of lasting assistance only to those who are determined to help themselves. One of the best ways for them to do this is to increase their production and their incomes. The plant nursery is designed to help them do just that.

A SEED BANK IN EVERY BARRIO

One of the chronic problems faced by farm families year after year is how to obtain seeds, cuttings, and other planting materials of high quality for the propagation of vegetables, fruits, and other products. The practice of securing seeds from the few who are far-sighted enough to keep more than they need for themselves has developed in many farmers a bad habit of unconcern about their own future requirements.

Basic Procedures

The basic procedures for producing superior seeds, and for processing and storing them, are fairly simple.

1. To produce good seeds, employ the same cultural processes as in producing good crops, with special attention to these additional points: (a) When desirable, use first generation hybrid seeds, but avoid seeds produced from hybrid seeds. (b) Harvest only the matured plants or fruits. (c) Harvest legumes, such as beans, patani, or mungo, during the cooler periods of the day to avoid the snapping of the pods and consequent waste of seeds.

2. In processing seeds, observe these practices: (a) For dry seeds--like batao, beans, corn, lettuce, patola, and patani--place the harvested pods or seed clusters in a warm, airy place. When the outsides are dry, free the seeds and continue drying. (b) For the seeds enclosed in moist flesh--like eggplant, squash, ampalaya, watermelon, sweet pepper, and upo--crush, squeeze, or break up the fruits in a vessel of water. The seeds will separate easily from the flesh. Spread them out on absorbent papers, like newspapers, to dry. (c) For wet seeds with flesh attached to them--like tomatoes, cucumbers, and muskmelons--crush or squeeze the seeds from the fruit. The flesh rots away from the seeds in 24 to 48 hours of soaking. Do not let the seeds stand in the water more than two days. Then dry them as in (b), above.

3. In storing seeds, these procedures are basic: (a) Protect them from insects. A simple method is to mix them with a small amount of 50 per cent DDT powder and shake in a closed container. Then, if the seeds are small, like pechay, put them into paper packets. (b) Store the seeds in sealed containers. An easy method is to get a glass jar (preferably a mason jar) with a tight-fitting lid. Fill it one-fourth full with a moisture absorbent such as newly crushed wood charcoal, or ashes, or calcium chloride, a chemical available in drugstores. Put a cardboard floor just above the absorbent, then lay the seed packets or loose seeds on top of the partition. Close the jar tightly and store it in the coolest place available. Seeds properly stored at room temperature will keep for a year or more. (c) After taking out any of the seeds for planting, close the jar immediately to protect the remaining seeds from moisture. (d) When seeds have been stored for six months or more, test their germinating capacity before using them. About two weeks before planting

time, sow 25 to 100 seeds of each variety in a box of good soil, and count how many come up; 65 per cent is considered a fair germination.

The Seed Bank Project

After trying several ways to help farmers meet their recurring need for planting materials, PRRM decided to experiment with the development of a "seed bank" for each barrio, run in conjunction with the plant nursery program and in cooperation with the PRRM extension farms.

A seed bank is a place where the collection, treatment, storage, and distribution of high-quality seeds and other planting materials can be performed in a convenient manner, at no extra expense to the barrio people. It supplements and complements seed production and storage by individual farmers. Only seeds of known varieties, quality, age, and viability are kept and dispensed to the farmers.

Advantages. The principal advantages of having a well-run seed bank in the barrio are: (a) It provides, near at hand, a ready supply of a wide variety of good seeds and other planting materials; since the project is managed by the farmers themselves as a community service, it involves no extra expense to the people. (b) As the project is developed, farmers are trained in scientific, practical methods of seed collection, treatment, and storage. They are also taught how to select the better-quality seeds for immediate propagation or storage and, later, for wide distribution among the farmers. These skills are not difficult to learn. (c) A program of seed exchanges between PRRM extension farms and plant nurseries can be carried out easily, in a manner designed to make the best use of available supplies. (d) Seed bank records provide a convenient way to keep track of improved or new varieties of crops introduced into the barrio. (d) The seed bank project as a whole is simple, economical, practical, and duplicable.

Implementation. In developing the seed bank project, RRWs have experimented with numerous approaches; these have proven most effective to date:

1. Learn what planting materials are already available in the barrio, and the types of plants that the farm families prefer to cultivate on their home-

PLANT PRODUCTION

lots, as well as on their farmlots.

2. Consult the barrio captain, members of the barrio council, and leaders of the three people's associations about a convenient location for the seed bank. In this way, it is possible to share with the barrio leaders, from the outset, the responsibility of establishing and maintaining it. In absence of a more suitable place, a part of the plant nursery or a corner of the barrio hall or health center may be used.

3. With the assistance of technical personnel of the PRRM Plant Production Department, teach and demonstrate in farmers' classes how seeds can best be selected and then stored, with proper protection from pests and plant diseases. During the demonstrations, discuss how a good seed bank benefits the entire farming community.

4. Distribute literature, preferably in the vernacular, on the importance of high-quality seeds.

5. Make personal visits to farm families in different parts of the village, and explain the benefits they would derive from having a good seed bank right in the barrio.

6. When it seems that sufficient interest has been generated, start on the project itself, in cooperation with a small group of farmers--preferably demonstration farmers. Some seeds that are relatively easy to produce, harvest, and store are the following: ampalaya, batao, cucumber, eggplant, kondol, kulitis, okra, muskmelon, mustard, patani, patola, pepper, seguidillas, sitao, snap beans, squash, sweet corn, and upo. Get each member in the initial working group to agree to take a specific responsibility in the development and operation of the seed bank.

7. To sustain interest and foster continuing improvement, organize one or more trips to other barrios in which seed banks are functioning effectively.

8. Promote programs for exchanges of seeds and other planting materials. What the farmers of one barrio do not have in their own seed bank may then be obtained from farmers of other barrios who have supplies in excess of their needs, and vice versa. Such exchanges increase the chances that farmers in each

PRRM-assisted barrio will have available the high-quality seeds and planting materials they most need.

9. When practicable, arrange to obtain from nearby governmental or other experimental farms and distributing centers additional seeds and planting materials that may be used to extend or replenish the supplies in the barrio seed bank.

Recurring Problems

The RRWs have encountered many problems in enlisting the farmers' support for the seed banks. These are the most common ones, with the solutions that have been found most effective so far:

1) <u>Little interest at first</u>. This may be because the farmers do not comprehend the benefits which they and their families can derive from a barrio seed bank, or because they are not accustomed to participating in this kind of community enterprise.

   <u>Response</u>: With the help of technical personnel from the Plant Production Department of PRRM, conduct meetings with farmers of the barrio, and explain to them the workings and advantages of a good seed bank. Demonstrations during these meetings of how to select and preserve seeds will convince the farmers of the practicality of the project. Then start a seed bank with a few farmers, enlisting especially the cooperation of the demonstration farmers; this will generate further interest. Take advantage of the increased interest by organizing field trips to nearby barrios or agricultural centers where successful seed selection and storage operations are underway. Finally, make friendly visits to families that seem indifferent. Try to persuade them by explaining the benefits to be derived from selection and storage of good seeds, and cite other farmers who are already active in the development and maintenance of their barrio seed bank.

2) <u>Location</u>. It may be difficult to find a suitable place for the seed bank.

   <u>Response</u>: A corner of the plant nursery or of the barrio hall may be adequate. If these are not available, try persuading your landlord or

PLANT PRODUCTION   145

another leader in the village to provide temporarily a small space at his residence or homelot. This will make it possible to demonstrate to other farmers how a seed bank is developed and how it functions. Then, among those who become most interested, explore the question of a suitable permanent location. If necessary, seek the assistance of the barrio captain and members of the barrio council, especially the chairman of the livelihood committee, in persuading these farmers to provide a satisfactory place where the seed bank can be established.

3) <u>Lack of containers and chemicals</u> for seed storage and preservation.

Response: Enlist wide cooperation in collecting empty cans and bottles. Members of the youth association (RRYA) can gather them directly, school teachers can ask their pupils to bring them in, and members of the barrio council can ask families to supply them. For seed preservation, cheaper materials will generally suffice. Demonstrate the use of charcoal, ashes, and naphthaline balls for the preservation of seeds. This may save the farmers the necessity of buying expensive chemicals.

4) <u>Lack of high-quality seeds, cuttings, and other planting materials.</u>

Response: (a) Cooperate with barrio leaders in requesting seeds and other planting materials from national and provincial government agencies, including provincial nurseries. Use these as basic stock. (b) Enlist the cooperation of officers and members of the youth association in collecting good-quality seeds for the seed bank from the farmers in the barrio and in neighboring barrios. Repeat this, whenever necessary, to replenish the seed bank. (c) Teach families in the barrio how to preserve, for future use, seeds they have bought in the market; this will lessen the demand on seed bank supplies.

5) <u>Lack of knowledge</u>. The farmers usually do not know how to select and store seeds. For many, it is a new activity.

Response: (a) Demonstrate, during farmers'

classes and seminars, how to select seeds and how to store them properly. (b) Distribute reading materials on seed selection and storage. (c) Organize field trips to other barrios or agricultural schools or nurseries at times when seed selection and storage are actually taking place. The farmers can learn much by observing and asking questions during these visits. (d) During talks with farm families, discuss as a subject of lively interest the best methods of seed selection and preservation.

6) <u>RRW's limited knowledge</u>. The RRW himself may not have sufficient knowledge of the techniques of seed selection and preservation.

   <u>Response</u>: Seize the first opportunity to participate in in-service training provided periodically by PRRM in this and related subjects. Participate in field trips to agricultural institutions where proper seed selection and storage are being performed. And seek extra guidance, as needed, from PRRM technical personnel until the main techniques are thoroughly mastered.

7) <u>Drought or excessive rainfall</u>. During droughts, few or no good seeds can be collected. When there is too much rain, the water destroys both plants and seeds.

   <u>Response</u>: After consultations, if necessary, with PRRM technical personnel, advise the farmers to plant only the types of crops that are well-adapted to the soil and the climatic conditions of the barrio. And after learning as much as possible about the climate of the area, advise the farmers about starting specific garden plots or main crops at times considered most favorable for their successful production.

8) <u>Consumption of the best seeds</u>. Farm families often eat the best seeds they produce, instead of saving and storing them. This is especially true of rice.

   <u>Response</u>: During farmers' classes and seminars, emphasize repeatedly the advantages of selecting and preserving good seeds. Point out that if the best seeds are multiplied, the increased production and income will enable the farm families not

PLANT PRODUCTION

only to eat better, but also to buy more supplementary foods and other necessities.

COMPOSTING

Most Filipino farmers are now convinced that fertilizers do supplement plant nutrients in the soil and improve crop yields. But many are discouraged by the limited supply and high cost of most chemical fertilizers. They often do not realize that they can produce a good substitute in the form of organic fertilizer. This is done by composting.

A compost pile is a collection of organic fertilizer produced by dumping together dried leaves, animal dung, rice straw, soil, and water into a pit. After a period of decomposing, the contents of the pit contain in organic form the food elements needed by a growing plant. The PRRM has included composting in its program so that farmers may learn to convert farm wastes into good fertilizer, thus increasing their production through use of a simple, inexpensive method.

Other benefits of composting are that it improves health conditions by providing a sanitary, as well as productive, method of garbage disposal; it thereby reduces the breeding places of flies, mosquitoes, and other germ carriers. And it enhances the farm family's self-reliance and civic responsibility. For all these reasons, composting is strongly encouraged.

Newer Composting Methods

The old method of making compost fertilizer was to pile up on the ground alternating layers of plant wastes, animal wastes, ashes, and lime until the pit was about 1-1/2 meters (5 feet) high, with the same width and length. In about three months, this pile would shrink to about a tenth of its original size, and would change into a mass of rich inorganic fertilizer for garden, planting bed, or field.

By newer methods, it is possible to convert the compost into superior fertilizer in three weeks instead of three months. The process may be summed up as follows:

1. Mix plenty of animal manure and household garbage with the leaves and straw; this will add more nitrogen. Pig, chicken, caribou, horse, and goat manure are all rich fertilizers. The best compost mixture is about 30 parts of carbon (from garden and plant wastes) to 1 part of nitrogen (from manures). However, it is better to have too much animal manure than not enough. If there is insufficient animal manure and garbage, add, if possible, commercial fertilizer containing nitrogen to the compost. This will speed the composting process, will make the artificial fertilizer easier for the plants to digest, and prevent the nitrogen from evaporating or being washed away by the rain. Chop the mixture into small pieces about 3 to 5 inches long, to speed the rotting process.

2. Turn the compost pile every few days. Without this, there will be over-heating at the center, over-drying, and a bad smell. For testing, push a bamboo stick to the center of the pile and, after three minutes, pull it out again. If it is quite hot, or is dry, or smells bad, turn the pile, rotating the materials from outside to inside.

3. Keep the compost pile moist (like a wrung-out rag), but not wet. This can be done by sprinkling enough water on the pile each time it is turned.

Promotional Techniques

The techniques which have been found most effective in promoting the practice of composting are similar to those previously discussed: full explanation of processes and advantages during farmers' classes and seminars, practical demonstrations, distribution of illustrated literature describing the principal techniques, and visits to other farms or barrios where the use of good composts has resulted in bigger and better crops.

In addition, many RRWs have stimulated improved composting indirectly by encouraging the people in their barrios to engage in mushroom growing and in poultry and swine-raising. These projects provide by-products such as used straw and chicken and swine manure, all excellent materials for making compost.

To popularize the process, some RRWs have also enlisted the cooperation of barrio school teachers,

PLANT PRODUCTION   149

by asking them to require their pupils to make small compost piles and use them to fertilize their little school garden plots. The good results are unfailingly reported by the children to their parents. The parents, in turn, are encouraged to make more and better use of composting.

Recurring Problems

1) <u>Doubt whether it is worth the effort needed.</u> Good composting requires considerable labor and attention which farmers may feel could be better devoted to the actual production of crops.

   <u>Response</u>: The basic answer to this problem, of course, is to provide convincing evidence, through demonstration and visits, of how better yields are obtained when composting is used. RRWs have also found that when the project is being initiated, further incentive can be generated by offering prizes or certificates of merit to farmers who achieve outstanding results from the application of compost to their garden or field crops.

2) <u>Time required to show results.</u> Composts are slower in taking effect than commercial fertilizers.

   <u>Response</u>: Explain that, while this is true, it is also true that the effect of composts upon the soil is more lasting. In addition, composts provide bacteria that hasten the decomposition of weeds, rice straws, and grasses in the fields.

MAKING FARMERS' CLASSES EFFECTIVE

As indicated in the foregoing sections, one of the most basic means used by PRRM to disseminate scientific information and technology is the farmers' class--sometimes called a seminar if the emphasis is on discussion, or a study group if the emphasis is on reading followed by discussion.

Ably conducted, the farmers' classes, seminars, and study groups may have lasting effects not only on the techniques they employ, but also on their outlooks and ways of thinking and acting. As learning progresses, superstition and fatalism tend gradually to give way to a more scientific attitude, and a more hopeful view of the future. The farmer gains a truer understanding of what he is doing, and a greater readiness to change his methods in order to achieve higher production and better living standards for his family. He also acquires, almost unconsciously, a greater willingness to cooperate with his neighbors in activities that will benefit the community. For all these reasons, PRRM lays great emphasis on efforts to make the farmers' classes effective.

Methods and Procedures

1. Far in advance of the actual organization and conduct of the farmers' classes, plan with great care the subjects to be covered, the timing of the classes in relation to the farm year, and the preparation of teaching materials. This preparatory work is a responsibility, chiefly, of the technical personnel of PRRM's Plant and Animal Production Departments. It is their task to help simplify and humanize the scientific concepts and the technical know-how to be conveyed to the farmers, and to prepare the teaching materials to be used, including audio-visual aids and illustrated literature.

2. Give sound basic training to the RRWs in the fundamentals of agricultural science and practice most relevant to the areas in which they will be working. Train them also to organize and conduct the farmers' classes, seminars, and study groups. This training is the responsibility of PRRM specialists and technical personnel.

3. At the agreed time, go to work on the organization of the farmers' class. This is primarily the RRW's responsibility. Talk with members of the barrio council and other village leaders, explaining the purpose of the farmers' class and urging them to support it fully. Then visit other individual farmers at their homes or in their fields, and invite them to attend the first session. If practicable, stimulate further interest by organizing tours to other barrios where effective farmers' classes are being held.

4. Make good use of technical and moral support by members of the PRRM Plant Production Department, and by other resource persons of scientific and practical competence who might be brought in to help. Such persons may be able to advise or assist during

PLANT PRODUCTION

the early stages of promotion and organization. Their backing may be especially helpful when complicated subjects are to be discussed, or when important demonstrations are to be made.

5. Encourage active participation by the farmers--through questions, or by stating their reactions to the scientific methods and practices being taught. Such questions and comments often provide needed opportunities to clarify points that have been made. They also give clues to doubts that must be resolved before the farmers will wholeheartedly undertake a technique that is unfamiliar to them. When you can answer a question, do so. When you are not sure, admit it freely. Then make a written note of the question as a reminder to find out the answer and give it at the next session of the class. Keep the class discussions easy, friendly, and informal.

6. Whenever possible, during class sessions or specially organized field trips, demonstrate the effectiveness of scientific methods under discussion. PRRM technical personnel will give all the assistance they can in planning and carrying out these demonstrations, enlisting frequently the cooperation of farmers in other barrios, and of governmental or other technical agencies in the vicinity.

7. When it is available, distribute after each class appropriate, easily understood literature on the subject that has been discussed. Be sure, however, that the literature is up-to-date and reliable.

8. Follow up the classes by frequent home and farm visits. It is important to give encouragement and practical guidance in trying out the new methods, from preparation and planting through cultivation and weeding and spraying until the harvest is gathered and stored, and the seed collected and treated for the next season.

9. Provide added incentives in the form of prizes and certificates of merit to especially deserving farmers. Such recognition is highly prized, and it brings into prominence farmers whose methods and performances are worthy of emulation. Rewards of this kind, tested by PRRM, may in time be taken up and applied on a much wider scale by municipal, provincial, and national government agencies.

Recurring Problems

Since PRRM first began experimenting with farmers' classes in 1952, many problems have been encountered. The most common ones, and the most effective of the responses tried to date, are as follows:

1) <u>Initial lack of interest</u>. The farmers may not show any desire to attend a class organized for their benefit. They may believe that they know all there is to know about raising crops or animals that their families have been growing for generations. They may feel that, in any case, there is nothing that a person relatively inexperienced in farming can teach them. They may be unaware of the degree to which they could improve their production by adopting scientific methods. Or they may feel that these methods are beyond their capacity to learn.

<u>Response</u>: Meet the farmer's skepticism with good nature and humility, remembering that his confidence must be earned. At the outset, (a) invite PRRM technical officers or other available resource persons in the vicinity to speak before the farmers on the benefits afforded by scientific methods in raising crops and animals; and (b) organize study tours for groups of farmers to other barrios where farmers' classes, seminars, or study groups are being conducted with good reactions among the participating farmers.

2) <u>Lack of facilities</u>. Farmers may lack the water supply or fertilizers or certified seeds or good breeds of animals or vaccines that they believe to be necessary to achieve improved production. They are therefore discouraged from participating in farmers' classes.

<u>Response</u>: Report to the Livelihood Department of PRRM the specific lacks which the farmers feel to be most serious. The department may then look for sources from which some, if not all, of the more urgent needs can be met. In addition, point out to those who are discouraged that, by joining the farmers' class, they can learn about ways to increase their production and income even <u>before</u> they acquire the additional facilities they need.

3) <u>Lack of needed teaching materials</u>, in the form of

PLANT PRODUCTION   153

   illustrated literature and audio-visual aids.

   Response: Be sure that you have a full, up-to-
   date kit of the materials provided by PRRM.
   Whenever you find that any important topic or
   question is not covered by these materials, request the assistance of the PRRM Plant Production
   Department in filling the gap, either by producing the additional literature or other teaching
   aids desired, or by obtaining the needed materials from the National Media Production Center.
   The RRW may also request materials directly from
   the Media Production Center.

4) Past irregularity in holding classes and seminars. This often discourages attendance.

   Response: Be sure to schedule all classes at
   times known to be convenient to the farmers,
   chiefly between planting and harvest. Once the
   schedule is set, make every effort to stick to
   it, regardless of minor difficulties.

5) Slowness in learning.

   Response: Remember that the farmers may not be
   accustomed to learning rapidly, and that it is
   not easy, especially for the middle-aged and older farmers, to change their ways of thinking and
   absorb the scientific information and technology
   being described to them. Take plenty of time for
   each class. Do not attempt to crowd too much
   into an hour or two. Try to achieve the leisure-
   ly, chatty atmosphere to which they are accustomed, with ample opportunity for questions and
   discussion.

6) Distractions during the classes, sometimes caused
   by discussions of political, religious, or other
   questions on which there may be strong differences of opinion. This is especially likely when
   village leaders helping the RRW to form the farmers' classes belong to a political or religious
   organization different from those to which a majority of the farmers in the barrio belong. If
   the result is a controversial discussion, interesting but unrelated to the farmers' class or
   seminar, the class may become ineffective and a
   waste of time for the RRWs and cooperating PRRM
   technical personnel.

Response: Avoid taking sides on any political or religious questions brought up by any of the farmers attending. Explain the real purpose of the class, and point out with humor and tact that if this purpose is to be achieved, the time together must not be lost in talking about irrelevant subjects.

7) Lack of coordination, between the RRWs and representatives of other governmental or private agencies doing similar work in the barrios. These representatives may regard the RRWs as their competitors. This situation may confuse the farmers, and render them indifferent to appeals by both the RRWs and the representatives of the other agencies.

Response: Instead of treating the representatives of other agencies as rivals, try to make partners of them by offering to be of assistance to them in their work, and by inviting their collaboration in developing farmers' classes and other projects being promoted by PRRM. Take the view that the needs of the barrio are so great that there is ample work for all who sincerely desire to help the people help themselves. This attitude is not only more generous, but far more sensible than a competitive one. By such an approach, RRWs have been able to develop cordial cooperation with representatives of other agencies in numerous barrios including, for example, Dolores, Santo Domingo, Cabucbucan, Llanara, and Nueva Ecija. The result in each case has been a higher regard for the RRW and much more effective work with the barrio people.

CHAPTER 7 ANIMAL PRODUCTION

According to statistics published by the government's Bureau of Animal Industry in February, 1965, the annual per capita consumption of meat in the Philippines is only about 2/5 of the amount needed for a healthful diet; the consumption of milk and of eggs is about 3/5 and 1/7, respectively, of the amount required to meet the people's nutritional needs. Moreover, nearly 80 per cent of the meat, milk, and eggs produced and imported is consumed in the cities, leaving the rural families even worse off in their protein diet than these figures would suggest. As a result, Filipino peasants generally do not have the full quota of energy needed for heavy farm work, and are less resistant to disease than they would be if they enjoyed adequate, balanced nutrition.

There is also a shortage of draft animals for farm work--due mainly to diseases and to indiscriminate slaughter of carabaos and cattle. This means that many farmers are forced either to limit the acreage they cultivate or to prepare their lands in an inadequate manner.

It is logical, therefore, that animal production should have an important place in the PRRM program.

EMPHASES IN ANIMAL PRODUCTION PROGRAM

From its early days, the PRRM Animal Production Department has sought to develop projects that are easy to understand, that do not require more capital than farm families can afford, and that meet their real needs. Such projects--simple, economical, practical--are as a rule readily duplicable, and therefore of potential benefit to many families.

After experimenting with numerous projects that seemed to meet these criteria, PRRM now emphasizes the promotion and expansion of seven main programs in the broad field of animal production, while testing

of other projects continues. These programs are:
(a) the hatching of purebred New Hampshire eggs by
native hens; (b) the caponization of cockerels; (c)
the use of purebred boars for swine breeding; (d) the
raising of breeding sows for upgrading purposes; (e)
the raising of fattening hogs for market; (f) mass
vaccinations of livestock; and (g) special training
courses and seminars in animal production.

HATCHING OF PUREBRED NEW HAMPSHIRE EGGS
BY NATIVE HENS

In earlier experimentation by PRRM, conducted
in cooperation with the Bureau of Animal Industry in
1960-62, 700 purebred New Hampshire and White Leghorn
cockerels of breeding age were introduced among the
barrios with the aim of upgrading the native stock.
This was only partially successful, but it led to a
simpler and more economical project that PRRM introduced in 1964--the hatching of purebred New Hampshire
eggs by native hens. Hatchability has now averaged
70 per cent and the project has become so popular
that it is now spreading rapidly. The cockerels produced are adapted from early age to local conditions,
and it is believed that the project will greatly improve the weight and quality of the chickens produced
in the barrios.

Introducing the Project

The main steps to take in introducing and extending this project can be stated very simply.

1. If a farmer has a native hen that is broody
or about to set, advise him to sell the native eggs
and buy, through the PRRM worker, New Hampshire
hatching eggs that can be hatched by the native hen.
If the farmer has doubts about the hen's willingness
or ability to hatch eggs that are not hers, assure
him that experience has shown she will. If he fears
that the hen will harm the young chicks when she discovers they have a different color from hers, or that
the new birds will not thrive under local conditions,
tell him that experience in other barrios has proven
these fears to be unfounded.

2. Before introducing or expanding the project,
be sure that the requisite number of New Hampshire
hatching eggs can be obtained from the Animal Pro-

ANIMAL PRODUCTION   157

duction Department or from a good nearby distribution center.

    3. If healthy New Hampshire chicks are hatched in about three weeks, as expected, call them to the attention of other farmers, and advise them to follow the same procedure.

Recurring Problems

1) <u>Faulty delivery</u>. Many of the New Hampshire eggs were delivered by motorcycle and did not hatch because they were subjected to too much jarring.

   <u>Response</u>: Try to deliver the eggs or have them safely delivered by car.

2) <u>Lack of cash</u>. The farmer lacks ready money with which to purchase the eggs.

   <u>Response</u>: Some RRWs and technical assistants have become so interested that they have personally advanced money to purchase eggs. But when the project grows, this is no longer practicable. PRRM has therefore set up a special revolving fund for this purpose. Apply for advances from that fund, as needed, and arrange with the individual farmers for repayment, keeping an accurate record.

CAPONIZATION OF COCKERELS

    Recently introduced, this project is also becoming increasingly popular among the farmers. Caponized cockerels fatten easily, put on more weight than the uncaponized birds, and command a much higher price when sold for meat.

    Although a chemical method is sometimes used, the least expensive means of caponizing cockerels is by surgical castration. The technique, easily learned, has been taught to most of the RRWs and to some of the young farmers in PRRM-assisted barrios.

Introducing the Project

    1. While making a home visit, if you should see cockerels nearby, call the farmer's attention to the advantages of caponizing them. When he is convinced,

offer to caponize these birds or have them caponized. If possible, make your initial efforts with barrio officials and officers of associations. Be sure to make a good first impression.

2. People are not hard to convince once they actually see the advantages of the project. When there are many farmers who want to have their cockerels caponized, try to train some youths to help you. It has been found that a regular schedule of caponization in the barrio helps to make this project popular.

Recurring Problems

1) <u>Prior interest in fighting cocks</u>. Farmers who raise fighting cocks may not allow caponization of their own or their neighbors' cockerels for fear of losing future fighters.

   <u>Response</u>: Instead of arguing the case, direct your attention to other farmers not so concerned about cock-fighting. As capons are raised and sold at a good profit, the practice of caponization will spread.

2) <u>Short life of capons</u>. Some farmers object that the capons die before they are one year old.

   <u>Response</u>: Point out that while capons usually do die of over-fatness around the age of one, they can be eaten much earlier, even at five or six months.

A PUREBRED BOAR FOR EACH BARRIO

The most encouraging swine-raising projects developed so far have been (a) the introduction of at least one purebred boar into a barrio; (b) the upgrading of unimproved breeding sows; and (c) the raising of market or fattening hogs.

When purebred boars are mated with native hogs, the mestizo offspring are fast growers, and they attain a much heavier weight at maturity than the native stock. The usual payment for the service of a boar is one weanling. The offspring, as piglets or grown pigs, sell at a good price. The project is profitable, therefore, to all concerned: the boar

ANIMAL PRODUCTION

owner, the sow owner, and the raiser of market pigs.

Promoting the Project

These promotion methods have been used with good effect:

1. Contact individual farmers and explain the advantages of having a purebred boar to improve the quality of their native pigs.

2. Hold a farmers' seminar, with personnel of the Animal Production Department as speakers and resource persons. This gives an opportunity for a full and authoritative explanation of swine raising, and of upgrading by the use of purebred boars.

3. Organize a special study group for the most interested farmers, and collaborate with PRRM technical personnel in teaching what needs to be known about the selection of breeds, feeds and feeding, disease control, and improved management.

4. For those whose interest is sustained, organize a field trip to see successful piggeries in operation in other barrios.

5. Then, if possible, convince at least one farmer in the barrio with the necessary capital to purchase a purebred boar for upgrading purposes. Or persuade the barrio council to buy a purebred boar and have it taken care of by a farmer under mutually agreed terms.

Recurring Problems

1) Delicacy of purebred boars. Farmers fear that the purebred boars require more delicate feeding and care.

Response: Explain that this fear is valid, and that many purebred boars do get sick because of faulty feeding and housing. Then, with the help of PRRM technical personnel, give to the person interested in procuring a boar careful instruction on care and management, including disease prevention. Follow this with assurance of your continuing assistance, backed by that of PRRM technical personnel.

2) High cost of commercial feeds. Many farmers are apprehensive that the project will lose financially because of this.

   Response: Advise them to use commercial feeds only as a stand-by, or as a supplement to a local mixture of rice, bran, salt, kitchen refuse, and animal protein sources in the locality such as meat scraps, gills and intestines of fish which are usually thrown away, fresh water mollusks, chicken, entrails, or tadpoles. Greens like ipil-ipil leaves, camote vines, kangkong, or kulasiman will balance the diet and also make it cheaper.

3) Lack of technical know-how in swine-raising. Many farmers are interested but unable to cope with some of the technical problems that arise.

   Response: Arrange with personnel of the Animal Production Department to conduct a seminar or special study group in the barrio, supplemented by individual instruction in meeting special problems. Improve your own technical knowledge by participating in these activities.

4) Faulty breeding and management practices. Daughters and granddaughters are frequently mated to the sire. And litters as well as grown hogs are raised in filth.

   Response: Explain that in-breeding generally causes retarded growth, poor body development, poor breeding performance, and abnormalities. Suggest exchanges with boars of neighboring barrios, or the procurement of other boars. As a health measure, advise that the pigs be raised on cement flooring that can be cleaned regularly.

5) Lack of capital to finance the project. An interested farmer may not have sufficient savings to purchase a purebred boar.

   Response: If the farmer is a member of a credit union, suggest that he secure a loan, to be repaid by funds received for the boar's services. If that source is not available, check the possibility of a loan from the National Cottage Industries Development Authority (NACIDA). Another possibility is to suggest that the barrio council

ANIMAL PRODUCTION

or some relatively well-to-do families in the barrio help to finance the purchase.

Investment from any of these sources may be encouraged by citing cases like that of a farmer in San Fabian, Santo Domingo, who bought a boar. At breeding age, the boar serviced 80 sows in one year, of which 60 had already delivered. The farmer was therefore richer by 60 weanlings handed to him as service fees and these he sold for 30 to 35 pesos each. Seeing the beautiful offspring, people in neighboring barrios were bringing their sows to be serviced by the boar during its second year of breeding.

6) <u>Fear of hog diseases</u>. Farmers may hesitate to raise hogs because they have experienced the ravages of diseases like hog cholera and swine plague. They have also noticed that pests like external and internal parasites make animals stunted and emaciated in spite of proper feeding and care.

<u>Response</u>: While this fear is valid, explain that most hog diseases can be prevented through proper sanitation. Emphasize that the two most destructive diseases, hog cholera and swine plague, can be largely prevented by vaccination; hence, they should have their hogs immunized periodically. Encourage them to attend seminars where the control of diseases and pests is discussed. Give them simple reading materials on these subjects, explaining the contents to them if necessary.

RAISING BREEDING SOWS FOR UPGRADING PURPOSES

The presence of a purebred boar in the barrio provides an incentive for raising healthy breeding sows. The breeding involves no cash outlay, since the breeding service fee is usually one weanling. The owners of breeding sows mated to purebred boars profit from the better price of the weanling offspring, and the greater demand for these weanlings.

Promotional Methods

1. Hold farmers' seminars, to which you invite technical personnel recognized as authorities. Ask them to discuss with the farmers (a) the advantages

of using a purebred boar to upgrade native stock; (b) the necessity of having healthy breeding sows for this purpose; and (c) instructions on proper feeding, housing, and care of farrowing sows and of newborn pigs, and on breeding practices and the prevention of diseases. Make use of available audio-visual aids.

    2. Follow up these seminars by frequent visits to farm families, accompanied if possible by technical personnel from the PRRM Animal Production Department. During these visits, encourage the farmers to push forward the upgrading of native swine stock. Distribute literature on the upgrading of native pigs through the use of purebred boars and healthy breeding sows.

    3. Encourage the barrio council or the people's associations to sponsor the upgrading project.

Recurring Problems

1) <u>Fear of hog diseases</u>. This problem is discussed above, under the topic, "A Purebred Boar for Each Barrio."

2) <u>Lack of capital</u>. There are many farmers who cannot engage in this project because they lack capital with which to purchase young sows.

    <u>Response</u>: If the family cannot afford to buy, or borrow capital for, a young sow (gilt), but is willing to take care of one, advise them to raise a young sow belonging to another, on the 50-50 share system (locally known as "iwihan"). Under this system, the sow owner and the caretaker share in the litter equally and have equal interest in the sow.

3) <u>Feeding difficulties</u>. Farmers fear that they cannot give proper feeds to the sows that have been mated to purebred boars.

    <u>Response</u>: Explain that the sows do not require special or commercial feeds. Remind the housewife that, if her family is of average size, the kitchen refuse, supplemented by some vegetables and forage, is enough. Emphasize that intestines of fish or chickens, pickled or salted fish or tadpoles, young mollusks, and cooked carcasses of dead birds should not be thrown away, but mixed

ANIMAL PRODUCTION

with the hog feed. Advise the family to plant camote and other forage in the back yard as feed supplements. The children may go to the fields to gather edible forage.

RAISING FATTENING HOGS FOR MARKET

This means raising hogs intended to be sold or slaughtered for pork. Since these animals are fed mostly with kitchen and farm wastes, they actually convert things that are usually thrown away into pork, or cash.

Many farmers, however, do not realize the benefits to be derived from this project. It should be the RRW's concern to convince each family to raise at least one fattening pig for supplemental income or for home consumption.

Promotional Methods

1. Always talk with the housewife. Convince her that the project is profitable in these ways: (a) Hogs convert kitchen and farm wastes into pork, thus furnishing additional income. (b) A hog is a live piggy bank that can provide the family with much-needed cash in time of emergency. (c) Hog raising provides work for the children, thereby fostering industry and responsibility, and reducing teen-age problems associated with idleness. (In this connection, the children should know that they will share in the sales if they take proper care of the pigs.)

2. When weanlings become available, advise the owner to sell them to other families in the barrio, or to distribute them to people who are willing to raise them on the "iwihan" system. Offer to help look for deserving caretakers.

3. During seminars for the women, talk about the project and offer assistance, especially in the prevention of diseases.

Recurring Problems

1) <u>Roving pigs</u>. For reasons of economy, some farmers prefer to let their pigs roam and search for their own food. The result is bad sanitation and wanton destruction of garden crops.

Response: Explain that this practice is unsanitary and that the pigs may pick up disease organisms and parasites. They also damage the neighbors' yards and plants. If necessary, suggest to the barrio council that it follow the example of other barrios and pass an ordinance prohibiting stray pigs, under penalty of a fine, and specifying that pigs must be tied, housed, or kept within fenced enclosures.

2) Several other problems that have arisen--fear of hog diseases, lack of technical know-how in swine-raising, lack of capital, and feeding difficulties--are discussed under the topics, "A Purebred Boar for Each Barrio" and "Raising Breeding Sows for Upgrading Purposes."

MASS VACCINATIONS OF LIVESTOCK

Large numbers of carabaos, cattle, hogs, chickens, and other livestock are lost every year due to diseases that are now largely preventable. Sometimes these losses reach epidemic proportions. The more common livestock diseases for which immunizing vaccines are now available include anthrax, homorrhagic septicemia, hog cholera, fowl pox, and illnesses caused by bird pests.

Individual and, whenever possible, mass vaccinations of livestock can greatly reduce the economic losses suffered by farm families because of these diseases.

Promotional Methods

1. In meetings of the barrio council and of the three people's associations, discuss the needs and advantages of this project.

2. Organize a mass meeting of carabao and cattle owners in the barrio, at a time when some technical personnel of the Animal Production Department of PRRM can be present to speak and answer questions. If possible, a field veterinarian from the government's Bureau of Animal Industry (BAI) should also be invited to speak. It is, of course, helpful if assurance can be given that vaccine and vaccinating services can be provided free.

ANIMAL PRODUCTION

3. Follow up this meeting by a well-organized vaccination of carabaos and cattle in the barrio, at a time fixed by the RRW after consultation with representative farmers and BAI personnel. Usually they are glad to cooperate in the PRRM-aided barrios because they know that there will be good preparatory work by the RRW, and a large turnout of animals for immunization. The RRW's preparatory work, in addition to the mass meeting, includes suitable publicity regarding the time and place, as well as house-to-house calls to explain further the advantages of immunization, and to urge cooperation in bringing out the animals.

4. If there seems to be uncertainty or reluctance among the farmers during the early stages of an immunization campaign, use additional means to promote understanding of the project and a desire to cooperate. Methods that have been used with good effect by RRWs include: (a) inviting personnel from the BAI to talk with the farmers individually or in small groups about the importance of having their animals immunized; (b) persuading members of the barrio council, officers of the people's associations, and other leading villagers to have their animals vaccinated first, knowing that others will then more readily follow; and (c) asking for the help of these leaders in convincing others to cooperate.

Recurring Problems

1) Misconceptions regarding the vaccines. Some farmers believe that the injected vaccines make the animals weaker. Others fear that they contaminate the meat of the animals so that it cannot be eaten.

    Response: Such misconceptions are difficult to eradicate. The method found most effective so far is to continue patiently the educational and promotional efforts described above.

2) Unavailability of free vaccines. This may deter farmers who would otherwise willingly have their animals immunized.

    Response: Explain that free vaccines are available only from the Bureau of Animal Industry, and that you can help to obtain them only if the BAI has stocks on hand. If farmers complain that they are being charged, report this to the Manila office of the BAI.

3) <u>Isolation of some sitios</u>. Due to distance or lack of roads, sitios of some barrios are so isolated that the residents do not have their animals vaccinated.

<u>Response</u>: Recommend to personnel of the Bureau of Animal Industry the training of auxiliary livestock workers from the isolated sitios. Once trained, these workers are able to vaccinate the animals in their own sitios.

SPECIAL TRAINING COURSES AND SEMINARS

Mention has been made, repeatedly, of special training courses and seminars as important means of transmitting scientific ideas and practices to the farmers. To keep sessions from being too long, classes and seminars in plant and animal production, which were once held jointly, are now conducted separately. The RRW plans and organizes each seminar to suit the schedules of the participants. Seminars are usually planned to convey basic information and encourage discussion. Classes are organized for more intensive study or training.

A special recent emphasis has been on organizing intensive three-day training courses for the specific purpose of developing animal handymen to work with the RRWs in the animal production program. Such a course, for 15 or more people in a barrio, is initiated by a PRRM team captain and an RRW, who approach the barrio council together and explain the advantages of conducting such training in the barrio. If it approves the project, the council, in consultation with the PRRM personnel, selects those to be invited to take the training course. The PRRM Animal Production Department then sets dates convenient for the participants. When the course is completed, special certificates are awarded to the new animal handymen.

Experience to date indicates that those who receive this training may themselves develop new poultry or swine-raising projects; and that when an RRW leaves a barrio, the animal handymen are able to take over most of his functions in the field of animal production.

CHAPTER 8 COOPERATIVES

One of the most serious obstacles to progress in the rural areas is unavailability of credit at reasonable rates of interest. The farmer needs money to fertilize and irrigate his land, to buy certified seeds and insecticides, to purchase implements and other capital equipment, to buy hatching eggs or piglets or a purebred boar, or perhaps to start a little home industry so that he can continue earning throughout the year.

Without credit, most of the farmers are caught in a melancholy cycle of poverty. Because they are poor, they find it difficult to save money for capital investments. Without at least simple capital investments, they are unable to increase their production very much. Without increased production, they cannot raise their incomes. And without larger incomes, they remain mired in poverty.

While waiting for the crops to come in, especially in a bad crop year, farmers may be forced to borrow at usurious rates of interest and thereby acquire a grevious burden of debt. To make matters worse, most farmers have never learned to practice sound budgeting.

These conditions are not peculiar to the Philippines. They exist throughout most the the newly developing nations. In many, the picture is much worse than in our country.

The most effective instrument yet devised to alleviate indebtedness and provide credit at reasonable interest rates in poverty-stricken rural areas is the credit union. However, around the world and in the Philippines, credit unions have both a bright and a dark history: generally bright when they have been well organized and soundly administered, generally dark when they have not.

PRRM-SPONSORED CREDIT UNIONS

PRRM recognized early an urgent need for the systematic promotion, organization, and development of credit unions in the rural areas. In 1954, it started a modest development of credit unions in two barrios with the following objectives: (a) to help stimulate among the barrio people habits of thrift, and of regular saving as a means of accumulating funds for economic development; (b) to make available a ready source of funds for sound credit, on a self-help, non-profit basis, to be used principally for productive capital investments; (c) to help free the farmers from usury; (d) to train them in the wise use of money; and (e) to provide a source of financial help in times of emergency.

During the intervening years, this program has expanded and matured. Notable advances have been achieved in all important phases of the cooperative credit business. In many of the PRRM-aided barrios, credit unions are now the principal sources of credit --chiefly for productive investments, but also for education and health and emergency needs.

The main functions of the cooperatives program are: (a) promotion; (b) organization, accompanied by continuous education; (c) administration and management; and (d) supervision.

In carrying out these functions, it must be remembered that cooperatives are not mere "hand-out" organizations dispensing credit on easy terms. Unless they are technically sound, and responsibly managed in accordance with strict business principles, they will fail. Every such failure does great harm-- to the credit union members, and to the cooperative movement as a whole.

PRRM has achieved a record over the years, not of spectacular growth, but of solid successes in developing credit cooperative unions. That record must be jealously guarded. Rural reconstruction workers (RRWs), as they participate in the cooperatives program, are advised to keep in close contact with technical personnel of the PRRM Cooperatives Department until they acquire a "sure touch" through practical experience.

PROMOTION OF CREDIT COOPERATIVES

There are two principal ways in which the RRW can participate effectively in the promotion of credit cooperatives.

1. After getting well acquainted with the people of a barrio in which there is no credit union, discuss with personnel of the PRRM Cooperatives Department these questions, in an exploratory way: (a) Is there a need for a credit cooperative union in the barrio? (b) If so, could responsible leaders for the union be found in the barrio, and trained? (c) Would there be enough dependable members to provide a worthwhile volume of business? (d) Would there be a real desire on the part of those interested to help one another?

2. If the preliminary answers to these questions are affirmative, begin gradually to inform some of the most responsible people in the barrio about the benefits to be derived from membership in sound cooperative unions. Among these benefits are: (a) The opportunity to borrow at a reasonable rate of interest instead of the usurious rates which, in the past, have often run as high as 50 per cent for eight-month loans of money between planting time and harvest, or, over the same period, 200 per cent for each cavan of fertilizer provided. (b) Freedom to use the low-interest loans for productive purposes that will increase the borrower's income by much more than the amount of his loan. PRRM-promoted credit unions have made thousands of such loans for use in purchasing certified seeds, or fertilizers, or insecticides, or improved farm implements, or healthy chicks and piglets to be raised for a profit, or for starting a small business. (c) An opportunity to use low-interest loans for other worthy purposes such as repaying old high-interest debts, or medical care, or environmental sanitation for the protection of health, or children's education. (d) The training of those who join the union to save and manage their incomes in a way that will enable them to have, normally, small "earning" surpluses instead of "dragging" deficits; and to help each other through the mechanism of the credit union.

ORGANIZATION AND EDUCATION

In the development of cooperatives, organization and education must go hand in hand. Thorough and continuous training of officers and members in cooperative principles and procedures is imperative, to ensure a successful operation. The formal training must be conducted either by a cooperative officer of the government or a cooperative leader recognized by the Cooperatives Administration Office. The RRW plays an important part in making sure that this training is fully understood, and that the successive steps in organizing a credit union are well carried out. These steps are considered essential:

1. Using forms prepared by the Cooperatives Department of PRRM, conduct a simple survey to ascertain whether there is a real need for a credit union in the barrio; whether competent, dependable leadership could be trained; and whether prospective membership warrants the establishment of a union. The survey should also cover related information, including the availability of other credit facilities, prevailing interest rates on loans, and current loan requirements.

2. If the results of such a survey are affirmative, work with officers of the PRRM Cooperatives Department to organize a study club of 15 to 20 selected men and women of the barrio. The group discusses and learns about the aims of a credit union, its administration and management, its sources of funds and how they are protected, its lending functions, the law authorizing its establishment, and its proposed by-laws.

3. When this preparatory education has reached a sufficiently advanced stage, and there has been a careful screening of prospective members, hold an organization meeting and prepare the required papers for registration. Detailed discussion of these procedures is contained in the PRRM manual on cooperatives. Among other things, the organization meeting carries out the following business: (a) adoption of a constitution, by-laws, and articles of incorporation; (b) election of a board of directors, and members of credit and supervisory committees; (c) certification of the availability of a competent bookkeeper; (d) certification of initial cash count signed by either the municipal treasurer or the gov-

ernment's cooperative officer in the area; and (e) bonding of the accountable officer of the credit union for an amount of not less than 500 pesos.

ADMINISTRATION AND MANAGEMENT

The supreme authority in a credit union is its general assembly, composed of all members in good standing. Administration and management are entrusted to a board of directors elected by the general assembly and consisting of not less than 5, and not more than 15 members. The officers--president, vice-president, secretary, and treasurer--are chosen from this number. The board of directors meets at least once a month or as often as the business of the society requires, and sets policies on collaterals for loans as needed, and on withdrawals of deposits. It approves membership applications and withdrawals, determines the interest rate on loans, specifies the duties and responsibilities of employees, declares dividends, and allocates and distributes net savings. The board is usually assisted in its work by a 3-member credit committee, a 3-member supervisory committee, and a 5-member education and information committee.

These are normally the RRW's principal duties in relation to the credit unions established in PRRM-aided barrios:

1. Attend meetings of the general assembly, the board of directors, and the principal committees, as a friendly consultant.

2. During the early stages of operation, assist the treasurer in the collection of regular deposits, which are the main source of the credit union's working funds. The by-laws usually prescribe a minimum fixed deposit (not withdrawable so long as the depositor's membership is maintained) of 50 pesos, and an interest rate on deposits not exceeding 8 per cent per year. After his minimum deposit has been completed, a member may also make regular interest-paying savings deposits, withdrawable on demand to meet unforeseen needs. (PRRM is now giving some assistance to credit unions in obtaining loans from banks and other credit institutions.)

3. In cases where members have difficulty in

raising the amounts needed for their regular deposits, help them to find ways of increasing their incomes--through such activities as cultivating a secondary crop, raising pigs and poultry, or starting a small business like a sari-sari store. Those who participate in the Minimum Additional Income (MAC) Project generally find that, through a combination of such efforts, they can increase their incomes substantially within less than a year, after which it is much easier to make regular deposits.

    4. When requested, especially during a cooperative's formative period, give counsel and assistance to the board of directors in its determination of policies on loans, and to the credit committee in its decisions on loan applications. A few points to keep in mind are: (a) Special encouragement should be given to granting loans for economically productive purposes, designed to increase the self-reliance and future well-being of the borrowers and their families. (b) Loan policies should be based on human understanding, taking into account impartially the credit needs of the members. (c) A constant effort should be made to distribute the loans so that they will serve the greatest good of the greatest number. (d) The board of directors' loan policies should be made very clear to all members, with indications of the types of loans that are normally given priority. Requirements that must be met in filing applications for loans should be stated clearly. (e) Each credit union's loan policies should be reviewed from time to time in order to make adjustments to changes that may be taking place in the conditions and needs of the members.

SUPERVISION

The supervision of credit unions involves three main functions. The first is <u>inspection</u>, to see whether the board of directors and the committees of the union are meeting regularly and discharging their duties as defined by the by-laws; to make sure that all transactions are promptly and accurately recorded; and to suggest remedies for any irregularities that may have developed. The second function is continuing <u>education</u>, to make sure that all officers and committees of the union understand their responsibilities and know how to discharge them. The third is <u>auditing</u>, to verify the correctness of the accounting

COOPERATIVES

records through standard procedures.

In PRRM-assisted barrios, the supervisory responsibility is shared by three groups. They are: first, the Cooperatives Administration Office (CAO), a national organization with representatives in cities and provinces; its representatives are called commercial cooperative officers (CCOs), and they are charged with general supervisory responsibility for all commercial cooperatives; second, the supervisory committee of the credit union within each barrio, which serves as a watchdog for the members; and third, the PRRM, which is represented in the barrios by the RRWs and the technical personnel of the Cooperatives Department.

The principal responsibilities of the RRW in relation to the supervision of the credit unions are:

1. To assist the PRRM technical cooperative personnel in carrying out their supervisory duties.

2. To give counsel as needed to the credit union's supervisory committee. The by-laws usually provide that this committee shall make quarterly audits of the union's books, and submit audit reports properly supported by schedules.

3. To work closely with representatives of the CAO whenever they visit the barrio, and to help ensure cooperation among all three supervisory groups.

Recurring Problems

Space does not permit mention of all the problems encountered while helping to promote, organize, administer, and supervise credit unions in the PRRM-assisted barrios. Some of the most common may be cited, with ways and means that have been found effective in meeting them.

1) <u>Fears due to past failures</u>. In the Philippines, as in other countries, the early history of cooperatives was featured by inept administration, numerous failures, and extensive losses. This engendered understandable fears of this type of organization, especially among the rural people. As a result, PRRM was confronted with the task of helping to demonstrate convincingly that credit unions could be developed on a sound basis, with

full protection of the interests of the members.

Response: Tell those who express such fears that there are now many credit unions that are not only safe, but of great benefit to their members. If possible, organize a visit to one or more other barrios in which such unions exist, giving the visitors from your barrio an opportunity to ask questions, and to listen to the opinions of the union's officers and members. Try to show them that with adequate training and sound organization, strong and secure credit unions can be developed. Point out that a credit union in their own barrio would be given every assistance in developing along sound lines; that it would be carefully supervised by government and PRRM personnel as well as by a committee in the barrio; that the accounting officers would be properly bonded; that the bulk of the funds would be on loan to the members, with dependable assurances of repayment; and that other deposited funds would be kept in a nearby bank or other secure repositiory.

2) Lack of self-confidence among the chosen leaders of the credit union. This is natural, for in most cases they have very limited education, and are called upon to carry responsibilities in which they have had no previous experience.

Response: See that they get thorough, unhurried training, so that they become thoroughly familiar with their duties and the basic principles by which they should be guided. Then stand behind them and give them frequent encouragement. Gradually, as they become accustomed to the work and see that they can do it, their confidence will grow.

3) Tardiness or negligence in making deposits and repayments on loans. Even if initial members have been chosen because of their known thrift and dependability, it is easy for them to put off making regular deposits as well as repayments on loans when they fall due. It is most important that this problem be met head-on from the very beginning. For deposits and repayments form the life-blood of the credit union, and must be maintained if the organization is to thrive.

COOPERATIVES

Response: The key to the solution of this problem lies in prompt and unfailing reminders whenever deposits or repayments are overdue. Suggest that the treasurer start by sending a written reminder. If this does not produce the desired result, join the treasurer in making a personal follow-up call, and tactfully stress to the member the importance of making all payments on time. Some larger credit unions, as a last resort, have posted in the barrio hall lists of those whose repayments are overdue. When this is done, the lists tend quickly to become shorter and shorter.

4) Delinquent officers. Occasionally, officers elected by their fellow members to positions of trust fail to carry out their responsibilities. Some may even set a bad example to other members of the credit union.

Response: This problem cannot be sidestepped, or the organization will suffer. Discuss the matter discreetly with other more responsible officers, and with PRRM supervisory personnel. A first step may be a private talk with the delinquent officer to make sure that his mistakes are not due to lack of understanding. If the offenses continue, the next step should be a thorough investigation by the union's supervisory committee, followed by appropriate disciplinary action, if needed. For lesser but persistent abuses, this action might be suspension from office. In more serious cases involving a violation of trust, or a constant disruption of the harmony and efficiency of the organization, it may be necessary to expel the offending officer from the union.

5) Jealousies caused by favoritism, real or fancied. Sometimes jealousies arise because some loan applications are approved and others are not.

Response: Try to assist the board of directors and the credit committee in making clear to all members the guiding principles observed in acting on requests for loans, and the types of loans to which a higher priority is normally given. At the same time, assist the supervisory committee in checking the impartiality of the loans that have been made, and in suggesting prompt remedies in any case where there is valid evidence of favoritism.

6) <u>Feuding groups</u>. If one political or religious group, for example, initiates the move to join the credit union in a barrio, a contending group may find some means of disturbing the proposed plan, instead of encouraging its members to join too.

<u>Response</u>: Stay above the battle. Do not take sides. Work for mutual understanding and participation in the credit union on the basis of the genuine shared interests of prospective members. In sponsored barrios, the help of the sponsors may be enlisted in mediating between the factions. In any PRRM-aided barrio, it may be possible to enlist the help of the men's or women's rural reconstruction association in bringing about an understanding between the opposing groups. In some cases, a full reconciliation has been effected, with leaders of both groups elected as officers of the credit union.

A LOOK AHEAD

Because of the necessity of starting slowly and building well, the Cooperatives Department of PRRM has concentrated so far on credit cooperatives, which appeared to be the type most urgently needed. A solid basis of experience has now been acquired in this field, and expansion in the number of credit unions and in their membership will continue on an accelerating scale.

At the same time, preparatory work is now being done with a view to launching, one by one in PRRM-assisted barrios, three other types of cooperative organization. These are marketing, consumers', and industrial cooperatives. The RRWs will be advised of these developments as they occur, and given needed instructions. For in initiating these significant activities, the informed participation of the RRWs will be vital.

Marketing cooperatives are designed to help agricultural and other producers become better businessmen by jointly selling their products without the intervention of middlemen. In this way, the farmers are able to sell in larger markets under more advantageous conditions, and to get better prices for their products. The work of a marketing cooperative includes the collection of the product, grading, processing, storing prior to sale, and then taking the produce in bulk to the best available market at the most favorable time. The products that are sold in this way lose their individual identity; the original producers are given receipts for so many units of produce at various grades. On the security of products deposited at the cooperative's warehouse, the society advances funds to members according to their needs, usually in amounts not exceeding 60 per cent of the expected selling price of the produce they have made available for sale.

Consumers' cooperatives are associations of persons who contribute brains, money, and skills for the purpose of organizing a store to serve the needs of the members at minimum cost. By making relatively large purchases, they can secure many goods at wholesale rates, and then pass on the savings to their members. They can protect their members against sharp practices such as short-weight selling or adulteration of goods. The savings to members are reflected in the lower prices which they pay for goods bought in the cooperative store, and in the store's net profits, which are distributed equitably among the members.

Industrial cooperatives are associations of small-scale producers--such as carpenters, masons, weavers, metal workers, or shoemakers--who organize in order to buy raw materials at wholesale prices and issue them to members at cost. Through the cooperative, members work together to improve their manufacturing techniques, standardize their products, produce goods of better quality, investigate available markets, and sell their products at advantageous prices. There are many present and potential small-scale industrial producers in rural communities who will benefit from this type of cooperative association.

CHAPTER 9 — RURAL INDUSTRIES AND VOCATIONAL ARTS

The inclusion of rural industries and vocational arts in the livelihood program may be attributed to three conditions that PRRM found in the barrios. The first was the low standard of living among a large majority of the people, and their consequent need for income-augmenting or income-saving activities. The second was the seasonal character of most rural work; both the men and women tended to be quite busy during some seasons, and not so busy during others. The third condition was the local availability of raw materials suitable for use in certain types of rural industries and vocational arts, and the existence of accessible markets for their products. There was also a recognition that exports of any of these products would contribute to the country's foreign exchange earnings.

RURAL INDUSTRIES

From the outset, the aim of the rural industries program has been to increase the earning capacity and self-respect of rural families by creating or expanding cottage-type, money-earning industries that could be operated with minimum capital, using locally available raw materials.

Evolution of the Program

Experimental beginnings were made in several barrios. For example, in Balatong, Laoag, Illocos Norte, a PRRM technical assistant introduced the making of a bamboo winnowing basket which could be sold for one peso. In hacienda Alegria, Negros Occidental, training was successfully developed for the production of abaca slippers, bags, and doormats. A start was made, in Sto. Cristo, San Antonio, and in Costallano and Mallorca, San Leonardo, Nueva Ecija, in the production of bamboo fish traps and buri mats.

Gradually, the objectives of the program became

RURAL INDUSTRIES AND VOCATIONAL ARTS

more specific. They are: (a) to continue exploring practical possibilities for the development of specific viable rural industries; (b) to acquaint the barrio people with these possibilities, and their potential value as sources of supplementary family income; (c) to learn and apply techniques of effective promotion for selected industries; and (d) to analyze the problems encountered and devise means for their solution.

Survey and Experimentation

Early surveys in a number of districts indicated that the following raw materials, suitable for use in cottage industries, could be found widely in the rural areas: abaca (the source of Manila hemp), buri (gathered from leafstalks of the talipot palm), bamboo, and various types of wood. A few semi-processed items, such as plywood, could be obtained at fairly reasonable cost.

Surveys were also made of "interested" human resources, and it was found that considerable educational and promotional work, as well as training, would be needed to achieve any substantial spread of new village industries.

In order to have a variety of industries among which the barrio people could choose, PRRM technical staff members--at the organization's field headquarters in Nieves--carried forward experiments in the production of both new and familiar items. They succeeded in developing, or refining, a range of items including fruit trays, peanut trays, hanging vases, table vases, winnowing baskets, fishtraps, fans, ladies' handbags, slippers, bamboo cases for transistor radios, stools, doormats, dining chairs, center tables, and bamboo beds (papags).

Briefing the RRWs

As the number of possible choices increased, those in charge of the Rural Industries Unit were asked to start briefing the RRWs on: (a) the types of industries that might appropriately be considered in their barrios, with information for each on quality, standards, design, style, and measurements; (b) ways of checking on the availability of materials, tools, and human resources; and (c) how to cooperate with PRRM technical staff members in gauging roughly the potential market for each type of product under consideration.

Promotion

The next stage was one of discussion and planning among the technical personnel concerned and the selected RRWs, to devise a method of promoting rural industries in the barrios. This was followed by experimental approaches in the field. Gradually, the following procedures were developed, for flexible use according to the circumstances in each barrio.

1. The initial approach is made, not during, but after, a busy planting or harvesting season. The RRW makes the first contacts, starting with people who are anxious to find some way of augmenting their incomes, and are willing to try something new. He discusses types of home industry that might be learned, and mentions the possibility of obtaining a skilled instructor at no cost, if there is sufficient interest.

2. If the response is encouraging, the RRW, often with the help of a technical assistant or technical worker in rural industries, undertakes a series of promotional steps. The following are typical: (a) He arranges a special meeting or seminar for a group of interested people, at which possibilities are further discussed and sample products of different types of household industries are exhibited. (b) He plans a field trip by the same group to a nearby barrio where one or more rural industries have been successfully started. (c) In talking further with the group, he makes use of available literature and visual aids. (d) He plans and organizes a demonstration, in the barrio, of how certain products are made, and invites questions and free discussion.

3. If sufficient response develops as a result of these promotional steps, the RRW then approaches the barrio council, and describes the interest shown to date. If the council so wishes, he then assists it in preparing a resolution, or a letter, requesting PRRM to provide technical training and assistance for one or two cottage industries, stating the anticipated number of students, and proposing a date for the beginning of training. (It may be desirable for

the RRW, before meeting with the barrio council, to make certain that PRRM would be able to comply with such a request in the near future.)

Instruction

If the request is approved, the specialized worker on bamboo (or buri or abaca) craft work proceeds to the barrio at the prescribed time, taking with him all his teaching aids. The RRW meets the instructor and introduces him to the prospective students, who are then formally enrolled. The instructor proceeds to brief the group on the projects to be undertaken, the materials and tools needed for the course, and the number of days and hours required to complete it. (A typical craft class lasts from five to ten days.) Agreement is then reached on a definite schedule, which is adhered to until the course is completed.

The course usually begins with a thorough demonstration by the instructor. After that, the emphasis is on the class members learning to do the work themselves, with guidance and suggestions from the instructor. Gradually they acquire the ability to make the product completely by themselves. If there are already present in the barrio any skilled workers in the craft being learned, it is usually desirable to invite them to cooperate in giving the training.

Three or four days before the end of the course, the RRW, the instructor, and leading members or officers of the class may jointly plan a graduation ceremony, to which the people of the barrio will be invited. Certificates are awarded to all the graduates, and special recognition is given to those who have done outstanding work. If an interesting program is planned--including an exhibit of products made by members of the class, talks by one or two leading citizens of the barrio as well as the RRW and the instructor, and some entertaining music and folk dancing--it will be a pleasant occasion for all. And it may well encourage others in the barrio to learn a craft and increase their family incomes.

Supervision

Experience has shown that, once a craft has been learned, the follow-through is important. It is the

RRW's responsibility to visit the graduates repeatedly, to give them encouragement and, especially, to make sure that they are meeting all specifications for measurement, quality, style, and design. If the work does not come up to required standards, it may not sell at all, or its market may gradually disappear.

The RRW's help or counsel is sometimes needed, also, in arranging credit that may be required to purchase tools or to facilitate the first sales. Such assistance is transitional, and the newly trained producer is encouraged to "stand on his own feet" as soon as possible.

A Look Ahead

PRRM feels that it has only made a start in the field of rural industries, and that a great deal more can be done. The next move planned is a survey of all existing industries in the PRRM-aided barrios to ascertain as clearly as possible why some have succeeded much better than others. The results of the survey will be discussed by both technical and field personnel, as plans are made for strengthening and expanding this program.

Specific steps now under consideration include: (1) engaging additional technical personnel for the Rural Industries Unit; (2) scheduling regular visits by members of this unit to all PRRM-aided barrios, to collaborate with the RRWs in supervising existing projects and sponsoring new ones; (3) experimenting further with types of industries that might be developed, using locally available materials, including industries that can make use of electric power where available; (4) systematic studies of potential markets; (5) a special in-service training course on rural industries for both team captains and RRWs; (6) systematic recognition for RRWs who are doing superior work in this field; and (7) the creation of a revolving fund for the further promotion of rural industries in PRRM-aided barrios.

VOCATIONAL ARTS

The vocational arts training promoted by PRRM extends to the barrio people benefits similar to those afforded by the rural industries. It provides a means of supplementing the family income, and helps to distribute this income more evenly throughout the year. It also enables the family to stretch its limited cash reserves, by producing at home essential items that would otherwise have to be purchased.

By providing supplementary employment, this program combats the idleness and sense of helplessness that often prevail during long rainy seasons or other less active periods in the farming year. People in many barrios have stated that the increased amount of productive, creative activity has reduced the incidence of juvenile delinquency in their communities. And the RRWs have observed that the development of individual skills has encouraged artistic expression, and instilled in the participants a new pride of craftsmanship.

Evolution of the Program

The PRRM vocational arts program was started in 1952, after a socio-economic survey that showed that the typical wardrobe of a rural family consisted mainly of a few old, ill-fitting garments. The survey showed that most farm families had very little money to spend on clothing, and that most of the rural women had little or no knowledge of how to make clothes at home. To begin finding an answer to this need, PRRM introduced a training program in sewing in nine barrios in Rizal province.

At that time, many embroidery factories in Manila needed skilled workers. Arrangements were made for them to furnish personnel who could teach sewing in selected PRRM-aided barrios. Women who did not attain proficiency in embroidery work were given training in dressmaking. When the training was completed, raw materials were delivered to the women's doors, and regular payments--ranging from 8 to 12 pesos per week--were made as the finished articles were collected.

With the skills acquired in this way, and with the help of the additional income they earned, the women participating in this program were able to make many useful and decorative articles for their own families at very little cost. And they were able to do this in their own homes. As a by-product, this work provided an emotional and recreational outlet for the women, which was reflected in their growing activity and the added interest they began to take in their homes.

In 1954, PRRM developed two vocational arts and rural crafts laboratories in barrio Nangka, Marikina, Rizal, and barrio Ganaderia, Laur, Nueva Ecija. The focus in these centers was mainly on loom weaving and bamboo crafts. The barrio trainees produced varied articles such as woven placemats, napkins, towels, materials for bedcovers, and women's handbags. When this special training was discontinued in 1956, due to lack of funds, the graduates of the classes were able to find jobs in the newly opened textile mills in Pasig Rizal.

Dressmaking and tailoring were then introduced in these pilot barrios. (PRRM hired a local tailor to serve as instructor in the tailoring course.) The program proved popular, and the ceremony held to honor the graduates of both courses stirred wide interest in neighboring villages. Requests for PRRM assistance followed from many barrios, and interest in the entire four-fold program was stimulated.

As the requests for aid increased, it was necessary for PRRM to develop its own team of skilled instructors to conduct the vocational arts courses in the barrios. A vocational mobile team was organized, made up of RRWs who became proficient in dressmaking, tailoring, embroidery, and crocheting. Due to financial limitations, the work of this team, and associated in-service training for RRWs, has been intermittent.

Today the vocational arts program is administered by a permanent team of five PRRM technicians. Each visits at least 12 barrios a month and conducts at least 6 vocational classes a year, graduating at least 90 students annually. As a result of the growing interest among the people, and the progress PRRM has made in training and finding skilled instructors, the graduates of the vocational arts classes now number in the thousands.

Organization and Conduct of Vocational Classes

PRRM's experience in conducting the vocational

arts program in the barrios has given rise to some basic guidelines which RRWs now follow in organizing classes. Conditions are considered favorable for a successful vocational training program if (a) at least 15 prospective students have expressed their interest in writing; (b) sewing materials, sewing machines, and classroom space can be made available; (c) technical assistance is given; (d) classes are scheduled at times that do not conflict with the essential work of the barrio people at home and in the fields; and (e) the three people's associations give active support to the project. When these conditions have been met, or are assured, the RRW can proceed with the organization of the classes.

One way for him to start is to invite the officers of the three people's associations to meet and discuss the needs and advantages of vocational classes, and how one or more such classes can be organized. If there is sufficient response, the group may consider immediately how responsibilities can be divided. For example, it may be decided that PRRM will provide the technical know-how and training, teaching aids such as charts and models, and, at the end, certificates to graduates. The people's associations might agree to take charge of recruiting and signing up students, encouraging their regular attendance, and providing for sewing materials and classroom space.

If no technical assistant or specialized worker from the PRRM staff is available to come to the barrio, the RRW may decide to organize a class by interesting a resident who is proficient in a skill to serve as a teacher. One very successful program was conducted in this way. A resident dressmaker agreed to instruct her neighbors in dressmaking, and the participants in the course benefited doubly because she was always present in the barrio and readily accessible when questions and problems arose. Some classes have been started with the organizing assistance of RRWs from neighboring barrios, and with the National Federation of Women's Clubs hiring the instructor. There have been occasions when the trainees themselves were able to contribute enough money to solicit the services of a professional teacher outside the PRRM staff.

Dressmaking

Dressmaking is one of the most popular courses. It meets a widespread need and it provides an opportunity for women with families to work in their homes, thus not interfering with other duties. It enables mothers from poorer families to provide sturdy, well-fitted clothing for members of her family that they would not otherwise have. And in many barrios, women have been able to supplement the family income by opening a dressmaking shop, or doing work in their own homes for neighbors.

The dressmaking course that has evolved over the years is now designed to cover, in 100 hours, the fundamental skills of taking measurements, making a pattern, cutting, and sewing. Sewing may be done either by hand or by machine. During the course, each participant must make four garments. Each is intended to provide a member of her family with an item of clothing that is truly useful, and gratifying to the trainee, and at the same time to give her varied experience in making different garments requiring special skills.

The four garments usually chosen are (1) a polo shirt (to be finished in 25 hours); (2) an ordinary girl's dress, made of new or old cotton cloth, cut with a round, square, or "v" neckline, with sleeves and a sheared, pleated, or a-line skirt (to be finished in 25 hours); (3) a dress for special occasions, made of colorful material, with sleeves and extra decorations such as lace or buttons (to be finished in 35 hours); and (4) a multipurpose item ingeniously designed to serve as a curtain, coffee table cover, patadyong, sewing machine cover, maternity dress, nightie, or baby hammock (to be finished in 15 hours).

The materials which each student needs for the dressmaking course, and their costs, are as follows:

Tape measure	₱ .30
Ruler	.20
Needle	.05
Paper	.35
Pins	.20
Notebook	.25
Pencil	.05

RURAL INDUSTRIES AND VOCATIONAL ARTS

Thread	.50
Total	**₱ 1.90**

The cost of the materials for the four garments comes to approximately ₱11.00, making a total cost of ₱12.90. The same garments, if purchased, would cost about ₱21.20. The actual cash savings, therefore, is about ₱8.30. In addition, the trainee learns a skill that she can use the rest of her life.

Tailoring

Tailoring, the art of sewing men's wear, has brought comparable benefits. Since relatively few of the barrio people have mastered this specialized craft, graduates of the tailoring course usually have no difficulty in finding a market for their skills, and this enables them to supplement their families' incomes.

The PRRM course in tailoring that is now conducted takes 100 hours, and covers the same fundamentals of taking measurements, making patterns, cutting, and sewing. Those who take the course normally make three garments: a polo shirt (25 hours); short pants (35 hours); and long pants (40 hours).

The materials needed by each student, with costs, are as follows:

Square and curve line	₱ 3.00
Tape measure	.30
Pattern paper	.30
Pins	.20
Notebook	.25
Pencil	.05
Needle	.05
Thimble	.05
Thread	.50
Total	**₱ 4.70**

The cost of the materials for the three garmets is about ₱10.00, making a total cost of about ₱14.70. The same garments, if purchased, would cost approximately ₱22.40. The cash saved by making the garments at home is, therefore, about ₱7.70. And, as in the case of dressmaking, a useful new skill is acquired.

Embroidery and Applique Work

Embroidery is the sewing of decorative stitches on cloth to enhance the beauty of the material. It can be done by hand or machine. Appliques are decorative patterns cut from cloth and sewn to a garment. Mastery of these arts enables people to beautify their own homes, and to make pieces for sale--such as cushion covers, bedspreads, curtains, shirts and blouses, pillow cases, scarfs, hand towels, and napkins. Not only does this increase the family income and stimulate interest in attractive homemaking, it also arouses the interest of young girls in appropriate dressing habits.

The PRRM course covers simple stitching, and the tracing of patterns or designs on cloth for embroidery and applique work. The following equipment is needed:

> Tape measure
> Cutting scissors, 6 inches long
> Embroidery scissors with curved tip,
>   4 inches long
> Embroidery frames
> Stiletto
> Pins and Needles
> Embroidery thread
> Paper (coupon bond)
> Stamping pad and eraser

Recurring Problems

1) <u>Lack of interest</u>. Sometimes the barrio people show little interest in organizing a vocational arts training course, even though the need for the skills and gains they would provide seems apparent. This may be due to a lack of understanding of what the training course would enable them to do for themselves and their families.

   <u>Response</u>: Make home visits to those who might become interested. Show them samples of finished products. This makes the goals visible and within reach. If possible, ask some graduates of vocational courses to join in these visits, and to tell about the benefits to them of completing the course.

2) <u>Lack of money and materials</u>. This problem often

RURAL INDUSTRIES AND VOCATIONAL ARTS

interferes with completion of the projects required for the courses.

Response: In many cases, substitute materials can be found. For instance, old clothes, remnants, and feed bags can be used as materials in the dressmaking class. If the problem is lack of sewing machines for the classes, sometimes it is possible to borrow them from civic-minded community leaders. Or if any of the trainees should already have sewing machines, they may agree to bring them to class. Printed materials for use in the classroom can be augmented by patterns printed in papers and magazines, and by charts prepared in advance by the teacher.

3) Lack of a market for the finished products. It may be that there is no readily apparent market for the items produced, especially if the barrio is a very poor one.

Response: The RRW may be able to help by finding sales outlets in other barrios, or among PRRM personnel and other friends. He may also be able to make practical suggestions to the trainees for advertising their wares, and for ways and means of finding buyers in nearby barrios or towns.

CHAPTER 10 — THE MINIMUM ADDITIONAL INCOME (MAC) PROJECT

The grass-roots test of a rural program is, of course, its effectiveness in individual families. Conscious of this fact, PRRM started experimenting some years ago with ways and means of gauging the impact of its livelihood program on families. The aim was to find a type of measurement that would be meaningful to the farm families themselves, and more stimulating to them than abstract, perhaps incomprehensible, statistics. The idea then developed of testing the effects of specific activities on the individual family's income level.

SIX WAYS OF INCREASING THE FAMILY INCOME

Under the livelihood program described in the foregoing chapters, there are six principal ways in which most individual farm families might increase their incomes. These six ways are: (1) improving their rice culture, so as to obtain better yields and better quality; (2) producing one or more well-selected secondary crops; (3) making use of homelots for vegetable or fruit growing; (4) raising more and better poultry; (5) raising swine; and (6) learning and starting a small rural industry, which can be carried on during slack seasons.

Cooperative organizations provide an additional means of increasing family incomes, but they are not included in the list because the cooperative societies do not operate separately, but in conjunction with the activities just mentioned. For example, a loan from a credit cooperative may be extremely helpful in starting or expanding any one of these activities. Similarly, the sale of a farm family's increased production through a marketing cooperative is likely to bring a better return in money than individual marketing. Thus membership in a cooperative organization may facilitate either more production or more income from the products sold.

THE MINIMUM ADDITIONAL INCOME (MAC) PROJECT

SETTING AN ATTAINABLE TARGET

From staff discussions, the further idea emerged that it might be useful to set a specific target for individual families, so that farmers taking up these various projects would have the incentive of a definite goal, stated in terms of increased income, that they could strive to reach--or surpass. The target, of course, would have to be an attainable one.

On the basis of previous experience, and after considerable deliberation, the livelihood departments selected as a reasonable target an <u>increase</u> of at least ₱200 in a family's annual income. This would mean, for an average Filipino farm family, a rise of between 25 and 30 per cent. To make the goal more specific, and to encourage diversification in economic activity, PRRM set the following subtargets as a standard:

Activity	Minimum Target in Increased Annual Income
Improved rice culture	₱ 80
Secondary crop production	40
Homelot gardening	40
Poultry raising	30
Swine-raising	10
Rural industry	--
	₱200

This standard set of subtargets was intended only as a broad guide, to be used with considerable flexibility depending on the conditions faced by each farmer. One might find it convenient, for example, to put more emphasis on swine-raising and less on poultry-raising or homelot gardening. No specific subtarget was set for income from a rural industry even though, in some cases, it might provide a significant portion of a family's total increase in income.

THE MAC PROJECT

After some experimentation with this approach, PRRM decided to inaugurate a definite program embodying the above targets, and to call it the Minimum Additional Income project. Someone thought that

"MAC" would be a more convenient abbreviation than "MAI," and others agreed. So, from the beginning, it has been known as the MAC project.

Demonstration Farmers as Pace-Setters

The next idea that developed was that it would be desirable to have, in all the PRRM-aided barrios, individual farmers who would serve as "pace-setters." They would be invited to undertake the several activities contemplated under the MAC project, and to help demonstrate to their neighbors that these activities could lead to an increased income for each family of at least ₱200.

As a result, the "demonstration farmer," as conceived by PRRM, had a special meaning. His role was wider than that of simply demonstrating better methods of producing a single crop. In PRRM, a demonstration farmer is one who demonstrates, through five or six activities, a diversified approach to the objective of substantially increasing his family's income.

Selecting the Demonstration Farmers

The task of selecting the demonstration farmers falls mainly on the RRW, who is advised to do this in consultation with discriminating leaders in the barrio--including members of the barrio council, especially the councillor for livelihood.

Information gained and acquaintanceships developed during the initial socio-economic survey of the barrio are usually quite valuable to the RRW as he begins his search for the best potential demonstration farmers.

The criteria to be used in making the selections have been developed carefully by the PRRM livelihood departments. Subsequent experience has shown that better results can be expected if selections are always made on the basis of these criteria, which are:

1. Willingness to engage in scientific methods of farming.

2. Willingness to undertake all the MAC project activities.

THE MINIMUM ADDITIONAL INCOME (MAC) PROJECT

3. Sufficient financial resources (including borrowing capability) to participate in the MAC program.

4. Membership, or prospective membership, in a local credit union.

5. Readiness of the farmer and his family to strive to become a model farm family. (See Chapter 21.)

6. Willingness to attend farmers' seminars, classes, or study groups, and to conduct or participate in farming demonstrations.

After making a tentative selection of prospective demonstration farmers—on the basis of the socio-economic survey, personal contacts, and discussions with selected leaders in the barrio—the RRW proceeds to talk personally with each man chosen. The purpose of these talks is to explain the MAC project and its purpose, to see whether the farmer is willing to work hard to become a demonstration farmer, and to satisfy the RRW that he meets all the criteria listed above. During each talk, the RRW makes sure that the farmer does not have false expectations of material aid, and that he is not afraid of responsibility.

After these exploratory conversations have been completed, the RRW, after further consultation with the barrio council members, reaches a definite decision on who will be asked to become demonstration farmers. He then invites them to a scheduled meeting.

Training of the Demonstration Farmers

The training of the demonstration farmers begins at this meeting. The first step is for the RRW to brief the groups fully on what a demonstration farmer is, and what he is expected to do. He explains the system of targets, the value of having specific targets at which to aim, and the benefits to each family of the increased income that can be earned. He emphasizes PRRM's readiness to provide guidance and technical assistance. And he tries to instill in each member of the group a determination to do his best to become a demonstration farmer who will inspire others in the barrio to follow his example.

Sometimes PRRM specialists, technical associates, or team captains attend these important first meetings. When present, they give their support to the RRW as he starts the special training program.

At the first meeting, a tentative schedule is set up for the demonstration farmers' training program. It includes farmers' training classes, seminars, or study groups, in which the main responsibility for training is carried by PRRM specialists, technical associates, and technical assistants. The training is given systematically, and progressively, in each of the types of activity included in the MAC project. While the demonstration farmers usually form the nucleus of those receiving such training, others in the barrio who are interested are often welcomed at the training sessions.

Thus the training is specifically geared to the objectives of the MAC project. An added feature, which was found to be necessary and is now regularly incorporated, is training in maintaining fairly simple farm accounts. Without such training, the typical farmer is not able to record accurately the gains in his family's income resulting from his participation in the MAC project.

The following form, made available to the demonstration farmers by PRRM, is used to record their total production and income, month by month, and to calculate the increase in their total income over that of the previous year.

FARMER'S INCOME RECORD
For the year_____ to_____

Name of Farmer_____ Barrio_____
Municipality_____ Province_____

Income Previous Year

     I. Rice   ₱ _____
    II. Secondary crop   _____
  III. Poultry   _____
   IV. Swine   _____
     V. Home garden   _____
   VI. Other sources   _____
              Total   ₱ _____

(continued)

M A C PROJECTS	Jan	Feb	Mar	(etc.)
I. Rice				
1. First crop				
a. Area planted				
b. Total yield in cavans				
c. Average yield per hectare				
d. Value in pesos				
2. Second crop				
a. Area planted				
b. Total yield in cavans				
c. Average yield per hectare				
d. Value in pesos				
3. Gross income (1 & 2)				
II. Secondary Crops				
1. Tobacco (or other crop)				
a. Area planted				
b. Yield				
c. Value in pesos				
2. Onions (or other crop)				
a. Area planted				
b. Yield				
c. Value in pesos				
3. Mushrooms (or other crop)				
a. Area planted				
b. Yield				
c. Value in pesos				
4. Gross income (1,2,3&4)				
III. Home gardening				
1. Vegetables and ornamental plants				
a. Area planted				
b. Yield in kilos				
c. Value in pesos				
2. Fruit trees				
a. Quantity of fruit sold				
b. Value in pesos				
3. Gross income (1 & 2)				

(continued)

IV. Swine Raising
   1. Income from:
      a. Meat, in pesos
         No. of heads
      b. Weanlings, in
         pesos
         No. of heads
      c. Services (boar)
         in pesos
         No. served
   2. Gross income
      (a, b & c)

V. Poultry Raising
   1. Income from:
      a. Meat (broilers,
         culls)
         No. of heads
      b. Eggs
         No. of eggs
      c. Chicks
         No. of chicks
   2. Gross income
      (a, b & c)

VI. Other Sources of Addi-
    tional Income
   1.
   2.
   3.
   Income (1, 2 & 3)

VII. Summary of I, II, III, IV,
    V & VI
   1. Total income from the
      above projects and other
      sources   _____

VIII. "ADDITIONAL INCOME:" Total income during current year (VII) less total income, previous year, as shown at the beginning of this table:

    Gross Income Current Year   _____
    Gross Income Previous Year   _____
    Additional Income During Current Year   _____

Effectiveness of the MAC Project

Since it was started as an experiment about ten years ago, the MAC project has convincingly proven the value of definite targets for increases in family income. It has also demonstrated the usefulness of relating these targets to diversified activities through which farm families in the Philippines have the best chance of augmenting their production and income.

With the exception of one year, in which PRRM was undergoing a reorganization, the number of demonstration farmers has increased year by year since the MAC project began.

After making due allowance for the effects of climate, price movements, and other variables, and for margins of error in the accounts maintained, it appears that practically all the demonstration farmers have increased their annual incomes by more than ₱200, and that the average increase is around ₱340.

In almost all cases, the families of the demonstration farmers--now numbering several thousand--have better food, better clothing, and better shelter than they had before joining the MAC project.

Most important of all, the demonstration farmers have stirred interest among other farmers--and their families--in learning new skills, in diversifying and improving their production, and in increasing their family incomes.

For all these reasons, PRRM plans to intensify and further expand its efforts through the Minimum Additional Income project.

FOUR-FOLD PROGRAM IN ACTION

II. EDUCATION

CHAPTER 11 HUMAN DEVELOPMENT AND THE FOUR-FOLD PROGRAM

The greatest asset of a nation is its people, and no national goal is more significant than the release of their potentialities--for individual growth, for productive work, and for enlightened citizenship. Human development is the key to all other development. And the essential ingredient of human development is education.

EDUCATION FOR WHOM?

It is sometimes said that the fundamental problems of education--such as the shortage of well-trained teachers, the shortage of money and facilities, and the need for curriculum reform--are the same the world over. This implies that there are only differences of degree or detail between the educational problems of one country and those of another.

This is, of course, an oversimplification. There are basic differences between the educational problems of the economically developed nations and those confronting the less developed nations. A tendency to regard them as fundamentally the same has led many emerging countries to imitate the educational patterns of the most economically advanced countries. This tendency, which may be unconsciously encouraged by educational advisers from the more developed nations, may lead to the neglect of serious problems--and of notable opportunities--in the developing nations.

Take, for example, a broad question: education for whom? The advanced countries have for many years had systems of universal education. As a result, a very large percentage of their adult populations have had at least seven or eight years of schooling. A high proportion have been through high school and perhaps had some vocational or technical training. And the numbers of those going on to college and university, and into postgraduate study and training, have been steadily rising.

In countries that are striving to "catch up," it is not surprising that educators are focusing their attention on the expansion and improvement of primary and secondary schools, vocational and technical schools, universities and professional training. The strengthening of existing educational systems, public and private, is costly and difficult--but essential to real progress in these areas.

But is it enough? PRRM believes that it is not --because in the Philippines, as in other developing countries, most of the adult and many of the teen-age population have had little, if any, opportunity for education. A large number never went to school at all. Many who did enter primary school stayed only one or two or three years. Only a very small minority of the people were ever able to go to high school or beyond. They are now entirely outside the formal educational system, with no prospect of getting back into it. Compared to the adult populations of the economically more advanced nations, they are gravely handicapped.

PRRM has found this picture to be both disturbing and exhilarating. It is disturbing because, without some additional education, the vast majority of the teen-age and adult population--who are the "present generation" in the Philippines--cannot participate intelligently in the modernization of the country; this means the loss of a tremendous potential asset. Nor can they provide home environments that are conducive to the best development of their children.

But the picture is also exhilarating, for several reasons. First, those between the ages of, say, 15 and 45 are fully capable of learning, and many have a burning desire to learn. Second, as PRRM has demonstrated, it is possible to give them, at minimal cost, the essentials of the education they need most. Third, when they do have opportunities to learn, in ways they can fully understand, they usually respond eagerly. Fourth, if the education they receive is relevant to their needs, it can have a tremendous effect on their outlook, their self-reliance, and their contributions to local and national development.

It must be remembered, of course, that adult and teen-age populations in the rural areas are working people. It is not feasible to think of their going back to formal school classes as children do, and in that way capturing all that they missed in their early years. It is necessary to be rigorously selective --providing not a formal array of subject matter, but information and skills that the people urgently need. To be effective, fundamental education for adults and teen-agers in the barrios must be highly germane and practical. Before this standard can be achieved, it is necessary to consider the question:

EDUCATION FOR WHAT?

PRRM's answer to this question is not an outgrowth of any complicated or obscure philosophy of education. It is rooted, rather, in the Rural Reconstruction Movement's own practical experience in pre-Communist China and in the Philippines: an experience of discovering at firsthand, by living among the rural people, their most pressing needs, and then shaping an educational program to help meet them. The needs found are those now defined in the PRRM four-fold program: better livelihood, to combat poverty; relevant education, to combat ignorance and superstition; more knowledge about health, to combat disease; and techniques of social organization and self-government, to combat civic apathy.

In each of these areas, moreover, the need is not only for information, but for specific skills, and for practice in applying new knowledge, so that the relatively little outside help the people receive will be a stepping-stone to a great deal of self-help. Education will then not only be for life; it will enable the people to remake their lives and, as they do so, to enter the mainstream of national development.

Looking at the problem of education from a broader viewpoint, one of the great needs of the contemporary world is a means of unlocking the potentialities of young people and adults in all the developing nations, including the vast majorities who live in the rural areas. This is a colossal task, and there is no simple key to its solution. But if the people's practical knowledge and capabilities can be increased through a system of selective education, by means that are manageable and economical, it will be an important first step--one that will give firmer ground for hope that increasing enlightenment, prosperity, and peace can be achieved within the family of man.

EDUCATION AND DEVELOPMENT

National development involves an expanding application of science and technology in virtually all fields. Anyone participating in this process--including the farmer selecting his seeds for the following year, or preparing a compost pile--needs some comprehension of what he is doing. This requires education.

Development is greatly facilitated by an effective assimilation of technical and economic assistance, when it becomes available. This, too, requires education--not elaborate, but rudimentary.

As development progresses, there is a steady shift in need and emphasis to higher skills and more specialized knowledge. Those in the adult population who are best prepared to acquire such additional skills and knowledge are, as a rule, those who have made a beginning--who have already acquired, through education and experience, some modern skills and knowledge.

The intimate relationship between education and development has not always been clearly perceived. Until quite recently, most economists tended to regard education as a consumer's luxury, nice to have if it can be afforded. But during the last decade, economists have increasingly come to view education as an "investment" of basic importance to an acceleration of economic growth. Dr. Phillip Coombs, a distinguished educator, noting this phenomenon, remarked wryly: "Labeling education an 'investment industry' implies that the development of people is as important as the development of things--which the educators have been hinting at all along."

There is now wide acceptance of the proposition

that the accumulation of intellectual capital is as important for economic and social development as the accumulation of physical capital, and, in the long run, perhaps much more important. This is borne out by a number of recent studies in both the more developed and the less developed countries, which show that charts of educational development and of economic-social development have approximately the same curves.

The pace of scientific and technical advance is now so rapid that education in all countries needs to be more and more a cradle-to-grave enterprise. This calls for new approaches, new techniques of teaching and learning. As one perceptive scholar put it: "The old forms and rituals of education will not suffice."

PRRM EDUCATION DEPARTMENT

It is with such an outlook, unimpeded by "old forms and rituals of education," that the PRRM Education Department approaches its task. Its work is not principally with the younger children of the barrios, since the government has assumed the main responsibility for primary education, but with the teen-agers and adults who have passed "school age."

The department has a dual role. The first is to conduct its own program among the people. This program, described in the next two chapters, consists of literacy work and cultural activities. The literacy work includes the teaching of literacy, the training of auxiliary literacy teachers, the promotion of reading centers and reading circles, and the production of appropriate reading materials. Cultural activities are designed to enrich the people's lives and make them more enjoyable. The activities include the promotion and teaching of folk dancing, folk music, folk drama, games and sports; and encouragement for the development of individual skills and hobbies.

The second role of the Education Department is to give assistance and support to all other PRRM departments. This is done through (a) collaboration in producing suitable illustrated literature for use in training and promotion, in all parts of the program; (b) assistance in the collection, from all sources,

of reading materials through reading centers and
reading circles; and (d) using the folk drama as an
additional means of conveying to the people new insights into the meaning of their development activities.

EDUCATION AND THE FOUR-FOLD PROGRAM

While it is true that the work of the Education
Department supports all segments of the PRRM operation, it is equally true that the other three parts
of PRRM's four-fold program are educational. The
work in livelihood is, basically, practical education
in better plant production, animal production, cooperatives, village industries, and vocational arts.
The health program is, primarily, education in hygiene and in the prevention of diseases. The self-
government program is, essentially, education in citizenship, leadership, and the development and operation of barrio institutions. In each area, PRRM's
aim is to evoke the interests and energies of the
people, and to give them tools--of knowledge and
skills--with which they can help themselves and their
communities.

As previously emphasized, PRRM's deepest interest is in human development. It is concerned not
only with education as the essential ingredient of
development, but with the effect of education on the
individual. It is concerned not only with "development" as such, but with what happens to people during
the process of development.

One lesson of the postwar period is that the initial impact of economic development may be an increase in social and political instability. In the
midst of change, many people may feel that events are
passing them by, leaving them uprooted, detached and
adrift, often amid unfamiliar and confusing surroundings.

The strength and appeal of the four-fold program
lie in its emphasis on development of the whole person, and on involving all the people, as far as practicable, in all parts of the development program.
This gives them a sense of belonging. They feel that
change and progress in their communities are in line
with their own aspirations and are, in a real mea-

sure, results of their own decisions and labor. Economic and social evolution is no longer something to be feared. It is, instead, an achievement of broadening significance to them and their children.

CHAPTER 12 — LITERACY AND LITERATURE

A recent study conducted by the United Nations revealed that, in many of the countries of Asia, Africa, and Latin America, the growth of literacy during the past decade has not kept pace with the increase of population. Literacy rates in these countries, instead of rising, have actually declined, despite the allocation of substantial funds for public education and literacy programs.

ILLITERACY IN THE PHILIPPINES

The Philippines share with all the newly developing nations the basic problem of illiteracy among the masses. Although the Filipino budget for education is notably higher than in most emerging countries, large numbers of children drop out of school after one, two, or three years. A high percentage of these dropouts quickly revert to illiteracy.

Studies conducted by the Research, Evaluation, and Guidance Division of the Bureau of Public Schools have shown that only about half the fourth grade children tested in nine major Filipino languages are literate in their own vernaculars. This is in spite of the fact that the public schools now teach children in their own vernaculars during the first two years of school, and introduce English only during the third year.

The problem of literacy education among adolescents and adults is equally serious. In these two groups are millions who have never learned to read and write or, due to lack of practice, have forgotten how to do so. Census returns in 1948 indicated that more than 5 million Filipinos past the primary school age were illiterate.

According to the census of 1960, the total number of illiterates was still more than 5 million, representing about 28 per cent of the population ten years of age and above. The percentage of illiteracy in rural areas is higher than in the cities.

PRRM LITERACY PROGRAM

Literacy is, of course, only a starting point for other education. If several millions of our people cannot read and write, we must assume that many more do not have the basic knowledge, or acquire the day-to-day information, that they need for intelligent citizenship.

The PRRM literacy education program, initiated in 1952, is based on the belief that inability to read and write is a great hindrance to social and economic progress, the establishment of good government, and the growth of democratic processes. An illiterate peasant is gravely handicapped in learning how to provide better for the health and sustenance of his family. And he is deprived of the opportunity to participate fully in the social, cultural, and civic life of the community.

As Dr. Y.C. James Yen has said:

> If the people are underdeveloped, the natural resources are underdeveloped. If the natural resources are underdeveloped, the country is underdeveloped.... It is not enough to make the world safe for democracy.... Self-government is not a gift from above; it is an achievement of the people.... For a healthy democracy, you must first have an informed citizenry.

Beginnings

In 1952, PRRM, then in its infancy, embarked upon two literacy projects in the barrios of Malanday and Maly, both in San Mateo municipality, Rizal province. The cooperation of barrio officials and local teachers was enlisted. The first task was to find out the extent of illiteracy in each barrio. In Maly, the barrio lieutenant and head teacher asked the school children whether their parents knew how to read a magazine, in Tagalog, called "Liwayway." The parents of those who did not raise their hands were listed as probably illiterate. In Malanday, the barrio lieutenant personally conducted a one-man census of the illiterates in his community.

The senior PRRM worker present then made house-to-house visits in both barrios, accompanied by the barrio lieutenant or a school teacher, in an effort to persuade people to join the first adult literacy classes. In Malanday, 28 signed up, and in Maly, 42. The classes were conducted by retired school teachers; PRRM paid each an honorarium of 25 pesos per month. In February, 1953, the first literacy class in Nueva Ecija was started, in Aulo, Laur. These were the small beginnings of PRRM's literacy program.

Syllabic Method and Teaching Aids

After completing the first training course for full-time workers in April, 1953, PRRM initiated a study to determine the simplest and most effective method of teaching literacy, as rapidly as possible with limited personnel, in Filipino barrios where different dialects were spoken. The conclusion reached, in early 1954, was that the syllabic method is most practical--because it facilitates rapid learning, and because Tagalog and other Philippine dialects are phonetic; that is, all letters and syllables are sounded.

The next step was to prepare a first primer, and a set of teaching aids designed to make up what is now called a literacy kit. The equipment developed for the kit included (a) printed syllable charts employing both small and capital letters to show all the syllables in their natural and inverted forms; (b) a set of syllable cards each showing a syllable in natural form on one side, and in inverted form on the other; (c) a packet chart; and (d) a small blackboard.

In the syllabic method, syllables are taught step by step, in alphabetical order. Instruction starts with the vowels--a, e, i, o, u. This is followed by teaching the syllables--ba, be, bi, bo, bu, and so on--until the last group of syllables--ya, ye, yi, yo, yu--is reached. First in capital letters, then in small letters, syllables are learned in their natural and inverted forms, with use of the following syllable charts:

Pilipino Syllables in their Natural Form in Capital Letters

A	E	I	O	U
BA	BE	BI	BO	BU
KA	KE	KI	KO	KU
DA	DE	DI	DO	DU
GA	GE	GI	GO	GU
HA	HE	HI	HO	HU
LA	LE	LI	LO	LU
MA	ME	MI	MO	MU
NA	NE	NI	NO	NU
NGA	NGE	NGI	NGO	NGU
PA	PE	PI	PO	PU
RA	RE	RI	RO	RU
SA	SE	SI	SO	SU
TA	TE	TI	TO	TU
WA	WE	WI	WO	WU
YA	YE	YI	YO	YU

Pilipino Syllables in their Natural Form in Small Letters

a	e	i	o	u
ba	be	bi	bo	bu
ka	ke	ki	ko	ku
da	de	di	do	du
ga	ge	gi	go	gu
ha	he	hi	ho	hu
la	le	li	lo	lu
ma	me	mi	mo	mu
na	ne	ni	no	nu
nga	nge	ngi	ngo	ngu
pa	pe	pi	po	pu
ra	re	ri	ro	ru
sa	se	si	so	su
ta	te	ti	to	tu
wa	we	wi	wo	wu
ya	ye	yi	yo	yu

Pilipino Syllables in their Inverted Form in Capital Letters

AB	EB	IB	OB	UB
AK	EK	IK	OK	UK
AD	ED	ID	OD	UD
AG	EG	IG	OG	UG
AL	EL	IL	OL	UL
AM	EM	IM	OM	UM
AN	EN	IN	ON	UN

ANG	ENG	ING	ONG	UNG
AP	EP	IP	OP	UP
AR	ER	IR	OR	UR
AS	ES	IS	OS	US
AT	ET	IT	OT	UT
AW	EW	IW	OW	UW
AY	EY	IY	OY	UY

Pilipino Syllables in their Inverted Form in Small Letters

ab	eb	ib	ob	ub
ak	ek	ik	ok	uk
ad	ed	id	od	ud
ag	eg	ig	og	ug
al	el	il	ol	ul
am	em	im	om	um
an	en	in	on	un
ang	eng	ing	ong	ung
ap	ep	ip	op	up
ar	er	ir	or	ur
as	es	is	os	us
at	et	it	ot	ut
aw	ew	iw	ow	uw
ay	ey	iy	oy	uy

After the mastery of the first and second lines of syllables, words are formed using the syllables learned. This process is repeated as additional lines of syllables are mastered. When used with the teaching aids, the syllabic method is both convenient and effective because the pupils understand clearly how each word is formed.

Role of the RRWs

The main responsibility for carrying out the PRRM literacy program rests on the shoulders of the RRWs.

During their pre-service training, all RRWs are prepared for this responsibility through instruction in various aspects of literacy work, including the identification of illiterates; methods employed to convince them to join literacy classes; characteristics of adult pupils; how to organize and conduct a literacy class; steps and techniques in the syllabic method; and how to cope with some of the special problems encountered.

Role of Auxiliary Literacy Teachers

Literacy teaching does not require a high level of education. By experimentation, PRRM confirmed a belief that some of the barrio people with a little education could learn fairly easily to teach others to read and write. This would afford a triple advantage. First, the burden of literacy teaching would not fall wholly on the RRWs, who have many other duties. Second, there would be greater participation of the barrio people in the actual conduct of the program. Third, the expansion of literacy teaching would be accelerated.

Accordingly, PRRM made an early start in training "auxiliary literacy teachers," individuals in the barrios who showed a willingness to help others, and who had the character and personality to do a responsible job. As an incentive, PRRM started the practice of awarding a certificate of merit to each auxiliary teacher who trained at least three others to read and write. The number of auxiliary literacy teachers in PRRM-aided barrios has now risen to more than a hundred.

Literacy Classes

The PRRM-sponsored literacy classes have been organized with the support of the barrio councils, the people's associations, school teachers, and other civic-minded individuals. The RRWs have served as stimulators, coordinators, and teachers.

Those enrolled usually attend the literacy classes for a total of 70 hours or more, distributed over a period of three to four months. As a rule, they can learn in that time to read easy printed materials, to write a simple message, and to do elementary arithmetic.

Additional Training for "Functional" Literacy

One painful lesson from PRRM's experience in this field is that those who learn to read and write may rapidly forget these skills if they are not put to use immediately. A survey conducted in 16 of the PRRM-aided barrios showed that, of a total of 481 graduates in basic literacy, 114, or 25 per cent, had reverted to illiteracy after an interval of two years or more.

To help remedy this situation, PRRM has now introduced a second stage in its literacy program, to help literacy graduates become truly "functional" literates. This second stage consists partly of additional training, but its chief emphasis is on providing stimulus and opportunity to put their new literacy skills to use.

The stimulus is provided partly through talks to the literacy classes, and to literacy graduates, on subjects that will broaden their interests and their appetite for learning. The talks may be on a wide range of topics including practical skills, current events, Philippine history, geography and government, and the rights and responsibilities of citizens in a democracy.

There are four principal ways in which PRRM helps to give literacy graduates more opportunities to use their new skills: (a) by acquiring and distributing suitable reading materials; (b) by establishing reading centers, which function as small libraries in the barrios; (c) by organizing reading circles or clubs, consisting of literate people who come together to make reading a regular activity under a supervised plan; and (d) by giving greater responsibilities to literacy graduates in the development programs so that their literacy can be put to work on the study of simple printed materials, or the keeping of records and accounts, or the preparing of reports.

The Reading Center

The reading center is a place where various types of literature are kept and displayed, and where the barrio people can go to read or borrow them. The center is managed and maintained by members of the reading circles. The RRW usually trains the members to take on these responsibilities, and sets up a schedule assigning those who live closest to the center to take charge, in rotation.

The main sources of reading materials are: (a) pamphlets and a monthly paper issued by PRRM; (b) magazines, pamphlets, and brochures from the government bureaus and offices, and the National Media Production Center; (c) reading materials secured from private agencies; and (d) magazines and newspapers solicited from civic-spirited people in the barrio.

The Reading Circle

A reading circle is an informal group of literate people in the barrio who endeavor to make reading part of their daily lives. An effort is made to see that every literacy graduate becomes a member of a reading circle. The group meets regularly to read and discuss various subjects, according to the members' interests and needs. A discussion leader is chosen for each meeting, and whenever possible a resource person is invited to attend.

The chief objectives of the reading circle are: (a) to provide an opportunity for the literate members of the barrio to form the habit of regular reading; (b) to develop each person's ability to express himself and communicate his ideas; (c) to prevent reversion to illiteracy on the part of literacy graduates and people who have completed only the primary grades; (d) to promote cooperative and friendly relationships among the members; and (e) to develop more active and enlightened citizens.

These steps are recommended to the RRW in organizing the reading circle:

1. Explain, at a meeting or through personal contacts, the benefits to be derived from membership in an active reading circle.

2. Invite all the literate citizens as well as the new literacy graduates to attend.

3. List the names of all who wish to join. Ask them to agree on a schedule for regular meeting.

4. Either post or announce the schedule.

The activities for a meeting will usually include group singing, news reporting, oral reading, group discussion, reporting on useful items read, and planning for the next meeting.

Preparation and Distribution of Literature

The PRRM departments have issued many publications that help to advance the aims of the four-fold program as they provide reading material for the literacy graduates. Brochures and pamphlets, which are prepared and distributed to the field from time to time, give the people selected information and practical know-how in the areas of livelihood, health, education, and government. The Education Department has prepared special reading materials for the literacy pupils and members of the reading circles. In addition, PRRM publishes a monthly paper in Pilipino, called "Tinig ng Nayon" (Voice of the Barrio), and distributes it free to the people. This paper contains articles on the four-fold program, and reports on interesting projects and activities in the barrios, as well as short stories and poems.

The reading materials that have been prepared and distributed in the barrios by PRRM include these titles:

1. Lives and Teachings of Great Filipinos
2. Four Freedoms for the Barrio People: Freedom from Hunger, Freedom from Disease, Freedom from Ignorance, and Freedom from Civic Inertia
3. Life and Liberty
4. Beginning to Read and Write
5. Exercises in Reading
6. Progressive Poultry Raising
7. Progressive Swine Raising
8. Masagana Rice Culture
9. Secondary Crop Production
10. Mushroom Culture
11. Orchard Growing
12. Homelot Gardening
13. The Rural Homemaker
14. Sewing for the Family
15. Simple Recipes for Every Home
16. RRMA Manual
17. RRYA Manual
18. Barrio Self-Government
19. The Barrio Charter
20. Primer on the Revised Barrio Charter
21. The Strength of the Rural Reconstruction Men's Association
22. The Strength of the Rural Reconstruction Women's Association
23. The Strength of the Rural Reconstruction Youth Association
24. Leadership Training Manual
25. Model Farm Family Manual
26. Note on How to Become a Model Farm Family
27. Water-Sealed Toilet
28. Blind Drainage for Every Home

LITERACY AND LITERATURE

29. Environmental Sanitation
30. First Aid Manual
31. Health Manual
32. Education Manual
33. Guide in Teaching How to Read and Write
34. Parliamentary Procedures
35. Household Hints and Tips

Recurring Problems

The fact that literacy has not spread as rapidly as population has grown, in many newly developing countries, is one evidence of the difficulties of literacy work. These are some of the problems that PRRM has faced, and the responses to them that have been found most effective to date:

1) <u>Need for public backing in the barrios</u>. It is not usually easy for illiterate peasant men and women to overcome their inertia, perhaps their shyness as well, and to commit themselves to the task of learning to read and write. In many cases, because their experience is limited, they do not appreciate the extent to which "book learning" may be of practical value to them. Under these circumstances, a favorable atmosphere must be created in the barrio for literacy education. One who is considering joining a literacy class needs to feel that others will approve his action.

<u>Response</u>: One of the best ways to develop a favorable atmosphere within the community is to enlist the open backing and encouragement of leading citizens. There are several ways to do this: (a) Attend a meeting of the barrio council and explain to the members the importance of the literacy program, and its need for strong support. Ask them to encourage people to join the literacy classes. (b) Make a similar appeal through personal calls on other influential people in the barrio. (c) Urge a substantial number of village leaders to attend the graduation ceremoney of each literacy class, and be sure that it is an interesting one. This will make it easier to organize the next class. (d) If additional persuasion is needed, inform members of the barrio council and other leaders that their barrio cannot hope to win a satisfactory rating on their progress toward becoming a "model village" unless

they show a rapid gain in literacy.

2) <u>Identifying the illiterates</u>. Many people are embarrassed or ashamed to admit that they are not literate. Some can read a little but cannot write; some know how to write only their names. Quite a number cover up these facts by dressing well, associating with educated people, or wearing fountain pens and carrying around reading materials. Some "detective work" may be needed to get the desired information:

<u>Response</u>: Get as much data as you can on the extent of illiteracy in each family during the socio-economic survey. Supplement this with information gleaned discreetly from friends and relatives, public school teachers, and others. Study the registered voter lists, which are supposed to include only persons who can read and write. Information may also be gained by asking those present at a meeting to sign certain forms; or by passing out reading materials (which illiterates may refuse to take); or by asking whether a person voted at the last election; or by noting incorrect pronunciations of words that a literate would know how to pronounce correctly.

If the members of a literacy class agree, allow curious onlookers to watch a class in session. This has sometimes led an onlooker to divulge the fact that he is illiterate, and would like an opportunity to study.

3) <u>Convincing people to join literacy classes</u>. Those who are shy and do not wish to study in the presence of others may plead that they are too busy, or can study only at night, or that they have poor eyesight, poor hearing, or an inability to control their hand muscles sufficiently for writing. Others may feel that literacy would not be much help to them, or that they are past the age when they should have schooling. Some may think it would be worth their while to join a class only if they could learn to read in a hurry. Others may not wish to be taught by anyone in the barrio except the RRW.

<u>Response</u>: (a) During the period of intensive preparation and promotion for a literacy class, make a list of the illiterate persons who might

be persuaded to enroll. Seek opportunities to befriend them and talk with them. The following imaginary conversation between an RRW and a farmer may be suggestive:

RRW — Good evening, Mang José. I came earlier to see you, but you were still in the field.

Farmer — Good evening, Maestro. You know, I never get back to the house these days much before dark. And I leave before sunup. Come, let's go up to the house. I am glad you came to visit us.

RRW — Well, I came to tell you that we've gotten a supply of superior onion seeds, and they will be distributed at the barrio hall tomorrow afternoon. Please sign your name here and indicate the number of pounds you would like to order.

Farmer — Kindly just write it down for me. I'll order two pounds.

RRW — And here is a sheet of instructions telling about the onion seeds, and the best way to grow them.

Farmer — Will you please read it for me? It's really difficult for one like me who did not have the chance to go to school.

RRW — I am sure you wanted very much to study during your younger days, but couldn't because of special circumstances. You know, Mang José, we are getting ready to start a new literacy class after the rice crop has been harvested. Join it and I assure you that in a few weeks you can learn to read, yourself.

Farmer — By the way, Maestro, will you tell me what's in this letter that came yesterday? I guess it is from a person who wants to buy some piglets from our sow's last litter. A man dropped by and inquired about them last week.

RRW — I would be glad to, Mang Jose. Now, what about signing up for our literacy class? Your cousin, Mang Eduardo, has agreed to join.

Farmer — I heard about that. Well, if he can learn to read, maybe I can too. Then, I hope I won't have to ask other people, all the time, to read things for me.

RRW — Good, I'll put your name down then. Don't forget to get your onion seeds tomorrow afternoon.

Farmer — I won't forget. And I'll be coming with Eduardo to the literacy class.

During this kind of conversation, it may be helpful to mention a few of the specific advantages of being able to read and write and do simple arithmetic. Indicate that there will be practically no expense, since the teaching materials will be provided free except for paper and pencils. Mention by name people who have gone through the course, and are now learning many new things because they know how to read.

If the person you are trying to convince is a young parent, point out that literacy makes it possible to help the children with their school work, and to understand what they are learning. If the Model Farm Family (MFF) program is making headway in the barrio, show the relationship of literacy to the rating of families under that program.

(b) If you find that some of the prospective pupils seem reluctant to attend class in a public or conspicuous place, arrange to convene the sessions in a more isolated location.

(c) Sometimes it is helpful to enlist the cooperation of others in persuading those who are undecided or may be fearful. Family members, friends, previous literacy graduates, or perhaps a teacher, a priest, or some member of the barrio council might gladly help. The purpose is not to exert pressure, but to make prospective pupils feel that others would like to see them learn, and are confident that they can.

(d) Let the termination of one literacy course be part of the preparation for the next, by having a graduation ceremony at which all who have completed the course are given certificates. Make the accompanying program as attractive as possible, and invite not only the leading people of the barrio, but also those who may enroll in the next literacy class. Through posters or notices, try to ensure good attendance from the barrio as a whole. All this helps to give added prestige to the acquisition of literacy, and thus prepares the way for further efforts.

(e) Try to make evident the rewards that come to those who complete the course. Some discover that by reading simple instructions, they can produce better crops. Some find better job opportunities. Many are able to participate more easily and effectively in organizations, or in group projects in agriculture, health, or self-government. Ask those who have had such experiences to tell others about them.

(f) A special technique that has been used with good effect in some barrios is to promote a folk drama portraying the advantages of being literate, and the disadvantages of being illiterate. The drama should not ridicule illiteracy, however, since this might make people reluctant to give evidence of their ignorance by joining a literacy class.

4) <u>Time and place for literacy classes</u>. One difficulty in getting classes under way is settling on a mutually convenient time and place.

<u>Response</u>: Find a mutually acceptable meeting place, preferably one that will be free from onlookers and other distractions. Choose a season of the year, days of the week, and hours of the day that will be convenient for all prospective members of the class. As a rule, it is best to have classes during off-working seasons, and to consult the members before deciding on the days and hours. Unless the barrio is quite small, organize the classes by blocks or "puroks." This will make it reasonably convenient for everyone to attend.

5) <u>Maintaining interest in a literacy class</u>. Some-

times, after a class has started well, interest begins to lag and attendance falls off.

Response: (a) Prepare thoroughly for the class. Know exactly what you hope to accomplish during the period, and how. Be well-groomed. Remember that the interest, sincerity, and warmth of the teacher may affect greatly the pupils' attitudes.

(b) Begin and end the class punctually. Group singing at the start may be a good way to create an easy, relaxed atmosphere before the work commences.

(c) Divide the period according to subjects: reading, writing, arithmetic, and special topics.

(d) Compliment good work. From time to time, make encouraging comments on the progress the class members are making. Mention occasionally the certificates they will receive upon graduation. Some RRWs have found it useful to hold little contests in each subject, and to give token prizes to the winners.

(e) If there is a marked difference between the slower and the faster learners, give differentiated assignments adapted to the capabilities of each group. This must be done skillfully, to avoid discouraging the slower learners.

(f) At appropriate intervals, give short examinations or tests in each subject, to check on the progress being made. Remember that a sense of accomplishment is the most important stimulus to continuing interest. Give members specific responsibilities, and opportunities to recite or report. A little recognition goes a long way.

(g) Ask members of the barrio council and others to give their personal encouragement to members of the class.

6) Selecting auxiliary literacy teachers. Experience has shown that the cause of literacy may be hindered rather than helped if good standards are not observed in selecting auxiliary literacy teachers.

Response: Those chosen for training should meet

these standards: (a) preferably a high school education, but at least a full elementary school education; (b) personality traits which include good moral character, a natural liking for people, patience, and some ability to lead a small group; (c) sufficient maturity: an age of 18 or more is preferred, and in no case should the auxiliary literacy teacher be less than 16 years old; (d) active interest, shown by willingness to take special training for the work, and to devote the time needed to make a success of it; (e) permanent residence in the barrio.

7) <u>Training auxiliary literacy teachers</u>. Experience has shown the fallacy of supposing that every literate person, without special training, can do an acceptable job of teaching others.

<u>Response</u>: It is essential that each auxiliary teacher acquire: (a) Skill in explaining the syllabic method, the reasons for using it, and the systematic way in which the syllables will be taught.

(b) Ability to explain, teach, and reteach, systematically, the successive groups of syllables in alphabetical order, with an appropriate amount of drill and review. The teaching of two-letter syllables is followed by the teaching of three-letter syllables. The tempo must be gauged to the learning ability of the students.

(c) Skill in the presentation and teaching of word-building, using only the syllables that have already been taught. After sufficient practice in word-building, "reading exercises" may be introduced. The rate of progress in the reading exercises must, similarly, be gauged to the capabilities of the group.

(d) Ability to synchronize instruction in writing with the reading lessons. As each set of syllables is taught, the pupils are asked to copy them. After they learn thoroughly how to write in printed syllables, they should be taught to write in script. Some RRWs are now experimenting with teaching the pupils how to write, first, in script, to save time spent in the transition from printing to script.

(e) Knowledge of how to teach number-writing and simple arithmetic.

(f) Knowledge of how to teach a pupil to write a simple letter or message.

8) <u>Making reading centers functional</u>. A reading center is considered "functional" when it is supplied with adequate interesting reading materials, when it is properly maintained and managed, and when the people make frequent use of it. But reading centers do not automatically become functional once they are established.

<u>Response</u>: (a) Ask the Rural Reconstruction Youth Association (RRYA) or the Rural Reconstruction Women's Association (RRWA) to assume responsibility for the maintenance and management of the reading center. This includes steps to make the center attractive, to keep records of the persons who read or borrow items from the center, to post simple reminders or notices on the proper handling and care of reading materials, and to solicit from all available sources additional reading materials that might be of interest to the barrio people. The RRW must help in getting these routines started.

(b) At meetings of the men's, women's, and youth associations, and of literacy classes, tell about the reading center and what it offers, and invite the people to make full use of it. Ask those who do to tell others about what they have seen and read.

(c) If there is a shortage of good reading materials, ask the barrio council to pass a resolution requesting donations of books, magazines, and other suitable items by public-spirited individuals. Ask members of the education committees of the men's, women's, and youth associations to follow up this resolution by soliciting contributions from PRRM headquarters and from other organizations such as the National Media Production Center, the Commission on Elections, the Presidential Assistant on Community Development, the United States Information Service, the Commission on Agricultural Productivity, the Asia

Foundation, the Department of Agricultural and Natural Resources, the Department of Health, the U.P. College of Agriculture, the Central Luzon State University, and other sources.

9) <u>Non-participation of the people in the reading center</u>. Many people who can read still do not know the value of reading, and prefer to spend their time in other ways, often far less profitable. Others may live far from the center.

<u>Response</u>: Make the reading center attractive and lively through posters, slogans, pictures, and other displays. It may also be possible to establish auxiliary reading centers in sections of the barrio far from the center--perhaps in homes, barber shops, or stores.

10) <u>Poor management</u> of the reading center, due to lack of training.

<u>Response</u>: Encourage members of the reading circle and the youth association to volunteer for training to manage the center. In one or two sessions, show them how to keep the shelves in order, how to keep systematic records of items borrowed and returned, and how to encourage everyone to take proper care of the reading materials.

A LOOK AHEAD

Further progress in the PRRM literacy program will probably depend largely on three main lines of development: first, an expansion in the number of auxiliary literacy teachers; second, an expansion in the production of illustrated reading materials tailored to the special interests and needs of the barrio people; and third, an intensification of PRRM efforts in this field.

More Auxiliary Literacy Teachers

Experience has shown that the growth of literacy in the PRRM-aided barrios does not attain a satisfactory rate unless the RRW shows considerable initiative and resourcefulness in "multiplying" his own efforts--by training auxiliary literacy teachers, helping them get started, and supervising their work.

Nearly every PRRM-aided barrio now has two or more persons classified as auxiliary literacy teachers. But this is not a sufficient number, and many have not been properly trained.

Plans are now being made for a more adequate standard training course for auxiliary literacy teachers, and for experimentation in giving this training at the Nieves center. RRWs will be given full information as these plans mature, and will be invited to add constructive ideas and suggestions growing out of their own experience.

Expanding Production of Reading Materials

There is now a clear need for more and better reading materials, in Tagalog, Ilokano, and other dialects, as well as English--materials well written, attractively published, and tailored to the interests, needs, vocabularies, and reading abilities of the literacy graduates. This does not mean that fewer publications will be obtained from sources outside the PRRM. It does mean there will be a growing nucleus of illustrated materials prepared and issued by PRRM specifically for the barrio people.

PRRM is planning to engage for this purpose skilled writers with a knowledge of the principal Filipino dialects. They will work with the various technical departments, and with administrative and field personnel (including RRWs), to produce the tailor-made pamphlets and other materials now needed.

These materials will be used not only to broaden the horizons of the people and enrich their general knowledge and cultural life; they will also buttress all segments of the PRRM integrated four-fold program. The RRWs will be requested to ascertain and report on the people's reactions to successive items as they appear. The information gained in this way will be used to improve the quality and usefulness of further publications.

Intensification of Literacy Program

In 1965, PRRM conducted experimentally, in 122 barrios, a project called "Operation Basa-Sulat" (or "Operation Reading and Writing") during a three-month period beginning in early September. An award of merit was given to each RRW, team captain, group

leader, and district field assistant who reached a
given level of achievement in the development of new
literates in their respective barrios or districts.
This special effort resulted in the graduation of
530 new literates, and led to a PRRM decision to continue Operation Basa-Sulat on a yearly basis.

CHAPTER 13 CULTURAL AND RECREATIONAL ACTIVITIES

The rural people of a nation are too often looked upon as impersonal "masses" of producers or consumers or political pawns. This is an artificial and distorted view. They, like any other group, are men, women, and children with greatly diversified needs and potentialities. As human beings, they need to be freed from their shackles of ignorance and superstition, poverty, ill health, and civic inertia.

It is essential that the people themselves take an active part in achieving these goals, instead of waiting to have things done for them and to them. They are more likely to assume active roles when they see that their lives can be freed from drabness and loneliness and boredom. These are dispiriting influences that make for fatalism and demoralization—sometimes evidenced by drunkenness, gambling, and other vices.

Each life must be seen as a whole, which needs for its full development a balance of interests. Without such a balance, conflicts and tensions are likely to arise. When there is incentive for rounded personal development, with adequate scope for differing tastes and aptitudes, both individuals and societies tend to be more integrated, more stable, and more versatile.

There is no need to postpone this objective to some future date when higher standards of living will prevail. The need is now. Cost is not a prohibiting factor. And PRRM experience indicates convincingly that all-round individual development facilitates economic and social development.

For these reasons, the PRRM education program aims to do more than promote literacy, literature, and useful knowledge. It also aims, through cultural and recreational programs, to help the barrio people find new enjoyments in life, and through them to achieve a lift of their spirits and a buoyant release from unending tedium and drabness.

CULTURAL AND RECREATIONAL ACTIVITIES

The cultural and recreational activities promoted through the PRRM educational program are folk dancing, singing, and drama; games and sports; and the cultivation of individual skills and hobbies.

These activities blend traditional and modern influences. They embody much that is inherited from the past--elements in Filipino culture that can be preserved, built upon, and expanded during the present era of dynamic social change. This continuity amid change gives our cultural life a more original and authentic quality; it also contributes to social stability in an era when greater stability is needed. At the same time, PRRM has found it useful to welcome elements from other cultures, when our experience shows them to be wholesome and congenial.

In the PRRM-aided barrios, cultural and recreational activities are promoted jointly by technical personnel of the education department, by RRWs working in the barrios, by officers and members of the people's associations, and often by special groups such as teachers in the local schools.

FOLK DANCING

The Philippines is rich in folk dance lore. We are a musical people who have long found rhythmic expression through songs and dances, and these have been passed on from generation to generation. The dances are mostly ritual in character. They exhibit a wide variety of themes such as agriculture and other occupations, courtship, marriage, religious observances, and war. Due perhaps to the local isolation caused by barriers of language and communication, the dances vary greatly according to district or region.

During modern times, there has been a marked decline in the traditional folk dances. Quite recently, however, there has been a renewed appreciation of their worth. They have been revived and quickened by the Bayanihan dancers and other folk dance groups, now of international fame, and at the barrio level by PRRM workers, school teachers, and others.

When PRRM first began its field work, folk dances were unpopular in the rural areas, perhaps because some younger people thought them old-fashioned, and some older people considered them degrading. To offset these attitudes, PRRM workers themselves, in a few barrios, learned and performed the folk dances of the area, demonstrating their inherent rhythm and beauty. Gradually the people regained an appreciation of their traditional dances, and began to participate.

An early turning point was a barrio group's presentation of a series of folk dances in Nangka, Marikana, Rizal, to commemorate the first anniversary of the PRRM Nangka pilot project. Since then, interest has spread steadily, though not without some active encouragement. Today there is folk dancing in nearly all PRRM-aided barrios.

Aims

In teaching and promoting folk dancing in the barrios, the PRRM Education Department has these aims: (a) to arouse among the people a better appreciation of historic Filipino melodies and folk dances; (b) to stimulate the interest of younger and older folk in performing and enjoying the traditional dances; (c) to help preserve for posterity the folk dances and music indigenous to different regions of the Philippines; and (d) to promote healthful relaxation and recreation, as well as bodily coordination, grace, and posture.

Teaching Methods and Procedures

For several years, detailed instructions for teaching folk dancing have been given to RRWs during their basic training. A summary of these instructions, in the form of a manual, may be obtained from the PRRM Education Department. It covers the fundamental positions of the feet and arms, the dancing terms used, the basic steps, and the patterns and sequences of the principal dances taught.

These general guidelines, derived from PRRM experience, are presented here for ready reference.

1. In teaching a dance, begin by giving its name and the region where it originated. Mention whether it is an occupational, courtship, marriage, fiesta, or war dance. If possible, tell something about the origin of the dance, and the customs, traditions, costumes, and mode of life of the people who

CULTURAL AND RECREATIONAL ACTIVITIES   231

originated it.

   2. Let the participants enjoy the music and analyze it with respect to tempo (slow, moderate, fast), mood (gay or sad, etc.), and count (1, 2, 3, etc.). Then repeat the music, and let everyone clap their hands or beat to the rhythm.

   3. If there is a song accompanying the dance, teach the words.

   4. Before taking up the dance itself, teach any intricate or unfamiliar steps. Be sure to give the names of the steps so everyone will become familiar with the terminology. Follow the written instructions and stick to the authentic traditional steps. Explain and demonstrate the steps in detail whenever necessary. Then let everyone try them with the teacher, and with each other. They learn best by seeing and doing.

   5. Get everyone into formation for the dance. Then teach the figures thoroughly, one by one, in succession. Always review previous steps and figures before taking up new ones. This avoids confusion and preserves the continuity of the dance.

   6. As the teaching progresses, encourage the participants to feel the music, and to give it expression and interpretation through the dance.

   7. When all the figures have been learned, perform the whole dance through. Repeat this until everyone can do it without strain, and enjoy it thoroughly.

Folk Dancing in the Barrios

   Learning the dances is the first stage; the next is putting them to use. There are four principal ways in which this is done in the PRRM-aided barrios.

   One is to have a folk dance on the program on special occasions in the barrio, such as a graduation, an induction of officers into a community organization, or a fiesta. It is now standard practice to have at least one folk dance performed on these occasions.

   Second, many barrios have now become fond of

holding occasional folk dance festivals, which all the people of the community are invited to attend, either as participants or onlookers. These barrio dance festivals are usually organized by one of the people's associations, or by two of them working together.

Third, in areas where PRRM has been operating for several years, larger-scale, competitive municipal folk dance festivals are organized from time to time. They involve weeks of practice, and the preparation of simple costumes by the competing teams from various barrios of the municipality. For the festival, one of the barrios serves as host to the others. Contests are held, impartial judges (selected from among PRRM personnel, or school teachers in the area, or prominent visitors) render their verdicts, and prizes are given for outstanding performance.

Fourth, similar sizable festivals are sometimes held for all the barrios to which RRWs of a single PRRM field team have been assigned. These festivals are quite similar to the municipal festivals, and are attended by dancing teams and visitors from each barrio. At these "team folk dance festivals," community interest and friendly rivalry are apt to reach new heights.

Promotion

These pointers have been derived from PRRM experience in promoting folk dancing in the barrios.

To cultivate initial interest: (a) Talk with the leaders of the three people's associations, and ask for their help. (b) Talk with parents of younger people who join the first folk dancing class. Explain the advantages to be derived. At the same time, try to persuade some of the older folks to join too; they may be as skillful as the young in some of the stylized traditional dances. (c) Tell about the Bayanihan folk dancers, and the prestige they have brought to the Philippines; explain that the beautiful Bayanihan dances are based on traditional Filipino folk dances in various parts of the islands.

To recruit members for a folk dancing class in the barrio: (a) Promote friendships among the prospective dancers. (b) Enlist the help of any in the barrio (perhaps including school teachers) who are already skilled in folk dancing. (c) Take the prospective class members to see folk dancing in another barrio. (d) Tell them that pairings will be according to their preferences; those who wish to may pair off with near relatives, and girls may choose their partners. (d) Discuss the prospect of friendly competition, after a while, with other barrios that are also starting classes in folk dancing. Appeal to community spirit and to love of competition, which is strong among Filipinos.

To organize the first barrio folk dance festival: (a) Consult technical personnel of the PRRM Education Department about prospective plans and dates. (b) Seek and coordinate the assistance of teachers or others in the barrio who may already be skilled in folk dancing. (c) At an early stage, involve the barrio council and leaders of the three people's associations. (d) After consultation with them, choose the time when the festival will be held. Off-working and dry seasons are usually best. Two of the favorite times are after the rice harvest, and after the milling season. A regular community fiesta may provide a suitable occasion. (e) Form committees to take care of various aspects of the preparations, such as music, costumes, lighting, sound amplification, prizes, refreshments (if any), finances, guest list, and program. Ask the committees on prizes and finances to solicit from public-spirited citizens the modest support needed. (f) Select the best dancers for the competitive numbers, and make sure they practice enough to put on a good performance at the festival. (g) Decide well ahead of time on those who will be invited. Issue the invitations early. Those invited may include senior PRRM personnel, friends from neighboring barrios, guests from the municipal center, and distinguished visitors.

Values

Every aim of the folk dancing program has, in some measure, been realized. There is a growing appreciation in the barrios of traditional Filipino melodies and dances; widening interest in active participation; preservation of folk dances and music indigenous to different districts; and healthful recreation for the people.

In many barrios, folk dances have also increased

mutual understanding and friendliness among the people. They have boosted, indirectly, participation in other parts of the PRRM four-fold program. And in some barrios they have reduced gambling, drunkenness, and vagrancy. Many barrio people have said that folk dancing has raised their spirits and lessened their sense of loneliness. An unexpected benefit has come to some barrios with the discovery that they could save money at fiesta times, with no loss in enjoyment, by having a "home talent" folk dancing festival instead of a performance by paid entertainers from the outside. The folk dance festivals organized on a municipal or "team" basis have led to new contacts between people of different barrios, reducing their isolation and contributing to the growth of neighborliness and cooperation among them.

Recurring Problems

Any program that aims to test new ideas and approaches in a social setting is likely to encounter some problems. The revival and expansion of folk dancing is no exception. But the problems are not insuperable. These are the ones PRRM has encountered most frequently, and the ways they have been met most effectively to date:

1) Slow start. It may be difficult to recruit members for the first folk dancing class.

   Response: Try to find out, tactfully, why there is reluctance to participate. If it is shyness, arrange to hold the class at some relatively inconspicuous place, perhaps one of the more spacious homes of the barrio after nightfall. If there is parental opposition due to misconceptions about folk dancing, talk to the parents and invite them to come and watch or participate. The reluctance of older folks to participate can sometimes be overcome by pairing them with others of their age group. Women sometimes prefer to be paired with their own husbands or sons or nephews, and men with their own wives or daughters or nieces. If there are cultural or religious differences tending to keep some groups apart, it may be wise to select, for the first class, participants who are known to be on good terms with each other.

2) Lack of money with which to pay for costumes and

CULTURAL AND RECREATIONAL ACTIVITIES

musical equipment.

Response: Fancy costumes are not essential. Patadyongs and saya't kimonos, which are easy to prepare and provide, are quite acceptable. If a turntable and dance records cannot be obtained in the barrio, a guitar and a banjo should suffice. It may be necessary to borrow them from a neighboring barrio, or to request a sponsor to provide them.

3) Lack of skilled supervisors. A qualified technical assistant may not be available, and the RRW serving in the barrio may not have an aptitude for folk dancing.

Response: If necessary, postpone starting a new class in folk dancing until a qualified technical assistant can be present to take charge. However, many RRWs are themselves qualified to take over the teaching, with a little self-confidence and the help of the dance manual. Another possibility is to find one or more persons in the barrio who know the traditional folk dances of the region, and would be able, with encouragement, to train a group to perform them.

4) Irregular attendance at rehearsals, due to conflicting interests and obligations.

Response: This problem may be forestalled, to some extent, by asking the participants to agree on days and hours and places for the rehearsals or practice sessions. Frequently, off-work hours and Sundays are most convenient. Some RRWs have found that participants welcome suggestions for budgeting their time so they can attend the practices regularly. Other RRWs have found it useful to ask a few members of the group to take responsibility for encouraging all the others to be sure to attend.

5) Inability of some participants to memorize the sequences of the dance steps.

Response: This inability is often more apparent than real. It can usually be overcome by patient and constant repetition of the steps in the right order. Make sure that each step is thoroughly mastered before the next is undertaken, and that mistakes are not repeated. Paying attention to changes in the music helps in reminding one of the next sequence of steps.

6) <u>Dropouts</u>, especially when participants get married or leave the barrio.

<u>Response</u>: This may make it necessary to recruit and train new members. But those who do drop out, when married, can often be persuaded to serve as assistants in teaching the dances to others.

FOLK MUSIC

From primitive to modern times, music has been a way of expressing man's feelings and thoughts about love, play, adventure, work, and worship. One of the most universal forms of expression has been folk songs, which vary greatly from culture to culture. They were not composed by professional musicians. They were not even written down. Many are thought to have been jointly composed, and passed along to succeeding generations which made their own adaptations and alterations.

Folk songs are spontaneous, unsophisticated expressions of human experience, imagination, and emotion. They do not disguise man's character and deeds, but picture him as he is--at his worst and best. Thus in folk songs we find expressions of the heart and soul of a people--their reactions to what they have thought and felt. And the songs help to preserve through generations a continuity in a people's traditions, attitudes, and outlooks.

The Philippines is rich in folk songs and music. There are work songs, cradle songs, love songs, patriotic and war songs, and many others. Through them one can gain a better understanding of the nation's cultural heritage, and of the nobler sentiments of the race. And they often lend deeper meaning to present living.

Choral Groups and Rondallas

PRRM seeks, through the promotion of choral groups and rondallas, to help revive folk music and make it a living reality in barrio life today. A

CULTURAL AND RECREATIONAL ACTIVITIES 237

choral group is simply a coming together of barrio people to learn and sing folk songs. There may be male voices, female voices, or both. A rondalla is a similar and perhaps smaller group of persons who come together to play music--mainly folk melodies--on stringed instruments.

Promotional Methods and Procedures

Although enjoyable, these activities do not develop without some effort. Encouragement is needed--to arouse interest, to convince people to participate, and to organize and train the choral groups and rondallas. The following methods and procedures have proven most successful, to date:

1. Begin by securing good moral support for the idea of organizing a choral group and/or a rondalla in the barrio. Talk with the barrio council, with officers of the three people's associations, and with other influential people, trying to win their genuine interest and support. Find out who would be good members of one or both groups, then make friends with them. Arrange for the prospective members to visit a neighboring barrio when a choral group or rondalla is scheduled to perform. Convince them that they can do as well or better, with practice.

2. Find someone who can be the leader of the group, responsible for recruitment, for practices, and for sustaining interest and morale. The leader may be a member of the group, or a sponsor from the barrio or nearby who has had some training in group singing or rondalla music. Sometimes a leader's contagious enthusiasm and natural aptitude make up for a lack of formal training.

3. If the members do not have musical instruments, try to help them secure some by purchase or gift. If this is not feasible, use a turntable with records.

In teaching songs, first let the participants hear and enjoy the music, getting the "feel" of its tempo and mood. Group singing may be taught by the rote method, that is, by having the group follow or imitate the singing of one or two lines at a time, with repetition until the entire song is learned. The leader should himself enjoy the music and, beating out the cadence, should seek to evoke the sing-ers' best efforts.

A group method of instruction has been effective in speeding up the training for a rondalla. Those playing melodic instruments such as the banduria, banjo, and piccolo rehearse separately from those playing the rhythmic or percussion instruments. When both groups know their parts well, they are combined, and practice continues until good coordination and harmony are achieved.

Folk Music in the Barrios

International appreciation of Filipino folk songs and melodies has grown, following the world tours of the Bayanihan dancers. At the same time, folk music has become increasingly popular in the barrios. This is evidenced not only by the growing numbers of singing and instrumental programs in individual barrios, but also by the eager participation of many barrio people in folk music festivals.

The value of these activities is now increasingly evident. They introduce wholesome recreation among the people, through activities which many now prefer to idleness, gambling, and drinking. They also frequently provide the added spice of friendly competition between groups in a barrio, or between barrios. They help to perpetuate many elements in Filipino tradition, and to inspire a deeper love of country among the people.

Recurring Problems

1) <u>Reluctance to participate</u>, especially when group singing or rondallas are new to the barrio.

   <u>Response</u>: Try to find out the real reasons for this reluctance. If it is uncertainty about what to expect, arrange a visit to a nearby barrio where a choral group or a rondalla can be seen and heard in action. If leaders in the barrio are hesitant about encouraging folk music, invite them to see for themselves how much it is enjoyed by people in the other barrio. If some are shy about taking part, invite them to come together with other prospective participants to discuss plans in a friendly, informal way. Mention the fun to be derived from the activities, and the zest added by competition. Make it clear that

CULTURAL AND RECREATIONAL ACTIVITIES

the practice sessions will be held at times convenient to everyone in the group.

2) **Lack of money and facilities** such as a turntable, records, musical instruments, song books, and sheet music.

   Response: This is a problem that, since time immemorial, has been overcome by the ingenuity of music lovers. After some searching, it may be found that there are instruments in the barrio that can be used. Or persons may be found who are willing to contribute some of the simple equipment needed. The RRW should be able to supply, from PRRM, enough copies of song sheets and musical pieces. After a good beginning, the group may be able to organize a benefit program, through a show or a raffle or a bingo social, as a means of raising the modest amount of money they need.

DRAMA

In 1959, after a few tentative experiments, the Senior Staff of PRRM decided to begin a systematic effort to introduce "home talent" dramatic performances among the barrio people. The objectives were similar to those that prompted the use of drama in the Ting Hsien program, in pre-Communist China, namely: (a) to introduce and encourage a stimulating and enjoyable form of entertainment, conducted by and for the people of the barrio; (b) to use drama as a medium of education; (c) to build up the self-confidence of the participants; and (d) to discover local talents.

Beginnings

Once the decision was reached, a technical assistant was asked to make a special effort to stage a play in barrio Papaya, San Antonio. She conferred with the RRW, then with members of the youth association (RRYA). Reactions were varied. Some were excited; others did not like the idea; a few were indifferent. Still others wanted to have a traditional sentimental comedy, known as sarswela, rather than a PRRM-promoted drama portraying the four-fold program. Some elders who were listening did not want their daughters to participate. Only after a lengthy discussion, in which parents were convinced that the proposed play had no indecent scenes, did they finally agree to go ahead. Participants were recruited from the group then and there.

Real problems began with the rehearsals. For various reasons, attendance was uneven; only rarely did the entire cast show up. Then, as show time approached, some of the cast wanted to back out; pleading words were necessary to keep them in.

Staging, too, presented its problems. Much effort was necessary to obtain simple building materials, props, backdrops, and a front curtain which consisted of a cheap cotton material sewed up by members of the cast. The RRYA president collected a few pesos from the barrio to cover the rental cost of an amplifier service.

Finally, on July 28, 1959, the play was staged before an audience of approximately 1,000 people from Papaya and neighboring barrios. Despite many defects, it was pronounced a success.

Drama in the Barrios

One reason for the relative success of this and other early attempts to promote drama in the rural areas was the past popularity of plays in the barrios, and the fact that so little has come to take their place. For many years, dramatic arts like the duplo, the balagtasan, the moromoro, and the sarswela have been widely enjoyed. Through them, especially the sarswela, the barrio folk had found expression for their desires and dreams. But now the heydey of these dramatic forms has passed. The duplo has disappeared. The balagtasan has been replaced by the radio. The moromoro is seen only in remote districts. And the sarswela appears only during fiesta celebrations.

But the latent interest in drama remains, and this has made it easier to promote drama as a feature of the PRRM cultural program. The people love plays. They enjoy seeing them. They also enjoy participating in them. Many possess a natural aptitude for acting, and can play the roles convincingly.

CULTURAL AND RECREATIONAL ACTIVITIES

Recurring Problems

Despite the latent love of drama and the presence of fine human resources for dramatic performances, PRRM has encountered several problems in promoting the production of good plays in the barrios. These are the principal ones, and the methods used so far to cope with them:

1) <u>Content of the plays</u>. On this question, PRRM faced a dilemma. In recent years, the most popular dramatic form in the barrios has been the sarswela, a comedy, usually in three acts, which lasts for three to four hours. It is highly didactic, showing the inevitable triumph of the virtuous over the evil, and of the humble and unfortunate over the proud and tyrannical. The theme usually centers around the romance, difficulties, and final marriage of a rich girl and a farm boy, or vice versa. In it are typed characters such as the ideal father, the ideal daughter, the wicked villain, and the earthy comedian --playing out their roles in a sentimental plot which gives ample expression to the elemental emotions of love, loyalty, hate, jealousy, fear, and anger. This, in a capsule, is the sarswela, which has been a dominant cultural form for generations.

PRRM wanted to follow the principle: "Start with what the people know." But PRRM wanted also to break away from a rigid mold, to inject new ideas, and to make the drama a voice for education as well as culture in the new day. As Dr. Yen has said:

> The old plays have done a great deal of good in helping to inculcate the four "cardinal virtues" of loyalty, filial piety, chastity, and friendship. They have also done considerable harm, however, in fostering superstitious beliefs and hindering the development of a scientific attitude toward natural phenomena and the problems of everyday life.

<u>Response</u>: It was felt that an effort must be made to reconcile the sarswela and the PRRM-inspired drama. This would have to be done by writing new scripts combining elements of barrio life and familiar dramatic forms with features of

the four-fold program. A playwrighting contest was opened with an offer of cash prizes, but there were no entries. Then a scriptwriter was hired; he produced one playlet. Since then, the technical assistant in drama has tried to meet the problem by:

(a) writing original plays on rural themes, infused with aspects of the four-fold program; (b) including in the collection historical plays that teach patriotism, plays that tell the stories of successful men and women, plays that deal with social problems and the rights and duties of citizens; (c) adapting plays from short stories; (d) translating selected English plays into Tagalog; and (e) encouraging barrio people with dramatic talent to write plays, with assistance and guidance from the RRWs.

From all these sources has come a variety of plays from which the RRWs and interested young people in the barrios can now select when they are planning to put on dramatic performances.

2) Holding rehearsals. Weeks of rehearsals, sometimes tedious and taxing, are needed before a play can finally be presented. Regular attendance is hard to achieve. The girls participating may not be allowed to attend evening rehearsals unless arrangements are made to fetch them and take them home.

Response: Make every effort to choose times and places for rehearsals that are convenient for all participants. Form a committee (usually of older members of the group) to encourage regular attendance and to escort the girl participants to and from each rehearsal.

3) Lack of equipment. Putting on a play requires a stage, costumes, curtains, and, since attendance is usually large, a public address system. The necessary materials and the 30 pesos or so needed to rent public address facilities may be hard to get.

Response: Devise props from available materials, preferably borrowed. Search for a sponsor or group of sponsors who are willing to provide needed facilities. In one barrio, the barrio

CULTURAL AND RECREATIONAL ACTIVITIES

council provided the stage, while the mayor of the municipality made a contribution for the public address system. Ask for contributions, in cash or in kind, from the people of the barrio.

OTHER RECREATIONAL ACTIVITIES

Recreational activities are needed, especially among younger people, for those who do not take part in folk dancing or music or drama. Between seasons of heavy work, the barrio people may have a lot of leisure time. Cervantes wrote:

> The bow cannot always stay bent, nor human frailty subsist without some lawful recreation.

When there is a dearth of healthy recreational activity, some may spend their time in idling and gossiping and, too often, in intemperate gambling and drinking.

Conscious of the many benefits of healthful recreational activities in the barrios, PRRM has included them in its education program. The activities most vigorously promoted are games, sports, skills, and hobbies. The aims of these recreational programs are: (a) to increase the availability and popularity of recreational activities; (b) to foster, among the youth of the barrio, a spirit of sportsmanship--fair play, teamwork, and friendly competition; (c) in this way, to help develop better citizens; and (d) to revive native games that have merit but are in danger of being forgotten in a period of rapid social change.

Games and Sports

The games that PRRM has helped to promote in different barrios include native games like sipa, patintero, the spider game, breaking the pot, striking the can, and kite flying; indoor games such as dama, sungka, chess, checkers; and parlor games including trip to Jerusalem, get me game, pig-tailing, and egg races.

The sports that PRRM has encouraged most are basketball, volleyball, softball, table tennis, and badminton. The following techniques have been effective in promoting these sports:

1. Seek the cooperation of good players, school teachers, and other competent persons in organizing or coaching particular sports.

2. Organize teams by puroks or blocks. Request the use of the school plaza or other available space for practices and games.

3. In the busier working seasons, have practices and games during off hours--in the evenings or on Sundays. A scheduling system may be needed if different teams wish to use the same space.

4. Organize inter-purok and inter-barrio athletic competitions. The more exciting contests may be well attended by people from the communities concerned. You might also encourage the invitation of friends from other barrios and distinguished visitors.

5. Ask civic-spirited citizens to donate athletic equipment, or promote benefit dances and raffles to raise funds to purchase balls, bats, and other items.

Skills and Hobbies

One may discover a great variety of aptitudes and interests in a small rural community. RRWs and members of the PRRM Education Department are on the lookout for opportunities to develop these aptitudes and interests by encouraging the cultivation of individual skills and hobbies. This requires no formal organization, and it may contribute significantly to a person's growth and peace of mind. It might also lead to the discovery of outstanding talents.

Among the skills and hobbies that PRRM personnel have sought to discover and encourage have been: drawing and painting, individual singing, instrument playing, or reciting of poems; craftwork, mechanical inventiveness; sewing and embroidering; flower gardening and landscaping. One of the most rewarding experiences of the RRW, as well as the rural teacher, is the discovery of unsuspected talent for such skills and hobbies.

FOUR-FOLD PROGRAM IN ACTION

III. HEALTH

CHAPTER **14** SCOPE OF THE
PRRM HEALTH PROGRAM

A basic assumption of the PRRM is that human development is the most important factor in a nation's social and economic development.

One of the major obstacles to human development is ill health. As Dr. M.G. Candau, Director-General of the World Health Organization, has said, countries cannot release the full talents of their people until they have healthy minds and healthy bodies.

Throughout vast areas of Asia, Africa, and Latin America, deplorable health conditions act as a heavy drag on all lines of human advancement. Unchecked diseases take a tremendous toll in death, in disability, in man-years of work lost. Malnutrition lowers the vitality of many who continue to work; chronic and debilitating diseases drain away the strength of many more.

Although numerous public health activities have been launched in the newly developing nations since the Second World War, health remains a primary problem. It takes different shapes in different countries. For while the biological phenomena of disease are the same everywhere, environmental factors affect greatly the incidence of particular diseases, and the extent and severity of health problems in any locality. Each country, therefore, needs its own system of public health, adapted to the nation's problems, requirements, and resources.

THE RURAL HEALTH PROBLEM

In the Philippines, shortages in health facilities and health personnel are most acute in the rural areas, where the great majority of the people live. Yet a high percentage of the illnesses that afflict the people in these areas are preventable by modern scientific methods. Dysentery, cholera, smallpox, diphtheria, whooping cough, malaria, measles, typhus, and other common diseases can be reduced to a minimum by known preventive measures. But, as every RRW realizes, a great deal of education, patience, persistence, and cooperative effort are required to bring about these results in any single barrio.

Public health legislation is important, but laws may have little effect unless ways are found to implement them. More than a century ago, in 1863, a law was promulgated in the Philippines for the regulation of water supplies and the control of human waste disposal. In 1909, the government's Division of Sanitation started a program for the regulation of water supply, excrement and refuse disposal, and insect and vermin control. But outside of a few cities, the influence of these measures was negligible.

Since 1946, the government has undertaken to improve and expand its health services, with assistance from the United States, three agencies of the United Nations (WHO, UNICEF, UNESCO), and the Rockefeller Foundation. Governmental health services are now on three levels: national, provincial, and municipal. Work at the national level is directed by the Secretary of Health, at the provincial level by provincial health officers, and at the municipal level by municipal health officers. A law designated as RA 1082 specifies that there shall be a rural health unit under each municipal health officer.

It was intended that the work of the rural health units would fan out into the barrios. But this has been accomplished only to a very limited degree, for several reasons—including shortage of funds, shortage of transportation, and, most important, shortage of personnel. Even with the best intentions, a small health unit staffed by one physician, one nurse, one midwife, one sanitarian, and one dentist cannot, by itself, cope with the health needs of the people in all the barrios of a municipal district.

The essence of the rural health problem is how—working through national, provincial, and municipal layers of government—to reach millions of people living in thousands of small, widely scattered barrios. It is easy to make broad plans. It may be easy to make superficial contacts with the barrios. But any serious attempt to help the rural people help themselves must be based on a foundation of confident person-to-person relationships. On that foundation must be built a structure of self-help programs in which the barrio people become interested, then involved, then committed.

Governments desiring to initiate a structure of self-help programs in their rural areas face a dilemma. They cannot afford to train and deploy the great armies of specialized personnel that would be necessary to provide every rural community with technical extension workers in literacy, public health, agriculture, animal husbandry, rural industries, cooperative organization, and self-government. Yet when small groups of specialists, like the municipal rural health units, try to reach all the barrios of their municipality, their efforts are spread so thinly that their impact is dissipated. Little is accomplished toward helping the people to help themselves. Is there any way to resolve this dilemma?

THE PRRM HEALTH PROGRAM

One of PRRM's aims is to develop, experimentally, effective institutional patterns and ways of working that can be adopted, at will, by governmental or private agencies. The PRRM pattern and working methods in the field of rural health are outgrowths of such experimentation. They are designed to reach entire rural communities, and to help them organize their own self-help programs now. They do not wait for a day in the distant future when large numbers of technical people can be deployed throughout the country.

At the heart of the PRRM approach is exceptionally close collaboration between two groups of personnel. One group consists of the multipurpose rural reconstruction workers (RRWs) who have received rudimentary but careful instruction in the main principles and techniques of rural public health work; each RRW lives in a separate barrio where his first responsibility is to win the confidence and friendship of the barrio people. The other group consists of a small number of specialists in medicine, nursing, and sanitation.

Health projects undertaken in the barrios are jointly planned, then initiated by members of the specialized staff with the active cooperation of the

RRWs and interested village leaders. After the projects are well started, the technical personnel return periodically to answer questions, provide counsel, and check on progress. But the day-to-day follow-up on the projects is primarily the responsibility of the RRWs, working closely with the barrio people concerned.

The health program which PRRM seeks to sponsor in each barrio has these specific objectives:

1. The establishment of a small but active barrio health center, to be used for promotion, education, and first aid.

2. The training and activating of a team of auxiliary health workers.

3. The conduct of other health training classes, especially mothers' classes in hygiene, nutrition, and maternal and child care.

4. Enlistment of all the people's cooperation in the construction and use of sanitary toilets.

5. Development of sanitary drainage and fencing projects throughout the barrio.

6. Provision and maintenance of pure drinking water for the entire barrio.

7. Mass immunization, conducted in cooperation with government health agencies.

In planning and developing a health program with the people in any barrio, PRRM tries to adhere to these principles: (1) Every project undertaken must be practical and economical. (2) Every program must not only answer the people's needs; it must also become _their_ program. (3) It must be a type of program that can be duplicated in other barrios. (4) It must complement and support the government's public health objectives. (5) It must fit into and strengthen the PRRM's over-all four-fold program.

The following chapters treat in some detail the various aspects of the PRRM health program.

CHAPTER 15   HEALTH CENTERS, HEALTH WORKERS, MOTHERS' CLASSES

This chapter deals with three of the principal ways in which PRRM works with the barrio people to improve their health conditions. The first is the establishment and operation of barrio health centers. The second is training and activating selected young adults as auxiliary health workers. The third is planning and carrying out urgently needed health education among mothers.

THE BARRIO HEALTH CENTERS

At an early stage in its development, PRRM discovered the advantage of having in each barrio a modest, centrally located building to serve as a focal point for the health activities of the community. Each of the more recently built health centers, put up and paid for by the barrio people themselves, has a small receiving and consultation room, and two smaller rooms for examination and treatment.

Purposes for Which the Centers are Used

A barrio health center so constructed, with simple equipment and proper maintenance, serves admirably as a place where visiting technical personnel from the PRRM, the rural health unit, the Philippine National Red Cross, the Social Welfare Administration, and even private physicians, can work with the barrio people. The most frequent technical visitors are from the rural health units and the PRRM Health Department.

Only a fraction of the work done by the visiting technical personnel is clinical in nature. This is because most of the illnesses among the rural people are preventable, and can be brought under control by preventive measures; and because the severely limited numbers of health personnel can accomplish more by prevention than by treatment. The clinical work done by visiting physicians, nurses, midwives, and dentists may be supplemented in their absence by first aid, which is administered at the center by the trained auxiliary health workers.

The greater part of the health center's work consists of training, education, and promotional activities. An important type of training is that of the auxiliary health workers, described later in this chapter. There are also mothers' classes, nutrition classes, and health seminars on subjects of special interest to the people of the barrio. Health promotional activities may range from a "baby contest," or a series of programs and events for a special "health week," to the enlistment of barrio-wide participation in an immunization campaign.

The health centers, when fully utilized, are much more than buildings alone. They are places where the vital health activities of entire village communities are organized and coordinated.

Management and Maintenance of the Health Centers

The physical features of a health center--building, simple furniture, equipment, and supplies--are of course essential. But the vitality and efficiency of the center depend upon people and organization. It is important, therefore, to understand the roles that have evolved for the groups of people concerned, as a result of PRRM experience over a period of years, recognizing that with further experience these roles may be modified.

Role of PRRM Personnel

These are the principal duties of the PRRM Health Department in relation to the barrio health centers:

1. To work closely with each RRW and RRWA in planning the individual barrio health programs.

2. To guide and assist the RRWs in training auxiliary health workers, and in conducting mothers' classes, nutrition classes, special seminars, and other projects in health education.

3. To guide and assist the RRWs in establishing and maintaining good relations with the rural health unit of the municipality, and with other health agencies in the area.

4. To visit every PRRM-aided barrio at least once a month--to give counsel and encouragement to the RRWs, to participate in health training and educational programs, to provide technical supervision of ongoing health projects, and to boost the morale of the barrio people engaged in these projects.

The work of the RRW is crucial to the successful operation of the barrio health center, especially during its formative stages of development. These are his principal duties and responsibilities:

1. To explain to the barrio people the advantages of having their own actively functioning health center, and to stimulate interest in the establishment or further development of the center. This can be done in talks with individuals during home visits, and at meetings of the men's, women's, and youth associations.

2. To help bridge the gap between the people and the agencies that can help them to improve health conditions in the barrio. These agencies include not only PRRM, but also the municipal rural health units, the Philippine National Red Cross, and the Social Welfare Administration.

3. To take central responsibility for organizing and conducting training classes for auxiliary health workers, and special health educational classes or seminars, as discussed later in this chapter.

4. To guide the men's, women's, and youth associations of the barrio in taking their full share of responsibility in the construction, management, and maintenance of the health center, pinpointing responsibilities (preferably in written form) and setting up schedules of activities.

5. To purchase medicines, using a revolving fund raised by the RRWA (mentioned below); and to supervise the sales of the medicine to the barrio people.

Role of Rural Health Unit (RHU) Personnel

While the responsibility for the administration of the health centers falls primarily on PRRM personnel and on the people's associations, the RHU, as a government agency, is legally responsibile for the health care of the people. In this capacity, the RHU provides technical supervision of the health centers, working closely with PRRM and the barrio people.

Specialists from the rural health units are expected to visit each barrio in their municipality at least once a week. The purposes of these visits are: (a) to provide such medical treatments and consultations as they can; (b) to give immunizations against cholera, dysentery, typhoid, diphtheria, whooping cough, tetanus, smallpox, and tuberculosis; (c) to furnish assistance in training auxiliary health workers and conducting health education classes; (d) to provide medicines as their supplies permit; (e) to cooperate in the technical supervision and maintenance of the barrio health centers.

Role of Other Agencies

The Philippine National Red Cross, the Social Welfare Administration, and private physicians operate in many rural areas. Their activities may include visits to a barrio (a) to give free medicines and sometimes food, in districts damaged by floods and typhoons; (b) to collaborate in carrying out immunization campaigns; and (c) to help supervise the distribution of aid they have provided.

Role of the Barrio People

Since it is PRRM's aim to do things with the barrio people, rather than for them, the people's role is of central importance. In the case of the health centers, it has been found desirable, whenever possible, to persuade each of the three people's associations to accept a special area of responsibility.

The Rural Reconstruction Men's Association (RRMA) may be asked to take over the planning and construction of the building itself, and to provide the necessary materials and labor.

The Rural Reconstruction Women's Association (RRWA) is asked (a) to raise a revolving fund for the purchase of medicines and equipment, which will be replenished through the sale of the medicines; (b) to administer and supervise the physical plant; and (c) to work with the RRW and the RRYA in planning the activities of the health center in relation to the total health program in the barrio. In addition, the president or treasurer of the RRWA audits the purchases and sales of medicines so that the revolving fund can be maintained and supplies replenished. All this is preparatory to the RRWA's eventual assumption of full responsibility for supervision of the health centers when PRRM withdraws from the barrio.

The Rural Reconstruction Youth Association (RRYA) is asked to provide young adults who will volunteer to be trained as auxiliary health workers. It is important that these volunteers understand that, after completing their training, they will take major responsibility for (a) providing first aid, at regularly scheduled hours, to people of the barrios; (b) handling the sale and distribution of simple medicines that they have been taught to administer, under the supervision of the RRW; (c) giving assistance to RHU as well as PRRM health personnel when they visit the barrio; (d) making records of cases, and keeping all records in good order; and (e) assisting in the collection and compilation of vital statistics for the barrio.

Recurring Problems

During more than a decade of work with the people to develop barrio health centers, PRRM has encountered many problems. These are the ones that have appeared most frequently, and the responses that have been found most effective to date:

1) <u>Indifference</u>. People are not usually indifferent to their own or their families' suffering. But they may doubt that it is in their power to improve their families' health, or to assist in improving the health of the community. They may never have received even the simplest modern health education. They may have a wholly fatalistic attitude toward disease. Or they may accept current superstitious beliefs and put their trust in herbolarios (quack doctors) or hilots (untrained midwives) whom they know, rather than in people with scientific training whom they do not know. If these attitudes are not changed, there is every likelihood that a barrio health center, even if constructed, will go unused most of the time.

Response: It is necessary to open the people's minds to some unfamiliar truths: that much has been learned through modern science about the control and prevention of diseases; that many illnesses from which they suffer are now preventable; and that if they will work together they can, with a little outside help, improve the health of the people in their barrios. But how are these truths to be conveyed to the barrio people?

(a) During home visits, especially when some member of the family is ill with a preventable disease, discuss the progress made in another barrio in preventing that disease, and tell how it was accomplished. (b) Plan with specialists from the PRRM Health Department the promotion, organization, and conduct of a mothers' class, or a class in nutrition, or a general health seminar, where visiting health personnel (from PRRM, the rural health unit, or other agencies) can teach fundamental facts about personal hygiene, home and child care, sanitation, nutrition, the causes of common diseases, and accepted health practices. The systematic scheduling of these classes is primarily the responsibility of the RRW, working in cooperation with the RRWA and, sometimes, the RRYA. A course in one subject may be followed, while interest is awakened, by a course in another subject. In arranging for speakers from outside, it is important, whenever possible, to secure persons who know how to talk with the rural people.

2) Shortage of competent women to maintain the health center. This problem may arise when the RRWA has never really assumed responsibility for the administration of the center. Or it may be that most of the women are busy working in the fields during planting and harvesting seasons.

Response: Discuss the matter again at a full meeting of the RRWA, indicating the importance of taking over the daily maintenance and administration of the health center, and helping them to organize to do so on a regular schedule, with a systematic rotation of responsibility. During the busy farming seasons, see that the assignments for care of the health center are given to women who do not have to be in the fields.

3) **Inadequate support from the youth association.** Without such support, the health center may lose its vitality. For the administration of first aid, the handling of medical supplies, the provision of assistance to visiting health personnel, and the maintenance of important records and statistics may all depend upon the RRYA.

Response: The RRW should consider these steps: (a) If the RRYA has never been seriously challenged to take a major part of the responsibility, arrange for a meeting. If possible, enlist the help of PRRM Health Department personnel or a team captain in putting the matter before the youth association in a strong and appealing way. (b) If there has never been a training course for auxiliary health workers, selected from the membership of the RRYA, work with PRRM Health Department personnel to get one under way as soon as possible. (c) If the lack of adequate cooperation from the RRYA is simply due to inadequate planning or faulty scheduling, work with the officers of the association to develop clear-cut scheduling and definite assignments of individual responsibilities.

4) **Insufficient revolving funds for the purchase of medicines.** It is not easy for members of the women's association to raise these funds, especially if the barrio is poor. They may need help.

Response: The RRW may assist in any of several ways. (a) Help the RRWA to organize a systematic solicitation among all the families of the barrio; even if individual contributions are quite small, the total may be sufficient to start the revolving fund. (b) Join the RRWA in requesting the barrio council to allocate to the fund a part of the 10 per cent of the barrio's real estate tax that it controls. (c) If the barrio people work on a hacienda, request the owner or manager to donate a part of the revolving fund needed for the purchase of medicines for the health center. (d) Ask the barrio council to adopt a resolution soliciting contributions of medicines from drug companies, civic leaders, the provincial health office, or the municipal rural health unit; assist the RRWA in following up with specific requests.

5) Absence of proper planning and scheduling. When several groups cooperate in the operation of a single health center, it is not easy to avoid misunderstanding and confusion. What is everyone's responsibility may be no one's responsibility.

Response: The RRW can do much to prevent this. (a) With personnel of the PRRM Health Department, plan carefully each successive stage of the health program to be promoted in the barrio. Reach a clear understanding regarding the division of responsibilities between the health specialists and the RRW. (b) Set up the schedules for health classes and seminars well in advance, adjusting them to the convenience of the class members and the specialists who are invited to assist; (c) Try to make sure that the roles of the RRWA and the RRYA in relation to the health center are clearly defined, and that individual responsibilities among the members of each group are thoroughly understood and agreed upon. (d) When the health center is well under way and running in good order, try to transfer to the RRYA and the RRWA the main responsibilities for continued planning and scheduling--standing ready to give assistance as needed.

6) Irregular visits by government health personnel. A barrio health center may depend heavily on regular visits by government health personnel, especially members of the municipality's rural health unit (RHU). Members of this unit may be the principal source of personnel for medical consultations, immunizations, technical help in training auxiliary health workers, and assistance in the technical supervision of the barrio health stations. They are expected to visit each barrio in the municipality once a week but, for various reasons, their visits are often much less frequent.

Response: This is a situation in which the RRW may have to exercise to the full his capacities for cooperation, diplomacy, and judgment. He must appreciate the responsibilities of the rural health units, and the size of the areas they are expected to cover. At the same time, he must do his best to help the people in his barrio obtain the assistance they need. Many responses to this problem have been tried out, with varying success. The RRW should choose from among these the ones he considers best, in a given situation:

(a) With the help of PRRM Health Department personnel, get acquainted with all the members of the RHU, and develop a friendly relationship with them.

(b) Try to get them to think with you about ways and means of developing a good health program for your barrio, and an effective health center. If any health projects are already well under way in the barrio, invite them to visit those projects.

(c) When they are willing, plan with them a schedule of regular weekly visits by their personnel, with a definite understanding as to the activities that will be undertaken during each visit. Invite them to attend meetings or events in the barrio, so they can get better acquainted with the people.

(d) If it should appear desirable or necessary, suggest to the barrio council that it adopt and send to the rural health unit, or to the provincial health office, a resolution requesting weekly visits to the barrio by RHU personnel. Alternatively, suggest that the barrio council appoint a delegation to make a call on the municipal government or the RHU, and formally request regular visits by the RHU specialists.

(e) Try to make each activity at the barrio health center so well planned and scheduled that it will stimulate the interest and enthusiasm of the RHU personnel.

(f) When they have participated in activities at the health center, share fully with the RHU the credit for whatever is accomplished, and encourage the people of the barrio to do the same.

AUXILIARY HEALTH WORKERS

Mention has already been made of the great need for auxiliary health workers in the barrios. The personnel of the rural health units, paid by the government, are too limited in number to cover adequately more than a fraction of the areas for which they are responsible. Many barrios are visited infrequently, if at all, by doctors and nurses. It is imperative, therefore, to help the people learn to help themselves in the field of health.

For these reasons young adult men and women are recruited, as volunteers, to receive training that will enable them (a) to assist the RHU and other technical personnel who visit the barrios; (b) to perform certain services such as the administration of first aid and the sale of simple drugs; (c) to maintain orderly records of cases treated at the center; (d) to assist in collecting and compiling vital statistics for the barrio; and (e) to continue the work of the health center after the PRRM program of intensive assistance is ended. Auxiliary health workers are, in effect, an extension of the PRRM health staff at the village level, increasing the number of those who can provide simple health services and convey essential information on health and hygiene to the barrio people.

Recruitment Criteria and Procedures

After several years of experience in recruiting candidates for training as auxiliary health workers, these criteria have been adopted: (a) at least a complete elementary school education, and preferably part or all of a high school education; (b) sufficient interest to be willing to undergo training and then to work without pay, during their spare time, as auxiliary health workers; (c) physical and mental fitness; (d) social and moral acceptance in the community; and (e) permanent residence in the barrio, so they can give regular time to this work.

The person primarily responsible for recruiting auxiliary health workers is the RRW. The timing of recruitment and the number of persons to be sought depend on the specific plans of the PRRM Health Department for training. Once these have been decided, the RRW proceeds with the recruitment, usually in three stages.

The first stage is one of searching for the best candidates. The RRW usually begins by consulting, informally, some member of the household in which he lives, or one of the school teachers in the barrio, or officers of the RRWA and the RRYA, or others who know the people of the community, to get their ideas as to good candidates. On the basis of these consultations, the RRW makes a preliminary listing of those who appear to be the best prospects.

Second, the RRW calls on these prospects in their own homes, to form his own estimate as to whether they would be good candidates. When the estimate is affirmative, he invites the person to enroll for the auxiliary health workers' training course.

The approach in such a discussion is important. After getting well acquainted and learning something about the interests of the young man or woman being interviewed, the RRW may start talking about the grim health conditions and needs of the barrio. He may then describe how PRRM collaborated with the people of another barrio in developing self-help programs. He may tell how various illnesses have been reduced in that barrio, and how those in need of medical assistance have been better cared for. He may then describe how PRRM collaborated with the people of another barrio in developing self-help programs. He may tell how various illnesses have been reduced in that barrio, and how those in need of medical assistance have been better cared for. He may then describe the way in which a few selected young men and women in that barrio, who volunteered to become "auxiliary health workers," received a short training course, after which they began to take an active part in various kinds of health activities. This will lead naturally to a mention of plans for training a new group of volunteers as auxiliary health workers. The RRW may speak of how he has consulted various people, asking for their ideas about who would be the best candidates for this training.

Through such an approach, the groundwork is laid for a direct appeal and challenge to the young man or woman to volunteer for the training course. Sometimes it has proven helpful to invite a member of the municipality's rural health unit staff to join in making these appeals.

Third, if a decision is not reached at once, but the person is definitely wanted, it may be helpful to ask some respected leader in the barrio, or a close friend, to encourage him to volunteer.

The Training Course

In training auxiliary health workers, the PRRM Health Department puts less emphasis on formal lectures than on practical demonstrations, which are repeated with the trainees themselves participating. The scope of the course is as follows:

1. <u>General first aid</u>. After a short discussion of basic principles in first aid, there are descriptions, accompanied by demonstrations, of how to identify and administer first aid to emergency cases commonly encountered in the barrios, including shock, fractures, wounds, burns, animal bites, and poisoning. This is followed by additional talks, with demonstrations, on artificial respiration, transporting patients, and the application of bandages, splints, and tourniquets.

2. <u>Prevention and control of communicable diseases</u>. Information is given on the most common communicable diseases, their signs and symptoms, and the ways in which these diseases can be prevented. Special emphasis is placed on specific preventive techniques: sanitation, the protection or purification of drinking water, and immunization. Flip charts and other teaching aids are used to make the subject matter vivid. Practical demonstrations include alternative methods for purifying water, and a simple, inexpensive method of constructing sanitary water-sealed toilets.

3. <u>Dental hygiene</u>. Information is given, with the use of visual aids, on the importance of sound teeth to general health, on the causes of tooth decay, on preventive methods including the proper way of brushing teeth, and on ways in which the people's interest in dental hygiene can be awakened.

4. <u>Practical home nursing</u>. After general training in home care for the sick, particular attention is given to the extra precautions that should be taken when there is any communicable disease in the home.

Toward the end of the course, participants are given detailed instructions on the specific duties and responsibilities of an auxiliary health worker in the barrio.

In-Service Training

This short course is only the first step in the training of the auxiliary health workers. It provides an introduction to the practical knowledge he will need.

The second step is in-service training in the barrio, conducted by visiting PRRM or RHU technical health personnel, with the assistance of the RRW. This phase of the training work usually gives added incentive to the auxiliary health worker as he comes in contact with the needs of the community, and discovers that he can render a useful service in the prevention or relief of suffering--a service that is welcomed and respected by his neighbors.

Recurring Problems

The problems most frequently encountered in recruiting and training auxiliary health workers, and the methods of dealing with them that have proven most effective to date, are as follows:

1) <u>Low educational background of some candidates</u>, who may have had only two or three years of formal schooling.

    <u>Response</u>: This is not an insuperable obstacle if they have good native intelligence and a will to learn. However, for such candidates, somewhat longer and more intensive training may be needed. It may be necessary to help them overcome a feeling of inadequacy due to their lack of formal education.

2) <u>Lack of enough permanent residents</u> in the barrio who are willing and qualified to become auxiliary health workers.

    <u>Response</u>: It may be desirable, under such circumstances, to recruit, train, and utilize a few non-residents who return during vacations to their homes in the barrios.

3) <u>Reluctance to volunteer for the work</u>. Good prospective candidates, otherwise qualified, may hesitate to sign up because of the lack of financial reward, or because their interest is not sufficiently stirred.

Response: Do not give up easily with these persons. If possible, take them to another barrio where a health program is under way in which auxiliary health workers are doing good work. Give them time to ask questions and see the work fully. Try to show them that a great deal of voluntary effort is essential in self-help programs, which are vital to progress in the barrios. Impress on them that they can help to show the way.

4) Reluctance of parents to permit their sons or daughters to participate.

Response: The best answer is patient, good-natured persistence. The idea of working voluntarily for the community may be a new one, which requires a little time to absorb. If they gradually come to understand the importance of the work, and the added prestige that will come to their children if they take part in it, their resistance may melt away.

5) Discouragement during the training period. Some trainees may begin to feel that what is being taught is beyond their capacity to learn, and that they will not be able to cope with their new responsibilities later on.

Response: Point out to any discouraged trainee that others are in the same boat. Discuss with him any questions he has not fully understood. Give him opportunities to show what he has learned. Be generous in recognizing the progress all the trainees are making. Explain how information that is new to them will soon become more familiar and manageable during their periods of continuing, in-service training in the barrios. It is also important to make certain that the trainees have some happy recreational hours between study sessions, and that they realize they are among good friends.

MOTHERS' CLASSES

One of the most important forms of health education in PRRM-aided barrios is that provided through mothers' classes.

Many young women are plunged into marriage unprepared and untrained for the responsibilities of motherhood. Their formal education is extremely limited, and they know almost nothing about personal hygiene or modern methods of pre-natal care and infant care. Many are still bound by primitive ways and superstitious beliefs. Partly for this reason, and partly because of the acute shortage of doctors in rural areas, a high percentage have their babies' births attended by hilots (midwives) who have no scientific obstetrical training, and no knowledge of basic procedures to prevent post-partum infections and hemorrhages. It is not surprising that maternal and infant mortality rates are high.

The mother, more than any other person, feels responsible for the health and nutrition of her family. She could prevent many of their illnesses if she understood better the importance of sanitary practices, pure drinking water, and a balanced diet.

Scope of Training Given

It is natural, therefore, that health education in many PRRM barrios began with mothers' classes. The aim of these classes is not only to reduce maternal and infant mortality. It is also to train mothers in their health responsibilities toward all members of their families, and toward the community.

Specifically, the classes aim to train mothers and expectant mothers in (a) personal hygiene and its importance for health; (b) pre-natal and post-natal care; (c) infant care; (d) home nursing; (e) the prevention of communicable diseases; (f) principles of nutrition; and (g) participation in community health projects.

Organizing a Mothers' Class

The RRW has an important role in organizing a mothers' class. These general guidelines are based on the previous experience of the PRRM Health Department, and of the RRWs.

1. Work through the Rural Reconstruction Women's Association. If an RRWA has not yet been organized in the barrio, or if it needs rejuvenation (see Chapter 18), that should be given a high priority.

2. Begin by discussing with officers of the

RRWA the idea of starting a class to train mothers in the fundamentals of health care in the home and community. Tell them what the mothers learn in such a course, and how vital this is to improving maternal and infant care and health conditions throughout the barrio. Try to win their enthusiastic support and their pledge of active cooperation.

3. Arrange with the officers for a general meeting of the RRWA, at which the proposal for a mothers' class will be put up to the membership. If possible, invite one or more senior members of the Health Department and/or your team captain and/or a key member of the municipal rural health unit to attend, and to join the RRWA officers in making a strong appeal to all present to participate. Then ask those who would like to attend the course to raise their hands. If the response is good, organize and schedule separate classes, according to sections of the barrio (puroks), so that all trainees can attend in their own locality. In some cases, it has been found advisable to have an initial class primarily for expectant mothers.

4. Cooperate with PRRM technical personnel and with leaders of the women's organization in the detailed scheduling of the classes. Sessions should not normally be scheduled during planting and harvesting seasons. In the less accessible barrios, do not try to hold the courses during the rainy season. Try to decide on hours and meeting places that are convenient for all concerned.

5. Informally, ask leading members of the barrio council and the Rural Reconstruction Men's Association to give their wholehearted moral support to the organization of the mothers' classes.

Conduct of the Class

1. Start all sessions punctually.

2. While the order of procedure at each class need not be rigid, these practices have been found useful: (a) Begin and end each session with group singing. This generates an atmosphere of friendliness and informality. (b) Have someone call the roll, so members will know they will be missed if they do not attend. (c) After the main talk or lecture at each class session, allow time for questions

and open discussion. (d) When a demonstration is given during the lecture or discussion period, follow this up immediately, if practicable, by a repeat demonstration in which members of the class participate.

3. During lectures and demonstrations, make full use of teaching aids, including flip charts, anatomical sketches, illustrated literature, and improvised equipment such as dolls (to represent babies), baby clothing, baby's trays, basins, and disinfectants.

4. Arrange if possible for the class to make one or two visits to hospitals, town clinics, or child care centers. Arrange in advance for responsible people at these centers to show them activities that fit in with their course of training.

5. At the end of the course, which usually lasts about ten sessions, give an oral or written test to each participant as a means of evaluating what she has learned and how well she has learned it.

6. The capstone of the course should be an interesting graduation ceremony which the people of the barrio, especially the husbands and families of the participants, are invited to attend. It is desirable to have at this ceremony some of the leaders of the barrio and of the municipality, and, if possible, some PRRM senior personnel and/or representatives from the Ministry of Health. Talks at the ceremony should give due recognition to the work of those who have taken the training, and should indicate what they have learned and what they will now be able to do for their families and the community. Certificates should be presented publicly to all who have finished the course. Small prizes are sometimes awarded, too, to those who have done especially well.

7. After the graduation ceremony, the expectant mothers in the group should be given kits of materials for use during their confinement.

Recurring Problems

These are problems most frequently encountered in organizing and conducting mothers' classes, and the responses which have been found most effective to date:

1) <u>Lack of interest</u>. The degree of interest, at first, may depend on how well the initial proposal for a mothers' class was presented to the women's association.

   <u>Response</u>: If there is a lack of initial response, try, with the help of good friends in the RRWA, to find out why. Then make individual visits to mothers in their homes and discuss with them the questions that may be in their minds. Sometimes individual talks will bring out more effectively the necessity of mothers being trained in the health care of their families, and will help to overcome any shyness that some may feel about attending the class. The certificates given at the end of the course may be mentioned. If, at first, the interest of those attending is not strong, try to bring in some good "resource personnel" to help conduct the earlier sessions of the class.

2) <u>Indifference of husbands</u>. If husbands do not care about their wives attending the classes, they may be discouraged from doing so.

   <u>Response</u>: Talk with husbands who are not enthusiastic, and try to enlist their interest in what their wives will be able to learn during the course. Or ask individual friends of the husbands, or appropriate leaders in the barrio, to talk with them. If this is a problem for several members of the group, plan one session to which all husbands will be invited, and make that session especially lively and informative.

3) <u>Irregular attendance</u>. Sometimes attendance is good at first, but falls off as the class progresses.

   <u>Response</u>: Tested remedies are house-to-house visits on the day of the class or just before class, by the RRW and officers of the RRWA, to encourage full attendance, and the ringing of a bell 10 or 15 minutes before the class is due to start. Attendance may also be improved if mothers are allowed to bring their babies, and if the place of meeting is rotated among different localities.

4) <u>Insufficient technical personnel</u> to help conduct

the course. If technical personnel from PRRM and/or the municipality's barrio health unit are prevented from being on hand as planned, for any of the sessions of the training class, they should notify the RRW as soon as they can and, if possible, arrange for alternative personnel to take their place. If that is not feasible, the RRW must meet the situation as best he can.

Response: Try to make arrangements for other "resource personnel"--members of the Health Department or local doctors or nurses--to give assistance when they are urgently needed. Sometimes the RRWs themselves, especially those who have had midwifery training, are quite competent to conduct certain parts of the course. If humanly possible, avoid cancelling or postponing regularly scheduled sessions of the class.

5) Persistence of old beliefs and practices. It may be found that information presented through lectures and demonstrations has not "sunk in," and that superstitious beliefs and backward practices persist among some members.

Response: Do not regard this as unusual or as reason for discouragement. It simply means that extra care must be taken (a) to present each topic clearly and persuasively, (b) to give ample time for questions and discussion, (c) to make the class demonstrations vivid and unmistakable, and (d) to review frequently what has been learned.

6) Presence of herbolarios and hilots. In many barrios, herbolarios and hilots are the only ones the people have been able to turn to, over the years, to treat diseases or attend deliveries. Since they are easy to call, and considerate in their fees, their services have taken root in the culture--and in the minds of some mothers are indispensable in times of need. But since these practitioners are not trained in modern medical techniques, they resort to all sorts of primitive, if not dangerous, practices. The methods taught in mothers' classes are counter to the practices and beliefs of the hilots, and may therefore meet with doubt and resistance on the part of the mothers; some may even leave the class as a result.

Response: There are several remedies to this problem, which the RRW should use his best judgment in applying: (a) the herbolarios or hilots may be asked to enroll in the class so they will learn modern obstetrical practices with the mothers; (b) they may be asked to attend obstetrical clinics and hospitals with class members, so that proper techniques may be demonstrated to them; (c) the hilot's practice should be brought under the close supervision of either the RRW, the RHU personnel, or the Health Department; (d) all deliveries attended by the hilots and illnesses attended by the herbolarios must be reported immediately, for proper recording and control, either to the RRW, the auxiliary health worker, or the barrio captain; and (e) the hilots and herbolarios must keep a complete record of cases attended and treatments given to patients.

CHAPTER 16 ENVIRONMENTAL SANITATION, IMMUNIZATION

Accurate statistics are lacking for the rural areas of the Philippines. But it is known that, apart from maternal and infant mortality, the principal causes of death in these areas are diseases of the lungs, diseases affecting the intestinal tract, diseases resulting from malnutrition, tuberculosis, influenza, tetanus, diphtheria; and eruptive fevers including smallpox, measles, typhoid, and typhus.

Probably three-fourths of the illnesses brought on by these diseases are preventable. Many can be prevented by immunization or other technical means requiring trained personnel. Many can be forestalled by sanitary measures and precautions which the barrio people themselves can learn to apply. Things that have not been learned in the home must be taught in the community.

ENVIRONMENTAL SANITATION

The most important aspect of environmental sanitation is the proper disposal of human excreta. Most intestinal infections common to men are transmitted by the fecal discharges of sick persons. Improper waste disposal allows tiny bits of these discharges to be carried to the mouths of the next victims by way of flies, drinking water, food, or soiled hands.

Disposal of Human Waste

To control the most common intestinal diseases, it is necessary to provide a barrier between the source of infection (the disease-producing organisms in infected excreta) and the susceptible hosts (the human population). The barrier must prevent the organisms from coming into direct contact with man or with his food or drinking water.

The Sanitary Water-Sealed Toilet

The most satisfactory means of human waste disposal is modern sewage. But the cost of community sewage systems, or individual family systems with septic tanks, is usually far beyond the reach of rural communities in the developing countries. It has been found that a water-sealed toilet bowl with an adjoining disposal pit, properly constructed, is one effective method of controlling fecal-borne diseases. They are inexpensive to construct and easy to maintain.

During the early days of PRRM, several kinds of toilets had been introduced in the country. But none had been widely adopted due to such features as inconvenience, improper functioning, failure to protect against flies, impermanence, excessive use of water, or high cost of construction and maintenance.

The PRRM Health Department conducted a series of experiments and tests with the aim of finding one or more types of water-sealed toilets that would be efficient, acceptable to the barrio people, and within their financial means. (A water-sealed toilet is superior to a trench latrine or borehole latrine not only because odor is eliminated, but because it provides much better protection against flies.) After developing and rejecting several experimental types because they proved inefficient or too costly, PRRM evolved an economical type which is now promoted in all PRRM barrios. A special model with a culvert or asphalt drum has also been developed for use in flooded or high-water-table areas. While the types now being made are far better than earlier models, they still do not meet completely the requirements of an inexpensive, convenient, sanitary toilet under all conditions, and research is continuing.

The PRRM toilet bowl is not very difficult for barrio men to learn to build. Detailed written instructions can be obtained from PRRM headquarters. The only tools required are a shovel, hammer, saw, and trowel. The only materials required are gravel, sand, cement, wire, used oil, water, and wood for use in making the mold.

The main advantages of this toilet bowl are that it is simple, economical, practical, and readily duplicable. It has stirred widespread interest, and both government and private agencies are now fostering its construction and use in rural areas.

Promotion

Promoting the construction and use of the water-sealed toilet in the barrios is not easy. Many barrio people, accustomed from time immemorial to using the open fields, have never seen a sanitary latrine. The poorly maintained public latrines they have seen may be repulsively filthy. They have never learned about germs and fecal-borne diseases. Even if they wanted a latrine at home, they would not know how to construct it. And they might feel they could not afford such a useless luxury.

These resistances must be recognized and faced. There is perhaps no field in which popular support is more essential than the field of sanitation. This support must be built on a gradual growth of understanding of the relation between sanitation and health. To develop this awareness, and then to promote the widening construction and use of the new sanitary water-sealed toilets, PRRM has experimented with many promotional techniques. Those that have proven most effective can be regarded as a "kit of tools" which the RRW can use selectively, working in cooperation with the PRRM Health Department and the barrio people. It is recommended that the RRW develop a master plan for a sanitation campaign, selecting from the following methods or techniques those he thinks will be most effective.

1. Work with the PRRM Health Department to organize a health seminar, in which some of the more open-minded people of the community can be given basic information about preventable diseases and their causes. Some unlearning as well as learning may be needed. For superstitions are still widespread, such as the belief that sicknesses are caused by evil spirits. As previously noted, the people often put more faith in "herbolarios" (quack doctors) whom they know than in modern-trained medical personnel they do not know. At the seminars, illustrated talks should be followed immediately by questions and discussion. Visual aids--such as flip charts, models, pictures, and illustrated literature--should be used liberally.

2. Make house-to-house calls on leading citizens to increase their understanding of the importance of a sanitation campaign in the barrio, and to win their active support.

3. Try to activate the men's and youth associations. It is important that groups from one or both of these associations should not only understand the importance of the sanitation campaign, but should also learn to construct water-sealed toilets for their own homes, and then help their neighbors to do the same.

4. Organize a field trip, for members of these two associations, to one or two other barrios where good progress is being made in installing water-sealed toilets.

5. Plan and carry out a demonstration of the actual construction and installation of a water-sealed toilet, making sure to set the time so that members of the men's and youth associations can attend. A second or follow-up demonstration may be needed. The teaching demonstration should prepare the men to begin immediately the construction of toilet bowls for their own families. Adequate tools and materials should be on hand for their use.

6. Organize a mass meeting to launch the sanitation campaign. Ask the barrio council and the men's, women's, and youth associations to join in sponsoring this meeting and to help bring the people out for it. Post notices at prominent locations in the barrio. The meeting should inform the people about the causes of preventable diseases, and what they can do to reduce or remove those causes. Speakers should include members of the PRRM Health Department and of the municipal rural health unit if possible, and perhaps a representative of the provincial health office as well. Sanitary water-sealed toilets already made by men of the barrio should be on display, and information should be given about how others can learn to construct them for their own families. Illustrated literature should be available for free distribution.

7. Follow up the mass meeting by a series of teaching demonstrations at which those who have learned to construct the toilet bowls give detailed instructions to others. It is desirable that sanitary engineers, technical assistants, or other personnel from the PRRM Health Department attend these teaching demonstrations, if possible; otherwise, the RRW should be present to help if needed.

8. At a subsequent mass meeting, give appropriate recognition, and perhaps simple awards, to those who have shown the greatest initiative and community spirit in carrying out the sanitation campaign.

De-Worming Campaigns

It has sometimes proved advantageous to link a general sanitation campaign in a barrio with a de-worming campaign, which also involves promoting the construction and use of sanitary toilets.

Intestinal infestation by roundworms and other parasitic worms is widespread in the country. The most common is a disease known as ascariasis; though not an immediate killer, its weakening effects are a real drag on the victim. The intestinal parasites offer strong competition to the human body in absorbing food. Sample surveys by PRRM have shown that the incidence of ascariasis among rural school children may be as high as 85 per cent or even 90 per cent, and that three months after treatment and cure, the percentage of children reinfected may be up to 45 per cent or 50 per cent, or more. While unsanitary toilets may not be the only cause of reinfection, it seems certain that they are the major contributing factor, and that treatment without attacking the source of infection has only a temporary effect. A PRRM de-worming campaign includes not only treatment, but also—and more important—prevention by promoting the introduction and use of sanitary water-sealed toilets.

The PRRM Health Department encountered so many difficulties in its first attempts to conduct de-worming campaigns that the effort was almost discontinued. However, persistent study produced new insights and led to a more effective, systematic approach involving six steps. The responsibilities of RRWs in helping to carry out these steps can be stated briefly.

1. Cooperate with PRRM technical personnel in organizing health seminars or classes to inform the people about the wide incidence of ascariasis, especially among children. Make clear that reinfection after treatment can be avoided by the installation and proper use of sanitary toilets throughout the barrio.

2. Help to organize a small group to assist the PRRM Health Department in conducting a survey to determine the extent of infestation by worms in different age groups in the barrio. The survey requires the collection and examination of stool specimens. Sometimes a preliminary survey is limited to a control group of about 100 children. Those found to be infected are given immediate treatment. The worms expelled by one or two children may be cleaned, bottled, and displayed in the barrio health center as dramatic evidence of the urgent need for the de-worming campaign. This may facilitate the collection of stool specimens from all age groups.

3. Cooperate with PRRM technical personnel in launching a simultaneous campaign for the construction and use of sanitary toilets throughout the barrio. This campaign may also include the promotion of "blind drainage" and fencing, discussed below.

4. Assist as needed in a wholesale treatment of worm-infected persons throughout the barrio. Preparation for each treatment includes a determination of any special susceptibility to the drug employed, and a determination of dosage according to the patient's age. To avoid evasion, each person given the medicine should be asked to take it immediately.

5. About three months after this wholesale treatment, cooperate in conducting a survey to determine the extent of reinfection. In all cases where reinfection has occurred, take follow-up action with the family concerned, urging those that have not yet made and installed sanitary water-sealed toilets to do so as soon as possible.

6. Continue with patient, persistent follow-up activity until all homes in the barrio have, and make proper use of, sanitary toilets. Make it clear that intestinal germs and parasites from a single person can rapidly infect others unless sanitary toilets are used by everyone in the barrio.

Blind Drainage Construction

Under or beside the typical rural home is a dirty-looking mud pool, formed by the water that drains from bathing and household washing of kitchenware and clothing. It is a spot where pigs and other animals may wallow, and it is a favorable breeding place for mosquitoes and other vermin. The people are not generally aware of the harmful effect these mud pools have on the health of the household and the community.

The method which PRRM has found most practical in attacking this problem is the construction, by each household, of what is known as "blind drainage." This consists of a pit at least one-and-a-half meters deep and one meter wide, filled with coarse gravel and sand, to which waste water is conveyed from the kitchen and washing space by a drainage channel made of metal strips or split bamboos. Every RRW should have at hand the illustrated detailed instructions issued by PRRM for building a blind drainage for a barrio home.

Even though the mud pools eliminated by blind drainage are unsightly and ill-smelling, there is usually considerable resistance at first to the idea of changing over to a blind drainage system. People are accustomed to the traditional way of disposing of waste water, and are reluctant to expend time and labor on a project that seems of dubious value.

Approaches the RRWs have used to win support for many other projects have been found equally applicable here. These have been particularly effective: (a) Hold preliminary meetings at which the project is discussed in an informative way--with emphasis on the types of sickness caused by the presence of stagnant mud pools under the home. (b) Conduct demonstrations of actual construction, which neighbors are invited to witness. (c) Ask the men's association (RRMA) to appoint a special interested group to take the lead in promoting the construction of blind drainage systems throughout the barrio. (d) Organize visits to other barrios where good progress is already being made in sanitary programs, including blind drainage construction.

Fencing of Homelots

The yards around poorer homes, rural as well as urban, tend to become dumping grounds for refuse and garbage. Any vegetable garden plots in these yards are apt to be overrun by chickens, pigs, or other livestock. Like other unkempt places, the yards are likely to be dirty and unhealthy.

For these reasons, and also because self-respect and beauty are important elements in a family's desire to improve, PRRM encourages rural families to clean up their yards, to enclose them with fences or hedges, to plant them with vegetables, and to beautify them with flowers and fruit trees. Many visitors have observed the striking contrast between these yards and the homelots that are still dumping grounds, with few if any protected vegetables, flowers, or fruit trees.

The most common materials used in building fences are split bamboos, wooden slabs, or occasionally, barbwire or hollow blocks.

Many approaches have been found useful in promoting interest in constructing fences and beautifying yards. One is to include barrio beautification in the curriculum of leadership training. In this way, civic pride may be generated and the enthusiasm of village leaders aroused. Another method is to ask local school teachers and visiting government personnel to lend their encouragement. Organizing group visits to other barrios that have made good progress in fencing and beautification has been one of the surest ways to stimulate interest. Another method used to good effect is to sponsor competitions in home and yard cleanliness and beautification, either separately or as part of the competitions sponsored under the Model Farm Family program. (See Chapter 21.)

Pure Water Supplies

Water is a prime necessity of life. Without it, the higher animals can survive only a few hours or days. Much water passes through the human body unchanged, but some of it also enters the structural composition of the body. Hence it is entitled to rank as food, although it does not itself build tissues or produce energy.

The bacterial pollution of water is one of the most common causes of gastrointestinal diseases such as diarrheas and dysenteries, and also typhoid. Unfortunately, much of the water used for drinking purposes in the rural areas is polluted.

The most common and practical ways to ensure pure water supplies in the rural areas are, first, to make sure that wells are at least 50 feet away from latrines--the distance should be greater if the soil is porous or if the land surfaces slope downward from the latrine toward the opening of the well; and second, to boil all water for 20 minutes before drinking. Other methods, usually less feasible in the rural areas, are chemical treatment and filtering. Whenever possible, drinking water should be taken from covered wells or relatively clean-looking streams, not from stagnant streams or pools. In all cases, unless a modern sanitary water system is available, water should be boiled before drinking.

These are the methods most readily available to the RRW in promoting the use of only pure water for drinking:

1. Be sure that health seminars held in the barrio include proper instructions on the purification of drinking water. Flip charts should be used when discussing the possible sources of drinking water and the best method (boiling) for destroying the disease-bearing bacteria in it. Literature on this subject, in the vernacular, should be distributed if it is available.

2. Ask all who participate in the health seminars, and all auxiliary health workers and members of the women's and youth associations, to cooperate in informing the barrio people on how they can protect themselves from gastrointestinal diseases and typhoid by drinking only boiled water.

IMMUNIZATION

As noted earlier, immunization is one of the principal means of preventing disease. Complete or partial immunity may be given to a person by an injection of vaccine which causes his system to produce antibodies that will resist the development of a particular disease or group of diseases.

The most important vaccines today are the CDT vaccine (against cholera, dysentery, and typhoid), the DPT vaccine (against diphtheria, pertussis or whooping cough, and tetanus), smallpox vaccine against smallpox, and BCG vaccine against tuberculosis. Some vaccines, such as those against smallpox, cholera, and typhoid, are highly effective. Others, such as those against whooping cough, diphtheria, and tetanus, give partial but not necessarily complete protection.

In the Philippines, the government assumes the major responsibility for immunization of the population against these diseases. Routine immunizations are intensified whenever an epidemic threatens or is under way.

Immunizing the population is a difficult job. Most of the people tend to be indifferent unless an epidemic is already spreading in a nearby barrio or town. Some of the people, especially children, are likely to run away when the health officer comes around, even though penalties are severe for anyone who refuses to be immunized. Why? The principal reasons may be that many do not understand the value, much less the mechanics, of immunization; that a large number are still superstitious about the causes of disease; and that injections are uncomfortable and may cause fevers, especially in children.

PRRM's objective, in its immunization program, is to cooperate with government health authorities to achieve high rates of immunization in all PRRM-aided barrios. The hope is that the methods used will be successful, and then prove applicable in all the barrios that the government serves. Some degree of success has been achieved. There are now, in the PRRM-aided barrios, high rates of immunization; smallpox, cholera, and typhoid have been completely eliminated.

The principal ways in which PRRM field workers can help to ensure maximum protection through immunization are:

1. Maintain continuous contact with government health authorities in the locality, especially the staff of the municipality's rural health unit. Make them aware of your willingness to assist in mobilizing the people for immunization campaigns.

2. Be alert to any significant increase of any kind of illness in your barrio; when this occurs, make sure it is reported promptly to the PRRM Health Department and the municipality's rural health unit.

3. Cooperate with the rural health unit in working out schedules for the days when they will ad-

minister various types of immunizations in your barrio.

4. Prepare for the scheduled immunizations by arranging a series of meetings where the mechanism of disease-prevention through immunization can be explained to the people in simple terms. Ask those present to pass along the explanation to their friends and neighbors.

5. When members of the RHU staff come to your barrio to give the immunizations, try to make sure that a maximum turnout of those who should be immunized will be waiting for them at the barrio health center. Enlist the help of barrio leaders in doing this.

RECURRING PROBLEMS

Sanitation and immunization are confronted by roadblocks of ignorance, misinformation, and superstition. A scientific program in these areas cuts across accepted ways of doing things, and aims at getting people to think and act in new ways. Progress is necessarily gradual at first, and problems are to be expected. Some have already been mentioned. Others are cited below, with brief comments on the methods that have proven most effective, to date, in dealing with them.

1) Indifference, which may be due to many factors, including lack of health education, adherence to superstitious ideas and beliefs, reluctance to alter habitual practices, and the difficulty of paying for any immunizations that are not given free.

   Response: Make sure that the talks and demonstrations at the first health seminar are highly interesting to those who attend. Then ask them to discuss with their neighbors what they have learned. This will make it easier to organize subsequent seminars with the help of those who attended the first one. During the seminars, and during home visits, distribute illustrated literature that will help to break down superstitious beliefs (such as the idea that worms are needed for good digestion), and will put in their place the beginnings of scientific knowledge about the causes of disease and what people can do to prevent them.

Try to enlist the help of school teachers in the barrio, as well as visiting PRRM and RHU personnel, in arousing the people's interest in health conditions and what can be done about them. Ask the barrio leaders to take an active part in the sanitation and immunization campaigns as they develop.

Organize field trips to other barrios where sanitation programs are well under way, with good participation by the people. Examples are contagious.

Try to make the installation of sanitary facilities throughout the barrio a matter of civic pride. Use expected visits of distinguished visitors as a spur for a speed-up in the program.

Find opportunities to recognize publicly citizens who have contributed the most, in leadership and effort, toward the success of the sanitation program.

2) <u>Excessive faith in immunization</u>. Some of the people have acquired the notion that immunizations give protection against all types of disease.

<u>Response</u>: Ask those who administer the immunizations to explain that they afford partial or complete protection only against certain diseases, and that sanitary facilities and practices are equally important in preventing other diseases, especially those of the intestinal track.

3) <u>Over-dependence on government</u>. Some barrio people say it is the government's responsibility to provide for sanitary facilities and other health needs.

<u>Response</u>: Try to convince leaders in the barrio that the people should not be over-dependent on the government, and that self-reliance is much to be preferred. Then ask the Rural Reconstruction Men's Association to show the way by building and installing sanitary water-sealed toilets and blind drains, and by encouraging others to do the

same.

4) People are "too busy" to attend demonstrations or to construct new sanitary facilities for their homes.

Response: Schedule seminars and demonstrations at times that will be most convenient for the men and youth concerned. They should not be held, normally, during the planting and growing seasons. Preferably, ask the people to set the dates themselves. Once they are convinced that sanitary toilets and blind drains are essential to protect their families against disease, farmers are likely to find time to construct them during the non-farming seasons.

5) Difficulty in obtaining materials such as gravel, sand, cement, wire, used oil, bamboo, or wood.

Response: Several ways of meeting this problem have been tried out, with varying degrees of success. The RRW can select those that seem most applicable in his barrio.

(a) Propose that each member of the RRMA contribute what he can toward the establishment of a revolving fund to be used for procuring these materials. The association should designate from one to three of its members to manage the fund. Those using the supplies then pay for them at cost, in order to keep the fund replenished.

(b) Suggest that the RRMA ask the barrio council to subsidize the sanitation program out of the 10 per cent of the land tax which it controls, by making funds available for the purchase of the materials needed.

(c) If there is a well-to-do, civic-minded resident of the barrio who owns a truck, ask him to make it available for hauling sand and gravel from a nearby riverbed for use in making blind drains and sanitary toilets.

(d) If certain materials are not available in your barrio, suggest that members of the RRMA try to obtain them from another barrio nearby.

(e) If bamboo splits or wooden slabs are not

available for fencing, suggest growing hedges, using an inexpensive, readily available plant such as garmamela or violeta or San Francisco.

6) Homelot boundaries uncertain or congested. Undefined homelot boundaries are most likely when the barrio is part of a hacienda. But in any barrio some of the homelots are likely to be quite small and close to one another. Either condition may discourage fencing.

Response: In cooperation with the barrio leaders, try to convince the hacienda owner to fix the boundaries of homelots in the barrio. In cases where two homes on small lots are close together, try to persuade the owners to cooperate in building a single fence between them. When homelots are large, it may be desirable to fence in only a part of each.

FOUR-FOLD PROGRAM IN ACTION

IV. VILLAGE SELF-GOVERNMENT

CHAPTER 17 — BACKGROUND AND AIMS OF THE SELF-GOVERNMENT PROGRAM

Two important lessons relating to self-government were learned during the great Ting Hsien experiment in rural reconstruction in pre-Communist China.

The first was that, even after vigorous and successful efforts have been made in a village, in the fields of livelihood, education, and health, a rural reconstruction program is incomplete. It is like a table with three legs. A fourth leg, local self-government, is essential to the growth of genuine self-reliance. Self-government is needed, too, for the removal of serious political obstacles to progress, and for the creation of a truly balanced program of development.

The second lesson was that before a rural community can be fully ready for self-government, the people must acquire some practical experience in working together in such areas as agriculture, cooperatives, education, and health. With even a limited background of experience in these areas, village leaders may show a surprising capacity to assume responsibilities of self-government at the local level.

EVOLUTION OF VILLAGE SELF-GOVERNMENT IN THE PHILIPPINES

That China experience has found a parallel in the Philippines. After PRRM had achieved considerable success among the villages where it was working, in programs of livelihood, education, and health, it found that its total effort was hampered by political indifference, lethargy, or even hostility. This was due chiefly to a political set-up in which the barrio lieutenant and his local council were merely appointees of a municipal official--a district councilor to whom (and to no other) they owed loyalty and responsibility.

So the PRRM embarked upon an experiment in democracy at the village level. With the consent of open-minded officials in the municipality of Marikina, Rizal province, a team of PRRM field workers conducted an election among all heads of families in the barrio of Nangka to choose a barrio lieutenant and members of the barrio council. After the election, the results were legalized through formal appointments by the municipal councilor concerned. Backed by PRRM advisers, the new barrio council went to work with enthusiasm.

The late Senator Tomas Cabili and some of his colleagues were so impressed by the results of this experiment that they introduced in Congress a bill providing for popular election, throughout the Philippines, of barrio lieutenants and other members of the barrio councils. This bill was enacted as Republic Act No. 1245, which took effect on June 10, 1955. Reflecting the experience gained from the PRRM experiment, it provided that there should be in each barrio a councilman for livelihood, a councilman for health, and a councilman for education.

Shortly thereafter, improvements in the law were embodied in Republic Act No. 1408, which took effect on January 1, 1956. Among other things, express authority was granted to the barrio councils, for the first time, to promulgate rules to promote the welfare of the barrio people. After the approval of this amendatory act, the first general election of barrio councils was held on January 17, 1956.

These events and the resultant quickening of activities at the barrio level contributed to an awakening of national consciousness to the significance of "democracy at the grassroots." Responding to popular demand, Congress passed, next, the Barrio Charter--Republic Act No. 2370, which went into effect on January 1, 1960. This law conferred legal personality on the barrio, making it an official unit of government. It created the barrio assembly. It invested the popularly elected barrio council with real governmental powers, such as the enactment of local ordinances and the imposition of certain kinds of taxes. And it granted each barrio a 10 per cent share of the proceeds of taxes imposed on real estate situated within its boundaries.

A revision of the Barrio Charter (Republic Act No. 3590, which took effect on June 22, 1963) strengthened the barrio government machinery and provided for larger direct participation of the people in their barrio government.

SELF-GOVERNMENT IN THE PRRM FOUR-FOLD PROGRAM

Within PRRM, the self-government program has become a pillar of the four-fold program as a whole. It is a medium for the creation of a community atmosphere, and for the mobilization of manpower, womanpower, and youthpower in the barrio.

The long-range objective of the self-government program is to find more and more effective means of ensuring to the barrio people village governments that, with their own active participation, will be truly dedicated to their well-being and that of the nation. Within this larger goal, more immediate objectives are (a) to foster among the people a strong sense of community responsibility, and (b) to mobilize the people more effectively for carrying out all phases of the integrated four-fold program of reconstruction.

Pursuant to these aims, PRRM's Self-Government Department is engaged in the following types of work, in concert with the other departments, and in close collaboration with the rural reconstruction worker and the village leaders in each barrio:

1. Organization and activation of associations for men, women, and youth in all PRRM-aided barrios.

2. Activation of the existing barrio government machinery.

3. Citizenship education and leadership training.

Succeeding chapters of this part of the manual deal with these three aspects of the self-government program.

A fourth aspect, newly under way, is a broad study of the progress of barrio self-government under existing laws, with a view to recommending, in due course, beneficial amendments.

CHAPTER 18 ORGANIZING AND ACTIVATING BARRIO ASSOCIATIONS

Giving assistance to village leaders in organizing and activating barrio associations of men, women, and youth is one of the RRW's most basic and important responsibilities. These associations have been a salient feature of the PRRM program since the early stages of its development. Their purpose is an active involvement of as many people in the village as possible in the essential tasks of reconstruction and development.

To this end, PRRM has fostered three principal types of associations known as Rural Reconstruction Men's Associations (RRMAs), Rural Reconstruction Women's Associations (RRWAs), and Rural Reconstruction Youth Associations (RRYAs).

The men's association, or RRMA, is an organization of adult men permanently residing in the barrio --mainly heads of families, but also widowers and bachelors. The women's association, or RRWA, is an organization largely composed of housewives, but widows and unmarried women freely participate. There is no hard and fast age line between these adult groups and the youth associations. The RRYA is an organization of unmarried younger people ranging in age from 14 to as much as 30.

The RRW knows well that fostering these groups requires much more than bringing them together and signing them up for membership. He has learned the importance of good organization and systematic procedures designed to promote the effective functioning of each organization.

The procedures which the RRW endeavors to follow, with variations according to local conditions in a barrio, are derived from experimentation and cumulative experience over a number of years. They are in no sense final. The RRWs are engaged in a continuing search for better methods. When new approaches tried are successful, the results are made available to the movement as a whole. The procedures which have been found most effective, to date, are summarized below for the main stages of work with the barrio associations: initial organization, continuing operation, and revitalization if and when needed.

ORGANIZING A BARRIO ASSOCIATION

Organization of each of the barrio associations usually falls into four distinct phases--those of exploration, promotion, pre-organizational gathering, and formal organization. Guidelines, derived from experience, for each of these phases, can be stated briefly.

Exploration

1. Search through the barrio for potential leaders and potential active members of each association. Through careful personal observation, and casual exploratory conversations with the more discerning people in the barrio, try to identify men, women, and unmarried younger people of both sexes who are known to be of good character and reputation, and who would make effective initial officers and members of each of the three associations. Seek individuals with qualities of industry and resourcefulness, who are friendly, personable, and respected; persons who are interested in leading, and who show an interest in the community. Do not limit yourself to the members of any particular group or clique.

2. Find out whether there have been any previous well-run activities in which people in the barrio played an active part. Learn who those people are, what they did, how it was done, and whether their work won the approval of their fellows.

3. Make lists of your findings within the three groups: men, women, and youth. Then re-check with a few of the wiser persons in the community to make sure, as far as possible, that your selections are as good as you can make them.

Promotion

1. Decide which of the three associations should be organized first. It is important that the first organization be successful so it will set an example for the others. Potential leadership and

interest within the group are therefore factors to be considered. It is also desirable to have in mind at least one or two projects, needed in the barrio, that the first association would be able to tackle with enthusiasm.

2. Once you have decided, embark on an informational and promotional campaign to sell the idea of organizing. Although the main emphasis is on the necessity of group endeavor for community benefit, you may find it desirable to cite also advantages that may accrue to individual members and their families. Many a family head has more readily agreed to help in forming a men's association after sensing that it might offer a prospect for cooperative construction of a schoolhouse that would enable his children to continue their studies after the fourth grade.

3. In the course of your promotional effort, watch for opportunities to discuss the idea of organization informally with the persons on your selected list, and with others who may become interested. These opportunities may come during special home visits, or at a casual meeting place like a barber shop, or at social gatherings such as fiestas, weddings, or christening parties. In chatting with a group of farmers, it is easy to ask one how he is faring with his farming, then to follow through with remarks on how, through an organization of their own, all the barrio farmers might take advantage of opportunities to learn more about secondary crop production, which could improve both their incomes and their land.

4. Suggest to those interested that they interest others. Without over-pushing, let the idea spread.

Pre-Organizational Gathering

1. When some real interest has been generated, ask prospective leaders and initial members to attend an informal meeting to exchange views on the objectives of the new association, and to begin thinking together about one or two initial projects.

2. At this preliminary meeting, aim for agreement on the appointment of a committee to work with the RRW in drafting a constitution and by-laws, and on setting a date for the establishment of a formal organization.

Note: Sometimes this pre-organizational meeting can be skipped. If there is already sufficient interest, and if potential leaders in the group have already pledged their cooperation, the first meeting may be convened for the purpose of formally organizing. In this case, the RRW should bring along a standard sample constitution, available from PRRM headquarters, for the group's consideration.

Formal Organization and Inauguration

1. At this meeting, take the initiative in getting matters started. Either preside or arrange with some competent person to do so, after discussing with him the purposes of the meeting. The principal purposes are: (a) discussion and approval of the new association's constitution and by-laws, (b) election of officers, and (c) selection of chairmen and members of standing committees on livelihood, education, health, civic affairs, and finance.

2. Shortly after the organizational meeting, even if the association has already begun to function, arrange for a well-publicized community program, to which high municipal and even provincial officials are invited. While this program may be featured by talks, music, and other entertainment, its main purpose is the inauguration of the new people's association. If the affair is well attended and impressive, it gives the officers and members of the association the feeling that the community expects much of them.

Essentially the same steps are followed in organizing all three people's associations.

Recurring Problems

In stimulating and encouraging the establishment of these associations, the RRW is sure to encounter problems. These are the most common, and the methods that have proven most effective in dealing with them:

1) Animosities. A potential leader may be reluctant to associate with some of the members of a prospective association because of past animosities. These may have arisen from personal or religious or political differences.

Response: Try to be alert to such animosities

and work quietly for reconciliation. A number of approaches have proven helpful. One is simply to bring the differing parties together, within the same group, and get them so interested in the new venture that past frictions seem unimportant. Another approach is to convey to one party anything good that the other has said about him, and vice versa; a little warmth may do much to melt past resentments. Still another approach is to get some mutually respected third party to mediate.

2) <u>Misgivings due to failures of previous community efforts</u>. A number of agencies have undertaken community organizational activities in the past. In numerous instances, these proved to be ineffectual or short-lived, or were outright failures. Barrio people who remember these attempts naturally have misgivings about similar new ventures.

<u>Response</u>: Through an intensive educational effort, try to acquaint the people thoroughly with the PRRM's four-fold approach to rural problems, and with the record of other communities where this approach has taken root and is moving ahead with the active collaboration of the people's associations. If possible, arrange a field trip to another PRRM-aided barrio to see the work that the associations are doing. Support this educational effort by distributing appropriate illustrated PRRM literature.

An additional technique that has often been used effectively is to get some interesting facts about the barrio, such as unpublicized data from a socio-economic survey, or figures on births and deaths from the municipal treasurer's office, or information about the barrio's boundaries from the Bureau of Lands. Then, at the first promotional meeting, make use of this information. When well done, this gives a strong impression that the PRRM, represented by the RRW, is informed and actively interested in the barrio's conditions, and that it therefore merits the people's confidence.

3) <u>Reluctance of some to be chosen as officers</u>. Whether the real reason is shyness, modesty, fear of failure, or a competing obligation, many good

officers are likely at first to beg off on grounds of being too busy.

Response: Before the organizing meeting, or during it, try to reassure the person regarding his abilities; if appropriate, mention what others have said about him. Express confidence that he or she will be given every assistance in getting started, by associates in the organization as well as the RRW and other members of the PRRM staff. If this is not enough, stress the challenge of the association's need for leadership in its work for the community. If needed, add an appeal to the individual's ego, by citing his particular talents or mentioning the prestige of leadership in the beneficial activities of the association.

ACTIVATING THE BARRIO ASSOCIATIONS

Of all the elements that breathe life into men's, women's, and youth associations, the most important is sustained activity. If the associations lag for want of lively interests and work under way, the RRW may feel he is failing, and he may be right. Perhaps he is not trying hard enough. Or he may be trying too hard, and doing so much for the officers of the associations that there is little challenge to their own initiative and sense of responsibility. Or the relative inactivity of an association may be due to factors for which the RRW is not at all responsible, but which he may be able to help remedy.

As Dr. Yen, the founder of the Rural Reconstruction Movement, frequently emphasizes, the acid test of the effectiveness of a rural worker is to be found not in how much he does for the people of the barrio, but in how much the people are doing for themselves and their community as a result of the RRW's inspiration, teaching, and leadership. The most effective leadership, oftentimes, is that which brings key barrio people to the fore and gets them, gradually but steadily, to assume increasing responsibility.

Much of the rural reconstruction activity promoted by PRRM is carried out by the people's barrio associations. No part of the RRW's task, therefore, is more fundamental than the activating of these associations. Following are some of the guidelines that have been found most helpful to the RRWs in doing this work.

Structure, Procedures, Morale

1. Try to make sure that the organizational structure is complete, and that each of the officers and committee chairmen is thoroughly familiar with his responsibilities.

2. Try to make certain that the constitution and by-laws are followed, and that the rules of procedure for the conduct of meetings, and such other rules as the association may approve from time to time, are fully understood and observed. These may seem to be routine matters, but many difficulties can be avoided by adhering to the "rules of the game."

3. Work with the leaders of each association in trying to instill in all its members a sense of belonging, and an atmosphere of friendliness and cooperation. This is, of course, more important than regulations and procedures. Group spirit and morale can be developed and sustained in many ways. Lively meetings are helpful. So are friendly, casual contacts and discussions outside the meetings, and occasional recreational activities and impromptu programs of entertainment in which maximum participation by individual members is encouraged. But the most important way to build the vitality of the organization is through action programs or projects in which the members are genuinely interested, and which they believe to be of value to themselves, their families, and the community.

Choice of Projects for Each Association

The selection of these projects is of the greatest importance.

1. Help the officers and committee chairmen, especially during the early life of the association, to choose projects that are appealing, useful, and manageable. It is important not to attempt too much at once, and to make sure that the first projects will be successful. Remember the PRRM criteria for all projects to be promoted among the people: they must be simple, economical, practical--and duplicable.

Generally speaking, projects for the different people's associations are selected in the light of the interests and abilities of the members. It is natural that the men's, women's, and youth associations should choose the types of activities suited to their particular groups. This may vary from barrio to barrio. It often happens that a plant nursery is conducted by a men's association in one barrio, but is run by a youth association in another; or that the barrio health center is operated by the women in one barrio, and by the youth in another.

The spontaneous interest of the people is so important that no hard and fast rules are practical in determining which association shall handle which type of project. However, it is possible to put before each group a preliminary list of projects which other associations of their type have conducted successfully, and which they may wish to consider, in consultation with PRRM personnel who can give technical assistance as needed.

2. To the RRMA, suggest some of the following projects and activities for consideration:

In plant production

Individual projects: improved rice culture; planting secondary crops; planting fruit and firewood trees

Group projects: barrio extension farm or plant nursery; seminars on scientific methods of plant production

In animal production

Individual projects: starting a piggery; constructing a carabao or cow shed

Group projects: immunizations of fowls and livestock; upgrading of fowls and livestock; seminars on animal production

In cooperatives

Individual project: membership in a credit union

Group project: organization and operation of

credit union

In health

    Individual projects: constructing a sanitary water-sealed toilet; digging a garbage pit

    Group projects: manufacture of toilet bowls; barrio drainage; barrio garbage collection

In education

    Individual projects: home reading; listening to worthwhile radio programs

    Group projects: literacy classes; musical programs; dramatic productions

In self-government

    Individual project: learning the fundamental rights and duties of citizens, together with important provisions of the barrio charter

    Group projects: construction of a barrio hall; campaign for the exercise of voting rights; leadership seminars

3. To the RRWA, suggest some of the following projects and activities for consideration:

In livelihood

    Individual projects: homelot gardening; milking goats

    Group projects: dressmaking class; cottage industries; campaign for credit union membership

In health

    Individual projects: cleaning of homes and surroundings; purifying drinking water supply

    Group projects: maintenance and operation of health center; mothers' class; nutritional seminar

ORGANIZING AND ACTIVATING BARRIO ASSOCIATIONS   299

In education

    Individual projects: home reading; listening to worthwhile radio programs

    Group projects: dramatic productions; folk singing and dancing; maintenance of a reading center

In self-government

    Individual projects: familiarization with lives of outstanding women in the country's history, and with rights and duties of all citizens

    Group project: educational drive for exercise of suffrage

    4. To the RRYA, suggest some of the following projects and activities for consideration:

In plant production

    Individual projects: home gardening; composting; developing a mushroom plot or a family plant nursery

In animal production

    Individual projects: poultry and swine raising

    Group projects: campaign for confinement of pigs; organizing a seminar for auxiliary husbandmen

In cooperatives

    Group projects: convincing parents to join credit union; participation in credit union projects

In home industries

    Individual projects: basketry; woodworking

    Group projects: organizing a rural industry class; promoting a cottage industry in the barrio

In health

>   Individual projects: building blind drainage for the home; fencing the homelot; training to become an auxiliary health worker

>   Group projects: maintaining cleanliness of the clinic; first-aid class; promoting immunization campaign in the barrio

In education

>   Individual projects: becoming an auxiliary literacy teacher; becoming an active member of a dramatic club; writing plays, stories, or poetry

>   Group projects: planning and conducting community programs, including folk music, drama, and dancing; organizing sports; building and maintaining a reading center

In self-government

>   Individual projects: learning the rights and responsibilities of citizens, and provisions of the barrio charter; learning how to get help from agencies concerned with community development; becoming familiar with examples set by national heroes

>   Group projects: cooperation in construction or renovation of barrio hall; taking part in an educational drive to convince the people to pay taxes and comply with ordinances; participation in the citizenship seminar

5. Do not yourself select the projects to be undertaken, individually and collectively, by members of each association. Merely suggest and advise. "Planning with the people rather than for the people" is the keynote. The principal considerations to bear in mind, in offering ideas, are (a) pressing needs in the barrio; (b) availability of human and material resources; (c) availability of technical know-how, either among the members or through technical assistance that can be provided; and most important, (d) genuine interest on the part of the participants.

6. Strive to avoid duplication or needless overlapping among the projects of the different peo-

ple's associations. This is not usually difficult in the PRRM-aided barrios, where the committee chairmen in the three associations--for the committees on livelihood, education, and health--are normally honorary members of the corresponding committees of the barrio council, and are allowed to participate in the council committees' deliberations.

Recurring Problems

Activating and maintaining the vitality of the three associations is generally more difficult than the initial promotion and organization. Cited below are some of the most typical problems, and ways of dealing with them which have been repeatedly tried and found most effective, to date:

1) <u>Failure of members to attend meetings</u>. This is one of the most common sources of the RRW's headaches and heartaches. For it is at these meetings that problems are discussed, new information is presented, ideas are exchanged, and activities are planned and evaluated.

   <u>Response</u>: Try to get the officers and committee chairmen to assume the main responsibility for promoting attendance. Help them, especially in the early stages of an organization's development, on such matters as scheduling, agenda, speakers (if any), choice of a central location, adequate notices, follow-up reminders, and perhaps the use of a community bell or gong shortly before each general meeting.

   Meetings of the associations and their committees should be regular, but not so frequent that they become repetitious or burdensome. Make sure they are well planned, with reports and other subject matter of real interest and concern to the members. Some association presidents, with the help of their RRW advisers, have succeeded in maintaining good turnouts by persuading small, enthusiastic groups of members to promote attendance at each meeting. To reduce competition from other sources, some RRWs have succeeded in inducing gambling promoters and owners of stores dispensing liquor to close up shop during the hours of association meetings. One well-established RRW even ventured to suggest that the men's association in his barrio meet a few meters from a gambling place. He then saw to it that the meeting was highly interesting and informative, with the remarkable result that the gambling broke up and most of the patrons attended the meeting.

The main task is to make every meeting educational and thoroughly worthwhile, with maximum group participation, so that each member will feel that it is his association, and that he is gaining something of real value from each meeting. If this is achieved, a nucleus of key members can usually be depended on to respond, and to get others to do the same.

2) <u>Incompetence of a presiding officer</u>. This may make for dullness, drabness, scattering of the discussion, or failure to accomplish the purposes of a meeting.

<u>Response</u>: Try to have the presidents and vice-presidents of the associations attend the PRRM inter-barrio leadership course described in Chapter 20. This course includes training in the art of conducting meetings.

Until this can be done, try to acquaint the principal officers with the elementary rules of parliamentary procedure. Discuss with them in advance the aims of the meetings. If necessary, give some tactful assistance in keeping the proceedings under control and moving ahead.

Drabness in a meeting may be countered, and interest revived, by brief interludes for impromptu songs or declamations, or for human interest stories and lively anecdotes, of which the barrio people are exceedingly fond. The RRW will do well to become a collector of stories and anecdotes, and to practice the art of telling them.

3) <u>The presence of filosofos or filosofillos</u> who argue against motions merely for the sake of arguing.

<u>Response</u>: Try not to show annoyance. A filosofillo can often be neutralized by the tactful expedient of agreeing with some of his points, then gradually getting him to agree, in a spirit of reciprocity, to the proposition at hand. If any of his arguments are valid, suggest that the

proposition be modified to take them into account. This kind of response may not only alter his attitude; it may also win the respect of others attending the meeting.

4) *A failure of expected resources to materialize.* Many a barrio association, having auspiciously planned and started a community project, suddenly finds itself unable to continue the project due to a failure of expected resources--for example, a promised donation for the construction of a barrio hall.

Response: Discuss with the officers the possibility of filling the need from another source. One method often used is to get the association concerned to undertake a fund-raising activity. This activity should aim for more than fund-raising alone. A benefit drama employing local talent, for example, may "shoot three birds with one stone" since it provides enjoyable recreation for the people, a form of education for the participants, and a means of raising funds.

REVITALIZING BARRIO ASSOCIATIONS

The young men and women who work with the barrio people in promoting and carrying out the self-government program are not deluded into thinking that every association will at all times be the constant, active instrument for reconstruction that it is designed to be. Knowing the hard facts of barrio life, they are well aware that any one of the people's associations may lapse into a state of weakness or dormancy at some time or other. They also know that the task of revitalizing dormant and weak associations is, first, a matter of determining the causes of the members' inaction, and second, attacking those causes.

Causes of Inaction

Experience points to the following as the most common reasons for members' inaction:

1. *Loss of interest in the projects initiated.* This sometimes stems from an absence of direct benefits from a project to an individual or his family. More often, it arises from a failure to involve the membership sufficiently in the conduct of the pro-

ject, and from a lack of immediate incentives.

2. An absence of team spirit, which may be due to personal differences and rivalries, or to factional disputes, or simply to a background in which there has been little experience of the benefits of cooperation and group action.

3. Indifference to community problems, which may be attributable to narrowness of outlook, or to the predominance of small group loyalties over any feeling for the community as a whole, or to habits such as gambling which may consume some members' attention, leaving little room for larger concerns.

4. An absence of good leadership for the association. This may be due to unwillingness on the part of recognized leaders to exert their influence for fear they will be accused of personal ambition. Or it may result from the impatience of existing leaders in dealing with recalcitrant members, so that they leave a trail of resentments. Or it may be due to incompetence on the part of the association leaders.

PRRM Response

PRRM does not accept these causes of inaction fatalistically or passively. They are problems to be dealt with. For the paralysis, or partial paralysis, which they produce is not only harmful to the members of the association; it also deprives the entire program of one of its main sources of vitality. In its efforts to cope with these problems, and to eliminate them as far as possible, various approaches have been tested. The following have been most effective to date:

1. <u>To revive interest in group projects.</u> Learn more about the members' individual talents, skills, and interests. Then ask them to undertake specific tasks suited to their own abilities, or put them in charge of specific phases of the work according to their interests and capabilities. This will give them a greater feeling of participation and sense of responsibility.

Be quick in expressing praise for each piece of work done well, and generous in according public recognition of accomplishments, at meetings and at

ORGANIZING AND ACTIVATING BARRIO ASSOCIATIONS

other public gatherings.

Further incentives may be injected through friendly competitions in relation to a project, with appropriate awards in the form of PRRM certificates or inexpensive donated prizes.

A visit to a nearby barrio, where a project similar to the one at hand has been successfully carried out, has also been used repeatedly to arouse further interest and a let's-not-be-outdone attitude.

2. <u>To restore a spirit of teamwork</u>. Find out some of the traits, and the likes and dislikes of the principal contending parties. Then endeavor to bring them together at some meeting or informal gathering where a conversation can be started on a matter they are likely to agree on. This, or some other simple move to "break the ice," may be the beginning of a more friendly relationship.

Many a conflict between two contending groups has been neutralized by asking leaders of both groups to serve on the same committee, or to participate in the same constructive project.

Another method repeatedly used with success has been to ask the assistance of an influential person acceptable to both groups to mediate quietly and try to bring about a reconciliation.

Even when there are no real frictions to divide the members, there may be an absence of team spirit. A standard method of coping with this situation is to hold socials and other recreational activities, with items on the program so planned as to increase camaraderie. This nurtures a group spirit and creates a better atmosphere for joint efforts.

3. <u>To revive concern for community problems</u>. In consultation with a few of the wiser and more influential citizens, organize one or more general meetings. Invite interesting visitors to speak, in ways that will awaken a sense of the community and an awareness of what other barrios have done, through joint efforts, to improve their conditions. These visitors may be drawn from the PRRM staff, or from some other well-known civic organizations, or from among enlightened government officials or distinguished citizens acquainted with the work of PRRM.

If possible, enlist some "home talent" to provide musical and other entertainment between the speeches. This will increase the enjoyment of all who attend.

At the gathering and in private talks afterwards, cite examples of the readiness of municipal and provincial authorities to assist in meeting barrio needs when they find a genuine civic spirit in the barrio; and conversely, their non-receptivity to requests if there is no evidence of the people's desire to work together in self-help programs.

Promote athletic contests, musical programs, and other activities that will draw people away from gambling and drinking places.

Organize visits by potential leaders--men, women, or youth--to other barrios where good projects are under way and a healthy community spirit has been developed.

With the cooperation of technical personnel from the PRRM Self-Government Department, promote and organize some citizenship training sessions.

Plan occasional joint sessions of the barrio council and its committees with the officers and committee chairmen of the three associations, at which reports are made on the progress of current projects, followed by a discussion of common problems.

4. <u>To strengthen or replenish leadership</u>. Organize leadership training sessions in the barrio. At the earliest opportunity, try to persuade the association's key officers to join one of the PRRM-conducted inter-barrio leadership training courses.

And, quietly, give all assistance possible to the association leaders who need it most in learning to do their jobs effectively.

If none of these measures produces results, discuss with personnel of the Self-Government Department ways and means of proposing reorganization of the association, with a new election of officers and the creation of new committees as needed. This, as a last resort, may be an effective means of replenishing the leadership of the association.

CHAPTER **19**   ACTIVATING THE BARRIO GOVERNMENT MACHINERY

The Revised Barrio Charter enumerates the powers and duties of the barrio council, the barrio assembly, and the individual barrio officials. It defines the role which the machinery of barrio government can and must play in the task of community development. In many barrios, however, this legally defined role cannot be fulfilled because of a lack of knowledgeable, competent, active barrio officials.

ESTABLISHING FRIENDLY RELATIONS

Awareness of this situation underlies an important part of PRRM's self-government program, namely, stimulating and training the elected officials in the PRRM-aided barrios. This activity is greatly facilitated by the PRRM policy of working only in barrios where its help has been requested.

Such a request is generally made by the barrio council, and it usually connotes good will and an open-minded attitude on the part of the barrio officials. They, as a rule, have had very limited opportunities for formal education. While their natural intelligence is in most cases good, they often feel acutely a lack of the knowledge and experience they need in order to carry out their official responsibilities.

For these reasons, the barrio officials are often very receptive to the offer of unofficial assistance and training provided by a private agency, like the PRRM, which has proven its value, remains in an advisory position, and has no political ax to grind.

The PRRM worker, however, does not simply assume that this is the case in his barrio. First, he endeavors to establish a cordial relationship with all the barrio officials. After this is done, the question can be tactfully explored--first with the barrio captain, then with the councilmen and other officials --as to whether they would welcome special assistance from PRRM's Self-Government Department in conducting a special training session with them. It is frequently helpful if a senior member of the department participates in these exploratory talks.

The training session, it is explained, deals with (a) the powers and duties of the council, the assembly, and the various officials of the barrio; (b) sources of funds; (c) financial procedures; (d) the drafting of ordinances and resolutions; and (e) the desired relationship, in PRRM-aided barrios, between the legally elected officials of the barrio and the officers and members of the three people's associations. During the training, it may be added, there is ample opportunity for questions and discussion.

If the suggestion is cordially welcomed, as usually happens, the RRW then cooperates with the PRRM technical personnel concerned in conducting the training session.

TRAINING OF BARRIO OFFICIALS

The training, given by members of the PRRM Self-Government Department in collaboration with the RRW, consists of a blend of group instruction and discussion-leading. The discussion-leading technique is used when the participants have some basic knowledge of the topic at hand.

It takes preparation on the part of the discussion leader to select and clearly define the points to be presented for discussion. He leads the discussion by directing questions to individual members of the audience, making it a point to distribute the questions as equally as practicable, for maximum audience participation. The questions should be thought-provoking, not ones which suggest an obvious answer or which call for a simple yes-or-no response. To ensure more productive discussion, answers elicited from one participant may be "thrown" to others for their assessment and comment.

Even though the course is brief, it includes an extensive coverage of the barrio charter provisions. This information, and the discussions it engenders, lead almost invariably to questions about other laws which relate to the barrios or are of some special interest to one or more of the barrio officials.

During the training session, the PRRM personnel present are sometimes called on to answer catchy questions, or to deal with thorny hypothetical problems. It is the aim of the technical personnel, or the RRW, to answer not only with level-headedness, a ready wit, and some knowledge of the law, but also with tact, patience, and understanding.

It is essential that every provision cited and every point discussed be reduced to the simplest, most understandable terms possible, taking into account the level of education of all the participants. With this in mind, the technial personnel and the RRWs make it a point to acquire beforehand a good working knowledge of Pilipino translations of words and phrases used in the law.

Recurring Problems

Among the problems that arise in the course of efforts to activate the barrio government machinery, two are of special interest to the RRW.

1) The indifferent barrio captain. Many of the barrio captains never really wanted to run for office, but were prevailed upon--perhaps reluctantly--to become candidates only because of a lack of other qualified persons, or because of their known acceptability to a majority of the people in their barrios. As a result, they did not have any kind of platform, or make any pledges as to what they would do if elected. In other cases, successful candidates seem to have been prompted to run by considerations of prestige more than by any desire to improve the life of the people. Under these circumstances, it is not surprising that a good many barrio captains are relatively indifferent to the problems of the community.

Response: In trying to cope with this touchy predicament, RRWs have found the following approaches especially helpful.

(a) After making friends with the barrio captain, try to persuade him to attend a PRRM leadership training course. This type of course (discussed in the next chapter) has been quite effective in developing new motivations and a heightened sense of responsibility.

(b) Encourage the barrio captain's attendance at public gatherings sponsored by PRRM. At these gatherings, speak about what public officials can do for the people who have elected them. Induce the municipal officials or influential citizens present to emphasize the same point.

(c) If the barrio captain's inattention to his responsibilities is due to a preoccupation with gambling or other unwholesome forms of recreation, try first to gain his full confidence; then, with tact and understanding, try to prevail upon him to take official measures to eradicate or at least minimize these practices in the barrio. If he does so, he will first have to set an example, and you will have accomplished your purpose. This approach, in a large majority of cases, has not been resented by the befriended barrio captain.

2) <u>Unconcerned barrio councilmen</u>. When a councilman for livelihood, or education, or health shows little interest in activities within his sphere of responsibility, the result may be not only a loss of needed leadership, but also an actual drag on the efforts of others. Common symptoms of a lack of concern are absences from meetings of the barrio council and other community gatherings, or half-hearted participation in discussions, or even opposition to constructive proposals.

<u>Response</u>: It is important to remember that each councilman is an elected public official and that the RRW is a friend and adviser to the council. Among the approaches tried out by the RRWs, these have proven most useful to date:

(a) Suggest to the barrio council that each councilman be assigned specific, well-defined responsibilities in connection with current projects, in addition to their general responsibilities as chairmen of standing committees.

(b) Arrange a visit by members of the barrio council to a nearby barrio where successful projects are in evidence, and where the constructive role of the barrio council members can be described or demonstrated in detail.

(c) Suggest to the barrio captain that he invite a prominent member of the community to some of the meetings of the barrio council, perhaps to give advice on a project being initiated. This will give to the councilmen a feeling of added importance, and help awaken their sense of official responsibility to the community.

Any approach should be employed against a background of cordial relationships with all the councilmen, developed through frequent contacts.

CHAPTER **20** CITIZENSHIP EDUCATION
AND LEADERSHIP TRAINING

For the people to participate effectively in government, it is essential that they know in a practical way what it means to owe allegiance to one's country, and to be entitled to protection and freedom under its laws. They need to know something, too, about the functions of government, and how it operates at different levels. They must be informed on the principal issues that affect their own well-being and that of the nation. They must be alert to the way in which elected officials are carrying out their responsibilities, and aware of their right and duty to take part in the election of these officials.

CITIZENSHIP EDUCATION

These are matters of education, which is fully as important in the rural areas as in the cities. It is just as important for adults who never had the opportunity for this education as it is for children in school.

Citizenship Forums in the Barrios

For all these reasons, education of the barrio people in citizenship is at the very core of PRRM's program in self-government. The emphasis is on citizenship at the barrio level.

The principal approach used is that of a short series of forums on citizenship, conducted by a member of the PRRM Self-Government Department in collaboration with the rural reconstruction worker, or by the RRW alone with the help of a detailed outline covered during his own basic training.

Each meeting of the citizenship forum is held at a time that will permit maximum attendance, usually during the late afternoon or evening of a weekday or at some appropriate hour on Sunday. The RRW keeps in mind the following techniques.

CITIZENSHIP EDUCATION AND LEADERSHIP TRAINING

1. Publicize each session of the forum. Ask the barrio council to assign to each of its members the responsibility of bringing the residents of their respective districts or sections of the barrio.

2. Punctuate each formal talk with examples that are familiar and vivid to the people.

3. When a topic is one on which a number of those present have some basic knowledge, draw out their information and ideas, using the discussion-leading method learned during your basic or in-service training.

Other Approaches

Two complementary approaches to citizenship education have been tested repeatedly, and are now being employed with generally good results.

1. Promote maximum registration of those eligible to vote, and, on election days, full exercise of their right of suffrage. This activity itself is an important aspect of citizenship training. During the days immediately preceding registration, and the period before elections, try to stimulate the officers and members of the people's associations to take the lead in urging maximum participation by the people. It may be mentioned that, in one barrio, where the people made nearly 100 per cent use of their right to vote, they succeeded in catapulting an honored favorite son into the position of municipal mayor, and then into the national Congress.

2. Encourage the cultural committee of one of the people's associations to put on a play which deals with a significant aspect of a citizen's privileges and responsibilities. Dramas of this kind may be written by someone in the barrio who has a flair for playwriting or story telling; or they may be drawn from PRRM's reserve supply of folk dramas. One of these depicts in a vivid manner, for example, the way in which a violator of the law brought not only a penalty upon himself, but also ill effects to others in the community.

Recurring Problem

<u>Awkward questions</u>. Citizenship training forums sometimes give rise to delicate situations. For

instance, a person aggrieved by an official act of a barrio captain or councilman may ask a question the correct answer to which might indicate that the official had acted badly in carrying out his duties.

Response: Be alert to the implications of such questions. They call for a combination of intelligence, honesty, and tact. A needlessly blunt answer might antagonize the official or lessen his prestige and effectiveness. An evasive answer might leave the questioner dissatisfied. One RRW, faced with this situation, managed to get across gracefully to the councilman the apparent arbitrariness of the action he had taken, and at the same time to convey to the questioner the RRW's belief that the councilman had acted in good faith and with a genuine desire to serve the interests of the community.

Some RRWs have found it useful to keep in reserve a few humorous stories that can be drawn on to produce a laugh and help "clear the air" if tensions develop during a discussion.

LEADERSHIP TRAINING

It is a basic PRRM principle that rural reconstruction is a task to be performed by the barrio people themselves, the RRW serving only as a guide and helper.

In line with this principle, the self-government program gives high priority to an effort to train individuals who can provide competent, interested, effective local leadership for the barrio associations and for all parts of the four-fold program: livelihood, education, health, and self-government. To this end, PRRM undertakes two types of leadership training, one within single barrios, the other for potential leaders from several barrios at once.

Training Sessions in Individual Barrios

Central themes in this type of training seminar are (a) the qualities of good leadership, (b) the planning of programs in the barrio, and (c) the art of convincing people. These specific procedures are recommended:

1. Invite to these sessions not only officials of the barrio government, key officers of the people's associations, and additional leading citizens of the barrio, but also any others who want to attend. Always remember that some natural-born leaders, not previously discovered, may be found.

2. To hold the interest of those attending, strive for maximum audience participation in the treatment of each topic. Distribute questions impartially among those present, and encourage a free exchange of ideas. This procedure has often proven helpful in drawing out those who are shy at first, and also in reducing the tendency of some "show-offs" to monopolize the discussion.

The Inter-Barrio Leadership Course

This is a six-day seminar conducted periodically at PRRM national headquarters. Five leaders from each of eight or nine PRRM-aided barrios are invited to attend as trainees, making a total enrollment of 40 to 45 in each seminar. The five leaders from each barrio are usually the barrio captain, the barrio secretary, and the presidents of the men's, women's, and youth associations. As a rule, the barrios selected for representation are from different areas in which different PRRM field teams are at work. All travel and living expenses during the seminar are paid by PRRM.

The purpose of the inter-barrio leadership course is not only to develop competent leaders, but also to deepen their interest in all aspects of the four-fold program. The training program is designed to impart, in a rudimentary but effective way, specific knowledge and skills in (a) parliamentary procedure, with proficiency in the proper conduct of meetings and in the exercise of group control, (b) the dynamics of leadership, with special attention to the requisites of good leadership, to methods of persuasion, and to effective techniques in planning community projects, (c) public speaking and communication, in a manner designed to promote interest and cooperation, (d) the conduct of the various parts of the rural reconstruction program, with special attention to key projects, and (e) illuminating reporting on the progress (or retrogression) of barrio programs.

Other phases of the course include a field trip to some of the barrios that have been most successful in carrying out the four-fold program, to whet interest, and to display techniques which the trainees can try out in their own barrios; socials which demonstrate to potential leaders the practical value of cultivating group spirit; and the organization of a leadership trainees' association, which provides camaraderie and affords practical training for the elected officers and committee chairmen in the exercise of leadership.

During the seminar, efforts are made to achieve a maximum of involvement on the part of the individual trainees. Formal lecturing is reduced to a minimum. The emphasis is on discussion-leading (when the subject is one in which the trainee group has some basic knowledge), and on demonstrations in which the trainees themselves are invited to take part. Each demonstration is followed by an analysis in which the trainees also participate. To climax each principal phase of the training, the participants undergo "practicals," which highlight learning-by-doing and role-playing methods. Role-playing consists of a trainee acting the part of a community leader in an imaginary situation calling for the exercise of leadership, such as presiding over a meeting, or persuading an indifferent head of family to join the RRMA, or delivering a public address on National Heroes' Day.

Although it is a comparatively new undertaking, the inter-barrio leadership training courses have had very encouraging results to date.

Recurring Problems

1) <u>The reluctant leader</u>. Some of those invited to attend the leadership training seminar are reluctant to leave their homes and their work for the six-day period required for the training.

   <u>Response</u>: Try to persuade the hesitant that the training course will be a new and valuable experience. Assure them that you will accompany them to the training center, and that their expenses will be paid.

2) <u>Dropouts</u>. These may occur because of concern over work to be done at home, or apprehension about the safety of carabaos or other property.

   <u>Response</u>: One approach, tried with some success, is to request, in advance, pledges from those who have agreed to attend that they will stay through the six-day training course. A more effective approach is to achieve and maintain a high level of trainee interest, involvement, and enjoyment throughout the training period. Animated discussions, field visits, learning-by-doing, role-playing, group singing, friendly associations, and a growing sense of "belonging" all contribute to this end.

FOUR-FOLD PROGRAM IN ACTION

V. JOINT PROGRAMS

CHAPTER 21 THE MODEL FARM FAMILY

One of the unique features of the Philippine Rural Reconstruction Movement is the Model Farm Family program. It developed spontaneously within the organization. It is a joint enterprise, requiring the cooperation of all departments. And it carries the work of the PRRM to a new level, or new dimension. Figuratively, it is concerned not only with the rice roots in the fields around each village, but also with the crucial smaller plots where the rice seedlings grow.

THE PROGRAM

The rationale of this program and the story of its growth can be summarized briefly.

Fundamental Concepts

The Model Farm Family program is based on these concepts: first, that healthy, cooperative family life is basic in the development of stable democratic societies; second, that nation-building is a task to be undertaken not only from the top down, but also from the bottom up--from the family to the barrio, to the municipality, to the province, and, finally, to the nation; third, that to have a strong, free, progressive nation, the family--which is the basic unit of a democratic society--must be made strong and progressive, freed from poverty, ignorance, disease, and civic apathy. When the family achieves adequate livelihood, a good start on the road to enlightenment, sound health, and some active participation in the affairs of the community, it can then play its important role in building a more prosperous, enlightened, healthy, and progressive nation.

The broad objectives of the MFF program are those of the Rural Reconstruction Movement as a whole: better livelihood, better education, better health, better citizenship. The special objectives of this program are (a) to encourage all members of the family--father, mother, children, and others in the household--to become involved and take an active part in projects suited to their individual interests and abilities; and (b) to make of this a cooperative venture in which each member supports the others in their activities, and in which the family as a whole takes pride in its collective achievements.

Occasionally, visitors have raised questions as to whether the barrio people did not resent such interest in their family life as an intrusion upon their privacy. It is a natural question. But the answer is that few among all the projects initiated by the PRRM have been more wholeheartedly welcomed. There appear to be three principal reasons for this.

One is that the family is a strong institution in the Philippines, which, as in other countries, has been subjected to new strains by the changes and pressures of modern life. There seems to be a wide realization that this has resulted in an increase in the stresses between parents and children, and some deterioration in the strength and wholesomeness of family life. A program, therefore, that focuses on things that family members can do together, or in support of each other, is widely welcomed.

The second reason is that many rural families, living in wretched poverty, have been demoralized, knowing that in their ragged clothing and poorly kept dwellings they must seem to belong in the lowest strata of society, but not realizing that they could do much about it. When, through the MFF program, they found they could change their situation perceptibly with a little guidance and some real effort on their own part, it gave them new hope and a new sense of dignity. Instead of resenting the challenge, many were eager for it.

Third, the PRRM workers have been trained for their jobs. They know the importance of respect for the people with whom they are working. They try to make sure that one step is understood and welcomed before the next is broached, and that even a family program, as it develops, has the support of leaders in the barrio, and of the people generally.

Evolution of Program

The MFF program had its beginnings in the early

THE MODEL FARM FAMILY

days of the PRRM program. It did not originate in plans drawn up in advance by PRRM personnel, but as a practical result of the RRWs' actually living in the barrios. Because the early RRWs did not pay for their lodging, they felt it was their personal obligation to share in the general cleaning and care of the home and premises. As they took on these routine chores, some of them began also to beautify the homes and their surroundings, especially by cleaning up trash and planting bougainvillea and other flowers there.

The results were so satisfying, and the transformed homelots became such a source of pride to the families and to the barrios, that this innovating initiative of individual RRWs gradually developed into a regular feature of the PRRM program. It was named, at first, the Model Home project.

In 1954, in Nangka, Marikina, Rizal, a PRRM pilot barrio, the Model Home project was launched with extra vigor by the barrio lieutenant and other leading families of the community, with the guidance of the RRW. The main objectives were to improve the physical appearance of the barrio, and to beautify every home. The results of this project were reported in the newspapers, and the praise of national leaders stimulated many more families in Nangka and other barrios to participate.

The next few years brought, gradually, a natural evolution in the project. The objective became not only beautification, but full, effective, participation of the family in the basic activities of livelihood, education, health, and self-government. It became the Model Farm Family (MFF) project, which was adopted as a definite program at the general conference of PRRM workers in 1959. The new project reached out to encompass the all-round development of the family members, not just the physical aspects of their homes.

What is a Model Farm Family?

A model farm family, as PRRM has come to define it, has several characteristics. It produces more than it consumes, through expanded and improved livelihood projects. It has a systematic plan of earning, spending, saving, and sharing. Its home is clean and has neat surroundings and a sanitary toilet. Its members are literate, law-abiding, tax-paying, healthy, and free from communicable diseases. They refrain from gambling and other immoral activities, and they participate actively in the barrio government and the barrio organizations that promote community projects and cultural activities. Since the MFF project also includes non-farm families (defining them as those who derive their main income from pursuits other than farming), appropriate modifications are made in the standards to be applied to them.

A love of friendly competition is deeply ingrained in the Filipino people--and beautification of homelots, as well as participation in many other PRRM projects, has brought it out. This has been exceptionally beneficial to the MFF program. It has provided new incentives for the families involved, and has helped to generate a great deal of interest in the program among the people.

This friendly rivalry made it necessary for PRRM to provide a clear, specific, standardized way of rating the families' progress toward model farm family status, to ensure a fair standard against which the people could direct and measure their efforts. The criteria chosen--and gradually refined--were intended to serve both as a test and as a guide. Besides providing a system of evaluating what a family had accomplished and what it had not been able to accomplish at a given time, it would specify concrete family goals in the context of the four-fold program.

The present program embodies specific criteria for a family in the areas of livelihood, education, health, and self-government. Achievement in relation to established goals is taken as the measure of progress toward model farm family status.

By the standards now in use, the model farm family is one that has attained a rating of 90 to 100 per cent, when its achievements are measured against the detailed criteria discussed later in this chapter-- _provided that_ (a) the family has no average rating of less than 75 per cent in any one of the areas of livelihood, education, health, and self-government; (b) the minimum additional income of the family over its previous annual income is no less than ₱200.00; (c) literacy is 100 per cent for the whole household, except for the small children; (d) a sanitary toilet has

THE MODEL FARM FAMILY   325

been installed and is being used properly; (e) qualified voters of the family voted during the last election; and (f) all members of the family are known to be of sound moral character. In short, it is a family that has shown decided, measurable progress toward overcoming the interlocking, basic problems of the rural areas: poverty, illiteracy, disease, and civic inertia.

Achieving the Criteria--A Family Enterprise

The activities and projects promoted to help families achieve model farm family status merge with all the rural reconstruction work going on in the barrio. For the most part, they are not separate activities under the MFF program. Some do have a family focus, such as homelot gardens, beautification and fencing, sanitary toilets, and blind drainage. But mostly, they involve the participation of family members in the activities promoted by the people's associations, classes, and other groups formed in the barrio to carry out projects in all four areas of the PRRM program. The man, woman, youth, and child of the family each participates in a way that corresponds to his individual interests and capacities. In doing so, he increasingly realizes his own potential while making a useful contribution to the progress of the family and the barrio.

Under the _livelihood_ phase of the program, a farm family practices improved, scientific techniques in their farming work, raising of livestock, homelot gardening, and perhaps a home industry. The man, for instance, might undertake to improve his main crop, cultivate a secondary crop, obtain New Hampshire hatching eggs, practice composting, attend farmers' classes, and arrange to get a purebred boar. In order to obtain the necessary capital for these undertakings, he might join a credit union and, as soon as he can, apply for a loan. The woman might start a homelot garden, to give the family a better diet and to provide surplus vegetables and fruits for sale. She might also feed the boar, using kitchen scraps and forage, and perhaps undertake a home industry such as dressmaking or basket weaving. The youth might take responsibility for part of the garden plot, help gather forage for the boar, and take part in the barrio's nursery project.

In the area of _education_, any member of the family who cannot read and write enrolls in a literacy class. Those who can already read join a reading circle, in which the members take turns practicing so that reading can become, naturally, a part of their daily lives. Reading in a group often stimulates lively exchanges of views on topics of general interest. The woman or a son or daughter might volunteer for training to become an auxiliary literacy teacher. The youth might take part in a folk music or dancing project, or a dramatic production in the barrio.

In the area of health, the man usually constructs a sanitary toilet and blind drainage for the home, after attending classes to learn why they are important and how they can be built economically, using available materials. The woman may attend a mothers' class and a health seminar, may learn to maintain a safe drinking supply, to serve a nutritious, balanced diet to her family with no increase in cost, and to seek medical advice in times of need. As a member of the RRWA, she might also help in the administration of the health center. The youth of the family, through the RRYA, might enroll for training as auxiliary health workers, then take their turns in doing voluntary work at the barrio health center. They may also help in maintaining clean, sanitary conditions around the home.

In the area of self-government, the man of the family is normally active in the RRMA. He might serve as an officer of the group, and participate in leadership classes. The woman belongs to the RRWA, and the older sons and daughters join in the activities of the RRYA. All participate in a family council. All are law-abiding. And those who are qualified are expected to vote in local and national elections.

Program by Stages

The Model Farm Family program is now promoted in every PRRM-aided barrio. PRRM has set minimum barrio targets, for half-year periods, as follows:

```
First Stage (1st 6 mos.)...  5 model farm families
Second Stage (2nd 6 mos.).. 10 model farm families
Third Stage (3rd 6 mos.)... 20 model farm families
Fourth Stage (4th 6 mos.).. 30 model farm families
```

When the program is started in a barrio, five

farm families are selected and invited to volunteer for the first stage. If they agree, the RRW assists them, at first, in recording the performance of the family members in all aspects of the PRRM four-fold program, as well as performance in special projects. The record is kept on a form, in Pilipino, which gives the criteria for a model farm family. Later, as a member of the family learns to do the recording, he or she will keep the record for the family, and the RRW will look at the record from time to time to see that it is being kept correctly. The same procedure is followed during the succeeding stages, with at least five additional families in the second stage; ten more in the third stage, and another ten in the fourth stage.

At the end of the fourth stage, or twenty-four months, it is expected that there will be a minimum of 30 model farm families in a barrio. Experience indicates that when as many as 30 families have attained the model farm family rating, the program acquires a general momentum, with more and more families deciding to follow the example of those who have set the pace, and to join the MFF program.

IMPLEMENTING THE PROGRAM

The MFF program takes strength from, and lends vigor to, the entire PRRM program. A family that achieves better livelihood, better education, better health, and better citizenship makes a significant contribution to the spirit and the progress of the whole barrio. PRRM technical and field personnel work closely together, therefore, to advance the MFF program.

Within this framework of cooperation, PRRM staff members have appropriate responsibilities. The specialist on the Model Farm Family program, with the help of a technical assistant, is responsible for general planning and supervision; also for continuous advisory help and counsel to the PRRM field personnel concerned and, at times, to village leaders who assist in initiating this program in their barrios.

The team captains provide guidance, as may be needed, to the RRWs and to the participating families as they work to achieve the MFF goals; they may also serve with the RRWs as consultants to the barrio councils and the chairmen of the three people's associations, who usually select the families that are asked to participate first in the program.

The RRWs, working through the barrio associations, families, and individuals, endeavor to win wholehearted acceptance and support for the program. As the PRRM staff members who live in daily association with the barrio people, they bear the main responsibility for conveying to them the meaning and spirit of the MFF program, so that its goals may become their goals. The ways in which the RRWs pursue these aims are outlined in the following sections.

Gaining the Support of Family Members

As he works with a family to gain their interest and active support for the program, an RRW tries to convey to each member a greater awareness of the importance of the family within the barrio, the municipality, and the nation. He encourages their sense of "team spirit" in the family, and builds on their natural enjoyment of friendly competition with their neighbors. At the same time, he remembers that each family member is an individual, and he tries to make everyone in the household--father, mother, youth, and child--see how his efforts in the MFF program will add to his own abilities and interests.

It is not always easy to gain a family's support for the program, particularly in barrios where there are few, if any, "model farm families" to serve as inspiration and example. Many approaches have been tried. From among the following, which have been the most effective to date, the RRW chooses those that he considers most appropriate in each case.

1. He makes frequent home visits to the family. During the visits he points out the advantages of participating in various community activities. He encourages everyone to ask questions and to join together in discussing problems and approaches to them. This strengthens the family's interest in discussing community problems that may stand in the way of their own progress.

2. He encourages the members of the family to join the three people's associations, and the head of the household to join the credit union if one has been started in the barrio. This involves them ac-

tively in the general rural reconstruction work of the barrio, and awakens their civic spirit. They also have a chance to see how problems can be dealt with practically and successfully by the barrio people, themselves, and this increases their self-confidence.

3. He organizes field trips for the family to other barrios that have flourishing MFF programs. These trips often inspire the participants to emulate what they have seen with their own eyes.

4. He encourages friendly competition among families. He describes, in a lively, engaging way the quarterly evaluation days, when judges--selected from among barrio teachers, members of the parent-teachers associations, and members of the barrio council and municipal council--rate the barrio families on their achievement in relation to the criteria described later in this chapter.

5. He uses visual aids to clarify the objectives of the program. This is particularly helpful in a barrio where no "model farm families" have yet developed, and when visits to neighboring barrios are not practicable. Pictures, in color, of well-kept homelots, containing vegetable gardens and adorned with bougainvillea or other flowers, have often proved very effective in convincing a family to achieve the same thing for themselves. The same effect has been accomplished with the use of moving pictures of successful "model farm families."

6. With the assistance of the technical staff of the MFF Department of the PRRM, the RRW organizes seminars and group studies on the Model Farm Family program. Well-known municipal or barrio leaders are invited to speak at these meetings in order to encourage the barrio families to participate.

7. Once a family's interest has been actively aroused, the RRW works with them in drawing up detailed plans designed to involve each member in a team effort to achieve the MFF goals. The plan entrusts specific projects to each member of the family, taking into account his individual interests and capacities, and helps to ensure balanced, well-paced progress.

8. The RRW encourages members of the families

to coordinate their activities, when possible, with those of organizations in the barrio. This facilitates cooperation, provides welcome opportunities for the free exchange of ideas, and develops a sense of mutual support.

Recurring Problems

1) Lack of materials and/or money to purchase them is often an obstacle. Many families do not have supplies needed--such as fertilizers to improve crop production--and cannot afford to buy them. Because of these handicaps, they are often reluctant to make a start.

    Response: Suggest, to begin with, projects that do not require money, after considering carefully any implements or materials the family may already have. Lack of money is a handicap, but a start can be made without it. Then try to plan one or two projects that will bring in some additional income, and encourage the family to earmark it to purchase specific needed materials. If there is a credit union in the barrio, suggest that the head of the household join it and, when he becomes eligible, take out a loan that will provide a little capital for investment. Point out to him that loans of this sort--used to increase production and income--are favorably considered in the credit unions.

2) Families do not own their homelots. Many families are tenants and are not interested in improving homelots that are not their own property, especially if the length of their tenure is uncertain.

    Response: Find out the tenant family's length of tenure. If it is practical, discuss with the landlord the possibility of making some adjustment to improve the tenant's position.

3) Transient families. In barrios where there are many transient families, RRWs find it difficult to promote the MFF program. For these families may not wish to invest their efforts and funds in projects or improvements that they will soon leave.

    Response: Pay visits to the homes of the transient families, and encourage them to undertake short-term projects from which they can derive some benefit.

4) <u>Topography of the barrio</u> makes improvement difficult. In some barrios, the land is so irregular that it is difficult for the RRWs to suggest feasible plans for improving the homelots. In these barrios, it may not be possible to implement all of the activities specified in the criteria for the model farm family.

<u>Response</u>: Enlist the aid of any member of the PRRM Model Farm Family Department in making appropriate adjustments in the criteria to be used in evaluating the progress of these families.

Sustaining Family Interest

When the RRW has gained the interest of several families, the Model Farm Family program is off to a good start. But the goals of the program are not easy to attain. There are bound to be frustrations and disappointments. When these come, the RRW has the responsibility of "standing by" the families, demonstrating his continuing support, and providing encouragement and advice as they continue to work toward the MFF goals.

If necessary, he is also ready to do this follow-up work with families who have already received the model farm family rating. For the goals of the program are not just tasks that can be done once and forgotten. They are a way of life, involving new habits and a new approach to problems. Once a family has achieved model farm family status, it is essential that they continue the daily activities they have undertaken to achieve this rating--applying scientific methods and practices to farming and animal production, keeping their homes clean and attractive, and participating actively in community projects.

Among the approaches used to sustain interest in the program, these have proven most successful to date:

1. Through the Model Farm Family Department of the PRRM, the RRW recommends that feature articles about model families be published in the newspapers. This makes the barrio people realize that the project

is not just a local affair, and that model families are playing a vital role in building the nation.

2. With the help of his captain and team associates, the RRW joins in encouraging the barrio councils of several communities to hold inter-barrio contests. He solicits donations to procure prizes for families that have attained the highest MFF ratings in their barrios. Some of these contests have elicited keen interest. They not only encourage families to participate fully in the MFF program, but also draw the councils of neighboring barrios into closer cooperation and understanding.

3. With the active assistance of the PRRM Vocational Arts Department, the RRW promotes a dramatic production depicting the activities of model farm families in some humorous or unforgettable way.

4. With the help of the technical staff of the MFF Department, he posts MFF placards and ratings in conspicuous places in the barrio. This stimulates the friendly competition that has worked so well in sustaining interest in this program.

5. He recommends special awards to families who maintain their status as model farm families for a specified period.

6. He continues his home visits to individual families on a regular basis, showing enthusiasm for progress made, and assisting in the planning of future projects.

Recurring Problems

1) The "ningas-cogon" attitude of some farm families. Some households that become model farm families lose their enthusiasm. Their interest tends gradually to fall off until eventually they return to a non-model status.

Response: To forestall this, encourage the parents in each household to assign specific responsibilities to everyone in the family. This makes it easy to detect who may begin to neglect his duties. On home visits, stress the necessity of continuing MFF activities if there is to be a permanent improvement in the family's way of life.

2) Some places in the barrio are flooded. Some barrios have low areas which are flooded during the rainy season. The model farm families living in these areas may be unable to continue their activities because their land is under water.

   Response: After looking over each situation individually, encourage farmers to continue any activities that are still possible, and to plan definitely for resumption of other activities when the land is dry again. It may be possible, during the rainy season, to suggest suitable new projects such as home industries.

3) Change of status of family members. Sometimes it is the unmarried members of the family who participate most actively in the MFF program. When they get married, they discontinue participation either because they move from the barrio or move to new homes within the barrio. It is then difficult for the RRW to sustain the family's interest in the program.

   Response: Encourage fathers and mothers, as well as younger people, to participate actively in the program. Advise the parents of young people who are getting married to reassign responsibilities to the members of the family who are still at home.

4) Changing assignments of RRW. From time to time, an RRW is withdrawn from one barrio and assigned to another. This interrupts the continuity of his efforts in implementing the program. Even though his replacement continues the tasks he started, the barrio people may have difficulty in adjusting to the way the new RRW performs his duties.

   Response: Before leaving a barrio, the RRW should inform his replacement fully about the progress made on the Model Farm Family program, acquainting him with the status of individual families and the ways in which he has worked with them. He should also give him a cordial introduction to the people of the barrio. It is advantageous if the new RRW can accompany the outgoing RRW on a number of home visits and observe him as he works with individual families.

5) <u>Disappointment over the evaluation of family performance</u>. Sometimes families are disappointed in the evaluation made of their progress, and lose heart.

<u>Response</u>: Talk frankly with the family about the evaluation, and be sure they understand the criteria so they will realize that objective standards, rather than favoritism, determined the rating. Take the opportunity to point out specific items that they can start working on immediately, so their rating will be higher in the next evaluation.

6) <u>Lack of time for maintaining projects</u>. Sometimes family members say they have no time to continue the projects required under the MFF program.

<u>Response</u>: Listen carefully to what they have to say. Try to help them plan their time so they can continue the projects they have started. Encourage them to use some of their leisure time for worthwhile projects, pointing out the benefits they will bring to themselves. Check also to see whether there is an equitable distribution of duties among the members of the family.

Persuading Reluctant Families to Participate

Experience has shown that when a good number of families in the barrio have achieved model farm family status, they tend to influence others to participate in the program. Despite this, there are always some families who are reluctant to commit themselves, for various reasons. They present a special challenge to the RRW. He can reach these families through many of the same techniques he has used with other families in the barrio--but a little extra effort may be needed. Here are some of the approaches that RRWs have used successfully in persuading reluctant families to participate in the program:

1. The RRW visits a family in their home to discuss the program. He emphasizes the advantages it will bring to everyone in the family, and describes the MFF goals in a practical, easy-to-understand way. He encourages all members of the family to ask any questions or express any doubts they may have, so they can be dealt with frankly.

THE MODEL FARM FAMILY

2. He follows up such home visits by distributing to the families illustrated reading materials about the MFF program.

3. The RRW invites these families to attend special meetings or study groups where resource persons from the technical staff of the PRRM Model Farm Family Department have been invited to speak. He makes sure that appropriate audio-visual materials, which have proven to be highly effective, are available at these meetings.

4. The RRW emphasizes the support that is being given to the program by the barrio captain, and members of the barrio council, the parent-teachers association, and the barrio school teachers. This is often effective in overcoming doubts that families may still have about the program's practicality and importance.

5. The RRW encourages members of doubtful or reluctant families to observe the progress being made in their own barrio by families participating in the program. He may also organize field trips on which heads of the non-model families may accompany barrio leaders to neighboring barrios and observe the accomplishments of model farm families there.

6. The RRW stresses the recognition given by PRRM to those who achieve MFF status, through the awarding of certificates of merit, placards, or prizes. He tells about the recognition day program, attended by important public officials, where the achievements of the model farm families are made known to citizens of the barrio and the municipality.

7. Once some of these reluctant families have begun to participate, the RRW posts rating sheets in conspicuous places showing their achievements. This provides an added incentive at an early stage, and helps to prevent dropouts due to initial frustrations or disappointments.

Recurring Problems

Many of the problems the RRWs face in working with these families are like those encountered in working with other families, and can be dealt with by the same basic approaches. Some additional problems, and responses to them that have been effective, are:

1) **Tribal differences**, as found in parts of Mindanao. In barrios in Cotabato municipality near Illana Bay, for example, there are distinct tribal differences among the people residing in the same barrios. These differences may give rise to jealousies and suspicions that obstruct the efforts of the RRW to involve families from all groups in the MFF program.

   Response: Explain to every family that PRRM is non-partisan, and that its aim is to help every family in the barrio to achieve a better way of life. Take great care to distribute home visits, time, and attention equitably among the families of the barrio, without preference for any particular group.

2) **Obstruction by overseers**, in some haciendas. In barrios that are located within large estates or haciendas, the overseer generally has control over the tenants' activities. If he is not sympathetic, it may present an obstacle to the MFF program.

   Response: Arrange to meet with the overseer and explain to him the purposes of the Model Farm Family program. Seek his cooperation in encouraging families in the barrios under his control to engage in the activities necessary to achieve model farm family status. If possible, call on the administrators or owners of the haciendas to enlist their support as well. It may be feasible to suggest specific instructions for them to issue to their overseers. In talks with overseers, administrators, or owners, the RRW may find it advisable to enlist the help of his team captain or a member of the PRRM Senior Staff.

3) **Limited space for homelot gardens**. In some barrios, particularly in haciendas, houses are very close to each other. There is very little space for homelot gardens, which discourages families from participating in the MFF program.

   Response: Urge the families to use what space there is to plant vegetables and ornamental plants. Ask for the help of plant production specialists in recommending to such families suitable plants for intensive cultivation in a small space. Suggest that these plants be grown

THE MODEL FARM FAMILY   337

in pots as well.

4) **Presence of vices.** Games such as "hweteng," poker, bingo, and "mahjong" are prevalent in some barrios, and may occupy too much of some families' time. Habitual gambling and drinking often makes it difficult for the RRW to persuade some family members to use their time for MFF activities.

Response: If the barrio is a sponsored one, the RRW may be able to recommend that the sponsors restrict gambling and the sale of liquor within the barrio. If it is not sponsored, he may suggest that the barrio council consider the passage of an ordinance restricting gambling and other vices.

5) **Indifference of some families** toward PRRM and the MFF program. Some families remain indifferent for a long period despite the usual attempts to interest them in the MFF goals.

Response: Patience and regular home visits may work in the long run. Do not expect all families to respond to the program with equal promptness. It is a good idea, with reluctant families, to ask the barrio captain or members of the barrio council to come along on home visits, and to speak in enthusiastic support of the MFF program. They may succeed in convincing a family where the RRW alone could not.

Gaining the Support of the Three People's Associations

The Rural Reconstruction Men's Association (RRMA), the Rural Reconstruction Women's Association (RRWA), and the Rural Reconstruction Youth Association (RRYA) can be of great assistance in promoting the Model Farm Family program. The following approaches have been used successfully by the RRWs in enlisting their cooperation.

1. Organize a meeting of the officers and members of the three people's associations to discuss with them the purpose and content of the MFF program. This serves to inform leading citizens of the barrio about the program and offers them the chance, at the beginning, to ask questions about any details that

they do not completely understand.

2. Request each of the three associations to appoint special committees to encourage their members to participate in the MFF program.

3. Meet with the officers and members of the associations on an individual basis, asking them to help take the lead by bringing their own families actively into the MFF program.

4. Organize a field trip for officers and selected members of the associations to one or two neighboring model villages. The good examples they see there may well be effective in stimulating the officers and other participants to promote the MFF program in their own barrio, and eventually to achieve model village status. (See Chapter 22.)

5. With the help of the technical staff of the PRRM Model Farm Family Department, plan a special seminar for the officers and members of the three people's associations, to present to them the general plan, purposes, and details of the MFF program. This enables them to back up the MFF program more effectively.

6. Encourage each of the three people's associations to join a municipal federation of the people's associations in PRRM-aided barrios. Such federations have given good support to the MFF program.

7. Encourage the officers of the people's associations to act as judges in home beautification and in crop and animal production contests.

Recurring Problems

1) Indifference of the people toward the barrio leaders. In some barrios, people may be indifferent to the officers of the three people's associations because they have not convinced the people of their sincere interest in improving the barrio.

Response: Establish good working relations with the officers and members of all three associations, as well as the members of the barrio council and other known leaders. Discuss with them the purposes of various MFF activities. When you make home visits to promote the program, encourage individual officers to accompany you. Try to see that they take an active part in discussing with the family any problems they may have in connection with the program. The sooner these barrio leaders work closely with the families, and gain their confidence, the more quickly the program will progress.

2) <u>Transient leaders</u>. In some barrios, there are leaders among the people who are not permanent residents. They may move from one area to another in search of better economic opportunities. This may complicate the problem of trying to gain the support of the associations.

<u>Response</u>: Encourage the officers of the people's associations who are permanent residents to work out a system so that some transient leaders can work on the program when they are in the barrio, and others can take over their responsibilities when they leave. Work out, if needed, special schedules that will enable transient members to participate in the program whenever they reside in the barrio. It is far better for them to work at improving the barrio part of the year than not at all.

Gaining the Support of the Barrio Council

The barrio councils have proven to be valuable allies of PRRM in rural reconstruction work. In barrios where the councils have actively supported the MFF program, families have generally achieved MFF status in a shorter period of time.

The RRW's efforts in promoting the MFF program are, in effect, "multiplied" when he gains the active support of the barrio council at the start. Here, as in his work with the people's associations, his success is greatest when he succeeds in getting the people to work most actively for themselves. No matter how conscientious he is, it is not possible for him, single-handedly, to provide constant guidance and assistance to every family that is working toward the MFF goals. When he succeeds in involving the barrio council, as well as other barrio organizations, he is putting many other hands--and heads--to work.

The following approaches have been used successfully by RRWs in enlisting the support of the barrio councils for the Model Farm Family program.

1. The RRW invites council members to attend seminars on the MFF program, so that each member may gain needed information and a sense of individual responsibility in implementing the program. When possible, PRRM experts, associates, and assistants are invited to speak.

2. The RRW visits the council members at their homes to discuss their leading roles in supporting the program.

3. He organizes field trips to other barrios where MFF programs are successful, and where the members of the barrio councils are taking an active part.

4. As indicated earlier, he may assist the council members in creating standing committees on livelihood, health, and education. These committees can be of great help in promoting the MFF program in their respective areas of interest.

Recurring Problems

In seeking the support of the barrio councils for the Model Farm Family program, two problems have come up frequently. They are cited below, with the responses to them that have worked effectively, to date.

1) Indifference. This problem may persist even though adequate information has been given about MFF activities and goals.

Response: Ask personnel from the PRRM Model Farm Family Department to come to the barrio and have heart to heart talks with the council members who show continuing indifference. Ask your team captain to assist you in talking with them about MFF projects already successfully completed, giving praise where praise is due. Try to increase the council members' morale and confidence by encouraging others in the barrio to give due recognition to their efforts.

2) Over-dependence on others. Some barrio council members tend to rely too much on municipal lead-

ers, or landowners, or PRRM experts, or others. Such over-dependence may prevent the council members from taking active leadership themselves in the MFF and other programs.

Response: With the team captain, talk with these council members about their responsibilities to the people who have elected them. Speak of their capabilities, recognize whatever they may have accomplished so far, and emphasize the prestige of the office they hold in the barrio. Point out that while it is perfectly all right to seek the help of other leaders, they have enough authority and ability to do a great deal on their own with fellow council members.

Gaining the Support of the School Teachers

Traditionally, school teachers are held in high regard in Philippine barrios. They are recognized as key community leaders and effective workers in community education. The barrio people often turn to them for help and advice whenever they are confronted with serious personal, family, or community problems. PRRM personnel have found them to be dependable sources of information about barrio conditions and, frequently, excellent partners in promoting the fourfold program.

The RRWs, therefore, usually seek the support of the local teachers, from the beginning, for the Model Farm Family program. If they are properly informed about its specific activities and over-all goals, they can lend their backing in many ways. When requested, for example, they may serve as advisers in the MFF program, give educational talks to parents about it, encourage their pupils to participate actively and then report at school on what they are doing. These approaches have been used successfully by RRWs in approaching the teachers:

1. Explain the MFF goals to them, emphasizing what this program can do to improve living standards in the entire barrio. Cover all the important features of the program, and point out how important the help of the teachers can be. Encourage their questions and answer them as fully as you can. Give them literature on the MFF program.

2. Encourage them to initiate programs on their

own to help implement the PRRM program, and especially the MFF project. If possible, arrange for them to meet teachers in other barrios who have cooperated actively in the MFF program.

3. In cases where the teachers become sufficiently interested, ask them to help supervise the MFF project in one or more sitios of the barrio. This delegates real responsibility to them, and involves them directly in the work of helping families achieve the MFF goals.

Recurring Problems

Despite the special contributions that teachers are often able to make to the MFF program, problems have arisen, at times, in gaining their support. These are the most common, with the responses that have proven most effective to date:

1) Full schedules. The teachers' days may be filled with school responsibilities.

Response: See if it is possible to agree on a schedule allowing for limited but regular time to be allotted to the MFF program. For example, a teacher might agree to spend an hour every Friday afternoon to visit neighbors and talk about the MFF goals. This kind of help has been effective in many barrios.

2) Non-residence. Many school teachers do not live in the barrios where they teach.

Response: Encourage these teachers to do what they can, with both pupils and parents, during the hours when they are in the barrio, and ask for their help in activating others.

3) Attitude of superiority. It is sometimes regarded as traditional for teachers, as members of the educated class, to show a superior attitude toward the barrio people. When such an attitude exists, or the people think it exists, this stands in the way of warm, cooperative relationships between a teacher and the families of the barrio.

Response: In discussions with the teachers, stress the value of a cooperative spirit among the people in carrying forward the MFF program. Let them know the importance of their contribution, and the barrio people's appreciation of their efforts. Encourage them to participate in the activities of the families working to achieve model status. The more they do so, the more quickly any "stand-offish" feelings will disappear.

4) <u>Political or religious differences</u> may prevent teachers from cooperating in joint efforts with other teachers and people of the barrio.

<u>Response</u>: Make it clear that PRRM is non-political and non-sectarian, that the MFF program requires the cooperation of all, and that it can benefit everyone living in the barrio irrespective of their political or religious affiliations.

EVALUATING PROGRESS

As mentioned earlier, the spirit of competition breathes life into the Model Farm Family program. Men, women, and children all share in the mounting interest as more and more families become participants. Evaluation of the progress of individual families is made four times a year, at the end of each quarter--that is, at the end of March, June, September, and December. Excitement mounts as these days approach, and reaches a peak when the ratings of the judges are finally announced.

MFF Selection Committee

The committee--or panel of judges--that makes the ratings is normally made up of members of the barrio council, the chairmen of the three people's associations, and other selected leaders, with the RRW and his team captain serving as consultants. On the day set for an evaluation, this committee visits the homes of all the contestants, and makes or reviews the detailed ratings for each as they see with their own eyes what the families have accomplished.

There is a holiday mood as the panel of contest judges weaves its way through the barrio. Good ratings are of course very pleasing to the families who have succeeded in attaining the goal of model farm family. For those that do not reach this goal, the evaluation serves the purpose of pinpointing what they still have to do, and showing them how model status is within their grasp.

It is significant that the evaluation is something done by the barrio people themselves, not something handed down from above. This generates a sense of warmth and enthusiasm for the program that would not otherwise exist. And the involvement of leading citizens of the barrio in the work of judging enhances their sense of participation and importance, and reinforces their continuing support for the MFF activities.

In rating the families, the committee uses detailed criteria, jointly developed over a period of years by PRRM staff members and barrio leaders. These criteria are posted for everyone to see, so every family may know that the standards are fair and objective, and the same for everyone.

The Criteria for a Model Farm Family

The criteria reflect the over-all goal of the MFF program--that each member of the family shall contribute in his own way to the family's joint progress in the four areas of livelihood, education, health, and self-government. They have evolved gradually, with many revisions reflecting practical experience as the program has developed. Numerical values are assigned to different activities and accomplishments to give a balanced emphasis to each segment of the program, and to provide a reasonably objective method of evaluating each family's progress. The criteria are not rigid and fixed for all time. As the program changes, they change.

It is now accepted that an average rating of 90 per cent or better, for the four segments of the program, is necessary before a "model family" award is given. Performance is rated against the following criteria, with which are shown the highest possible scores for the various categories of activity.

In livelihood

    1. Practice of scientific methods of

         a. Plant production.................... 25%

      b. Animal production.................... 20%

  2. Participation in

      a. Cooperatives........................ 20%
      b. Rural industries.................... 5%
      c. Livelihood seminars and classes..... 5%

  3. Attainment of minimum additional income ("MAC")....................... 20%

  4. Wise use of income..................... 5%

                                          Total 100%

<u>In education</u>

  1. All members literate................... 20%

  2. Literature read, considering quality and quantity

      a. At home............................. 30%
      b. In reading circle................... 10%

  3. Participation in

      a. Cultural activities................. 20%
      b. Recreational activities............. 20%

                                          Total 100%

<u>In health</u>

  1. Family health

      a. None suffering from communicable diseases.............. 25%
      b. All members immunized............... 15%

  2. Environmental sanitation

      a. Installed sanitary toilet and its proper use................ 15%
      b. Constructed blind drainage.......... 10%
      c. Maintaining safe drinking water..... 5%
      d. Maintaining clean and sanitary house and premises................ 10%

  3. Reporting all births, deaths, and

                communicable diseases................. 10%
        4. Participation in health
             seminars and classes................. 10%

                                        Total   100%

In self-government

        1. Active participation in

            a. Barrio organizations (RRMA, RRWA,
                 RRYA, and barrio assembly......... 40%
            b. Community projects................. 25%

        2. Active family council................... 15%

        3. All members law-abiding................. 10%

        4. Qualified voters vote during elections.. 10%

                                        Total   100%

                    How Families are Rated

    To arrive at a rating, the judges check the family's accomplishments against the criteria and give a percentage rating for each activity and each area. The average of these four area figures is the family's general rating under the MFF program. In other words, the four subtotals are added and divided by four. If the quotient is 90 per cent or better, if no subtotal is less than 75 per cent, and if the minimum additional income has been attained, then the family has achieved model status.

    The members of the MFF selection committee may call on the RRW to give them general guidance as they make their evaluations. The standard form they use, provided by PRRM, is entitled "Criteria for a Model Farm Family" (PRRM Form Number 14). It is set up as shown on the opposite page.

    How is this form used to record all the activities undertaken by an individual family? Say we are recording the activities of the family of a certain Mr. Juan Diaz. We start with the first category, "livelihood." Mr. Diaz is the head of the family. He does the farming, so his name is written on the line for plant production in column 2, under the

PRRM Form No. 14   MODEL FARM FAMILY   To be accomplished
                                                                       every quarter

Head of Family............ Barrio........... Municipality.......... Province..........
Date of entry in MFF........... Mother and Children (ages)............, ...,
..............., ..., Others (ages) ....

1	2	3	4	5
	UNDERTAKEN BY	FIRST STAGE	SECOND STAGE	THIRD STAGE
		Quarters Ending	Quarters Ending	Quarters Ending
CRITERIA FOR A MODEL FARM FAMILY		(Mo.) (Mo.) 19 19	(Mo.) (Mo.) 19 19	(Mo.) (Mo.) 19 19
I. LIVELIHOOD.....100%				
1. Practice of scientific methods of				
a. Plant production........... 25%				
b. Animal production........... 20%				
2. Participation in				
a. Cooperatives................ 20%				
b. Rural industries............ 5%				
c. Livelihood seminars & classes. 5%				
3. Realization of "MAC"............ 20%				
4. Wise use of income.............. 5%				
SUBTOTAL FOR THE QUARTER				

The complete form continues with sections for education, health, and self-government, using the standard criteria. It also extends to the right, providing columns for the fourth stage and one additional stage (a total of seven columns).

347

heading "undertaken by." If he practices all the scientific techniques that have been taught for plant production, the figure 25 per cent is entered in column 3. If he does not, partial credit is recorded. (A guide for arriving at specific figures is given in the next section.)

To continue, who in the family devotes the most time to raising the pigs and chickens? It is Maria, the eldest daughter. Her name and relationship to the head of the house is written on the line for animal production, in column 2. The entry reads, "Maria, daughter." If she practices all the scientific methods that have been taught for animal production, 20 per cent is entered in column 3. If not, she too gets partial credit.

After all the items of the criteria are rated for the livelihood section, the percentages are totaled. This gives the subtotal for the section. The same procedure is used to record the rating of the family's achievements in education, health, and self-government.

The completed forms for the families who have achieved model status should be filed with the RRW. The Pilipino version should be completed and posted by the committee, preferably on the wall of the family's receiving room. The RRW submits the names of the families to the PRRM office, which in turn prepares plaques and certificates of merit for presentation during the recognition day program.

Guide in Evaluating Performance

PRRM has prepared the following detailed guide for the members of the selection committee. It corresponds to the categories of the form, "The Criteria for a Model Farm Family," with a detailed breakdown to give the weighted value of each activity. By following this guide, the judges can give percentage ratings to each family to indicate their progress toward the MFF goals--and enter these ratings on the evaluation form.

Livelihood - 100%
---

1. Practice of scientific methods of:

      a. Plant production......................... 25%

In evaluating the performance of the farm family in plant production, 25 per cent is the maximum rating; it is apportioned as follows:*

Rice production............................ 9%
Secondary crop production................. 9%
Home gardening............................ 7%

The maximum rating that a farm family can obtain from each of these projects is again apportioned, as follows, according to the scientific practices or steps involved in carrying out each project:

1) Rice production   (9%)

    a) Selection of good seeds........... 1%
    b) Proper seedbed preparation........ 1%
    c) Proper sowing of seeds............ 1%
    d) Proper care of seedlings.......... 1%
    e) Proper land preparation........... 1%
    f) Proper transplanting of
       seedlings........................ 1%
    g) Proper care of growing crops...... 1%
    h) Application of fertilizers........ 1%
    i) Harvesting the crop............... 1%

2) Secondary crop production   (9%)

    a) Selection and use of high
       yielding quality seeds.......... 1%
    b) Thorough land preparation......... 1%
    c) Cultivation and weeding........... 1%

---

*Non-farm families that are not engaged in rice production and secondary crop production may participate in the MFF program if they follow the basic scientific practices involved in the major industry they are engaged in (including fishing). The maximum rating to be obtained from the major industry is 18 per cent; that is, the equivalent 9 per cent from rice production and 9 per cent from secondary crop production. Non-farm families, shall, however, participate in home gardening, animal production, cooperatives, livelihood seminars and classes, attainment of "MAC" (Minimum Additional Income), and in wise use of income, as well as in education, health, and self-government.

- d) Fertilization........................ 1%
- e) Control of pests and diseases....... 1%
- f) Crop rotation....................... 1%
- g) Green manuring...................... 1%
- h) Planting off-season crops........... 1%
- i) Special practices, such as ratooning, inter-cropping, succession cropping, etc. 1%

3) Home gardening (7%)

- a) A diversified garden of leaf, fruit, and root vegetables; planting, preferably, some of the plants named in the "Bahay Kubo" song, such as sincamas, talong, sigadillas, mani, sitaw, batao patani, kondol, patola, upo, kalabasa, labanos, mustasa, sibuyas, kamatis, bawang, luya and linga; including kamote or sweet potato, ampalaya, igos or okra, gabi, and kangkong in low places; malunggay, katuray, kamoteng-kahoy or cassava, papaya, and other trees providing vegetables, such as as kamias and tamarind (sampalok). The home garden may be supplemented by mushroom growing 3%

- b) An ornamental garden of flowering and decorative plants, such as sampaguita, dama de noche, bougainvillea, kamia, azucena, rosal, santan, canna or Bandera Espanyola, San Francisco, gumamela, etc...................... 1%

- c) Fruit and firewood trees, such as kalamansi, dayap and other citrus trees, tamarind, kamias, atis, santol, guayabano, duhat, nangka, siniguelas, ratiles, balimbing, kaimito, kasoy, tiesa, mabolo, avocado, madre de cacao, ipil-ipil, pakiling, etc. If space is available, the planting of bamboos for building materials and as sources of vegetables (bamboo shoots) is encouraged................................ 1%

- d) The lot has at least 2 compost pits, each measuring 2 meters long, 1 meter wide, and 1 meter deep. The second pit is dug when the first pit is about to be filled with composting materials............................ 1%

    e) The lot is fenced, with a pergola at the gate, and has flowering plants like bougainvillea. When the fence is made of temporary material, such as bamboo, there must be an immediate planting of garmamela, kamachile or damortis, ipil-ipil, or bougainvillea, distanced not more than 1 foot apart and close to the fence line, in order to have permanent living fences. When planted between the posts of the fence, malunggay or katuray will strengthen it, as well as provide vegetables for the family... 1%

b. Animal production........................ 20%

In rating the efficiency of the family in animal production, the scientific methods they employ in swine and poultry raising are considered. If these methods and practices are very satisfactory, the maximum rating of 10 per cent for piggery and 10 per cent for poultry is given. A rating of less than 10 per cent may be given for each item, depending on how many requirements have been met.

1) A piggery project which consists of at least 1 pig, either for breeding or fattening, regularly immunized against hog cholera and swine plague, and provided with suitable and sanitary pig pen.... 10%

2) A poultry project consisting of at least 5 laying hens and 1 rooster (preferably purebred), or 10 broilers, or 5 capons per stage of 6 months, or 6 (1 male and 5 females) ducks or turkeys, regularly immunized against avian pest, and provided with suitable and sanitary poultry house................................... 10%

2. Participation in:

    a. Cooperatives............................. 20%

For purposes of evaluating the farm family's participation in cooperatives, based on membership and attendance at meetings, regularity in making deposits, promptness in repayment of loans, and wise use of loans, the following criteria are used:*

1) Membership in credit unions   (4%)

    a) If 91 to 100% of eligibles
   in family are members............. 4%
    b) If 71 to 90% of eligibles
   in family are members............. 3%
    c) If 51 to 70% of eligibles
   in family are members............. 2%
    d) If 50% or fewer of eligibles
   in family are members............. 1%

If, however, in a given barrio 80 per cent or more of the members of the credit union are the only ones from their families who belong, these families are given a rating of 3 per cent, regardless of the total number of eligibles.

2) Deposits in credit union   (4%)

    a) If a member deposits
   from ₱51 and above in 1 year...... 4%
    b) If a member deposits
   from ₱41 to ₱50 in 1 year......... 3%
    c) If a member deposits
   from ₱31 to ₱40 in 1 year......... 2%
    d) If a member deposits
   from ₱21 to ₱30 in 1 year......... 1%

3) Attendance at meetings of credit union   (4%)

    a) If a member attends
   91 to 100% of all meetings........ 4%

---

*Families shall be evaluated on participation in cooperatives only in barrios having registered credit unions. When there is no credit union in the barrio, the 20 per cent rating is distributed equally between participation in rural industries and livelihood seminars and classes. Each of these sections then has a maximum rating of 15 per cent (original 5 per cent plus 10 per cent from cooperatives).

        b) If a member attends
              81 to 90% of all meetings......... 3%
        c) If a member attends
              71 to 80% of all meetings......... 2%
        d) If a member attends
              61 to 70% of all meetings......... 1%

   4) Promptness in repayment of loans (4%)

        a) If a member is never delinquent
              in repayment of loan.............. 4%
        b) If a member is delinquent in repay-
              ment of loan for 1 month only..... 3%
        c) If a member is delinquent in repay-
              ment of loan for 2 months only.... 2%
        d) If a member is delinquent in repay-
              ment of loan for 3 months only.... 1%

   5) Wise use of loans granted to members
        of credit unions   (4%)

        a) If the loan is used for
              livelihood to increase income..... 4%
        b) If the loan is used for
              education of any family member.... 3%
        c) If the loan is used for medical
              care of any family member......... 2%
        d) If the loan is used for
              civic purposes or an emergency.... 1%

       If the loans granted to a member are 2
       or more:

        a) If the loans implement
              the four-fold program............. 4%
        b) If the loans implement
              3 phases of the four-fold program. 3%
        c) If the loans implement
              2 phases of the four-fold program. 2%
        d) If the loans implement
              1 phase of the four-fold program.. 1%

  b. Rural industries........................ 5%

If there is at least 1 member of the farm
family engaged or employed in a rural industry,
such as bamboo craft, woodcraft, rattan craft,
buri craft, pottery, loom weaving, needlecraft,
or ceramics; whether the income derived is in
cash or in kind, they are given the maximum

rating of 5 per cent.

 c. Livelihood seminars and classes........... 5%

When the adult members and the youth of the family who are residing permanently in the barrio (except for those who are studying) have attended classes and seminars in livelihood conducted in the barrio, the family is given the maximum rating of 5 per cent; otherwise, appropriate deductions are made.

3. Attainment of "MAC" (Minimum Additional Income)..................................... 20%

When the farm family obtains ₱200.00 or more additional income from the "MAC" projects, such as rice production, secondary crop production, home gardening, piggery, poultry raising, and home industries, the maximum rating of 20 per cent is given. When additional income falls below ₱200.00, the rating is reduced accordingly. This formula is used to compute the rating in "MAC":

$$\frac{\text{Additional income}}{₱200.00} \times 20\% = \text{Rating in per cent}$$

Examples: $\frac{₱200.00 \text{ (MAC)}}{₱200.00} \times 20\% = 20\%$

$\frac{₱190.00 \text{ (MAC)}}{₱200.00} \times 20\% = 19\%$

$\frac{₱150.00 \text{ (MAC)}}{₱200.00} \times 20\% = 15\%$

$\frac{₱ 40.00 \text{ (MAC)}}{₱200.00} \times 20\% = 4\%$

$\frac{₱ 10.00 \text{ (MAC)}}{₱200.00} \times 20\% = 1\%$

$\frac{₱ 1.00 \text{ (MAC)}}{₱200.00} \times 20\% = 0.1\%$

4. Wise use of income........................... 5%

When the farm family income is used for projects and purchases that benefit the family, such as construction of a new house, house repairs, home appliances, utensils and furniture, clothing, food, work animals and farm implements, education of children, medical fees, wholesome recreation, or when it is invested in profitable projects, the maximum 5 per cent rating is given. Otherwise, appropriate deductions are made. Unwise uses of income include gambling, lavish preparations for fiestas and parties, and other unnecessary expenses that drain the family treasury.

Education - 100%

1. All members are literate................... 20%

    The following formula is used to compute the family's rating in literacy:

    $$\frac{\text{Number of literate members}}{\text{Number of literates and teachable illiterates at least 13 years old in family}} \times 20\% = \text{Rating in per cent}$$

    Examples:

    $$\frac{5 \text{ (literate members)}}{5 \text{ (literate and teachable illiterate members of the family)}} \times 20\% = 20\%$$

    $$\frac{4 \text{ (literate members)}}{5 \text{ (literate and teachable illiterate members of the family)}} \times 20\% = 16\%$$

    $$\frac{3 \text{ (literate members)}}{5 \text{ (literate and teachable illiterate members of the family)}} \times 20\% = 12\%$$

    $$\frac{2 \text{ (literate members)}}{5 \text{ (literate and teachable illiterate members of the family}} \times 20\% = 8\%$$

    $$\frac{1 \text{ (literate member)}}{5 \text{ (literate and teachable illiterate members of the family)}} \times 20\% = 4\%$$

2. Literature read by family:

    a. At home................................... 30%

1) The family buys or subscribes to daily or weekly newspapers or magazines..... 10%

2) There are at least 5 kinds of books or pamphlets or magazines containing articles on scientific methods in such fields as crop production, animal production, cooking, household management, child care, and health practices...... 10%

3) Literate members of the family read the above materials and apply to their activities the knowledge and skills they have learned......................... 10%

b. In the reading circle.................... 10%

1) Literate members of the family are members of the reading circle.......... 5%

2) The family helps in the upkeep of the reading center and in providing and securing suitable reading materials................................. 5%

3. Participation in:

   a. Cultural activities...................... 20%

   1) One or more family members have participated in such activities as a literary-musical program, folk dance, or drama. 10%

   2) One or more adult members of the family have attended the last literary-musical program, folk dance, "balagtasan," drama presentation, or other cultural program held in the barrio............ 5%

   3) One or more adult members of the family have actively participated in constructing a stage or in preparing materials for a program........................ 5%

   b. Recreational activities.................. 20%

   1) One or more adult family members participate regularly in athletic and parlor games, and other recreational activities............................ 10%

2) One or more adult family members regularly attend athletic and parlor games, and other recreational activities in the barrio............................ 5%

3) The family actively participates in promoting athletics and other recreational activities, giving financial support or any other form of contribution.............................. 5%

Health - 100%

1. Family health:

   a. No suffering from communicable diseases.. 25%

   This formula is used to determine the family's rating with respect to communicable diseases:

   $$\frac{\text{Number of members who are not suffering from communicable diseases}}{\text{Total number of family members}} \times 25\% = \text{Rating in per cent}$$

   Examples:

   $$\frac{5 \text{ (well members)}}{5 \text{ (total family members)}} \times 25\% = 25\%$$

   $$\frac{4 \text{ (well members)}}{5 \text{ (total family members)}} \times 25\% = 20\%$$

   $$\frac{3 \text{ (well members)}}{5 \text{ (total family members)}} \times 25\% = 15\%$$

   $$\frac{2 \text{ (well members)}}{5 \text{ (total family members)}} \times 25\% = 10\%$$

   $$\frac{1 \text{ (well member)}}{5 \text{ (total family members)}} \times 25\% = 5\%$$

   b. All members are immunized................ 15%

   This formula is used to determine the family's rating in immunization:

$$\frac{\text{Number of members who are immunized}}{\text{Total number of family members}} \times 15\% = \text{Rating in per cent}$$

Examples:

$$\frac{5 \text{ (immunized members)}}{5 \text{ (total family members)}} \times 15\% = 15\%$$

$$\frac{4 \text{ (immunized members)}}{5 \text{ (total family members)}} \times 15\% = 12\%$$

$$\frac{3 \text{ (immunized members)}}{5 \text{ (total family members)}} \times 15\% = 9\%$$

$$\frac{2 \text{ (immunized members)}}{5 \text{ (total family members)}} \times 15\% = 6\%$$

$$\frac{1 \text{ (immunized member)}}{5 \text{ (total family members)}} \times 15\% = 3\%$$

2. Environmental sanitation:

   a. Installed sanitary toilet and proper use. 15%

   1) The family has installed a sanitary water-sealed or funnel (Antipolo) type of toilet........................ 10%

   2) The toilet is being used properly..... 5%

   b. Constructed blind drainage.............. 10%

When the farm family has a well-kept blind drainage, covered with stones, with water draining through a covered canal running into a covered pit, full credit of 10 per cent is given.

   c. Maintaining safe drinking water.......... 5%

Full credit of 5 per cent is given to a farm family that maintains safe drinking water by observing these practices: water is kept in a clean, well-covered container, provided with either a faucet or a dipper; no hands are used to draw out water; if possible, each member of the family has a separate drinking glass.

    d.   Maintaining clean and sanitary house and and premises............................... 10%

    1) Clean and sanitary house............... 5%

    2) Clean and sanitary premises........... 5%

3. Reporting all births, deaths, and communicable diseases............................... 10%

The family is evaluated as follows on their reporting of vital statistics:

    1) Reporting vital statistics promptly... 10%

    2) Delayed reporting..................... 5%

4. Participation in health seminars and classes. 10%

    1) Active participation.................. 10%

    2) Fair participation 5%

Self-Government - 100%

1. Active participation in:

    a.   Barrio organizations (RRMA, RRWA, RRYA, and barrio assembly).............. 40%

The family is given credit as follows:

    1) Regular membership and participation in the meetings of the RRMA, by the adult male................................... 5%

    2) Active performance in individual projects by the RRMA member........... 5%

    3) Regular membership and participation in the meetings of the RRWA, by the adult female................................. 5%

    4) Active performance in individual projects by the RRWA member........... 5%

    5) Regular membership and participation in the meetings of the RRYA, by the youth 5%

    6) Active performance in individual

projects by the RRYA member............ 5%

7) Regular membership and participation in the meetings of the barrio assembly.... 5%

8) Active cooperation and participation in the affairs and projects of the barrio council................................ 5%

b. Community projects...................... 25%

The family is rated as follows for participation in community projects:

1) Regular participation of RRMA member.. 10%

2) Regular participation of RRWA member... 5%

3) Regular participation of RRYA member.. 10%

2. Active family council....................... 15%

The development of a model farm family requires an active family council. Family councils are rated according to the degree of their participation in the model farm family projects, as follows:

1) Active family council................. 15%

2) Fairly-active family council.......... 10%

3) Not-so-active family council.......... 5%

3. All members are law-abiding................. 10%

The members of a model farm family must all be law-abiding, with no record of criminal conviction in any court. This does not include barrio residents who have been charged in court for rebellion during the war and are now law-abiding citizens. All members of the family must be known in the community to be of sound moral character.

4. Qualified voters vote during elections...... 10%

A farm family whose qualified voters all vote during elections is given the maximum rating of 10 per cent; otherwise, the family is rated according to this formula:

$$\frac{\text{Number of qualified voters who voted}}{\text{Total number of qualified voters in family}} \times 10\% = \text{Rating in per cent}$$

Examples:

$$\frac{5 \text{ (voters who voted)}}{5 \text{ (qualified voters in family)}} \times 10\% = 10\%$$

$$\frac{4 \text{ (voters who voted)}}{5 \text{ (qualified voters in family)}} \times 10\% = 8\%$$

$$\frac{3 \text{ (voters who voted)}}{5 \text{ (qualified voters in family)}} \times 10\% = 6\%$$

$$\frac{2 \text{ (voters who voted)}}{5 \text{ (qualified voters in family)}} \times 10\% = 4\%$$

$$\frac{1 \text{ (voter who voted)}}{5 \text{ (qualified voters in family)}} \times 10\% = 2\%$$

RECOGNITION DAY PROGRAM

The recognition day program enables the whole barrio to take stock of the progress made by families participating in the MFF program. The program is held (a) to recognize and honor all the families that are selected as model farm families by the model farm family selection committee, (b) to inspire these model families to continue their projects and activities; and (c) to encourage the others to participate more actively in the program, and achieve the MFF goals.

The program is sponsored by the model family selection committee, with the assistance of the RRW and the team captain. The leading citizens of the barrio, as well as visiting PRRM personnel, participate. Certificates of merit and model farm family plaques are awarded to all the families who have newly attained model status.

The program affords a good opportunity for the PRRM representative to speak to the barrio people about the MFF program, and to praise and encourage the families who have worked so hard to achieve their goals. He may point out the general improvement in the barrio, and speak about the possibilities for further achievements in the near future. He may suggest to the model families that they frame their certificates and hang them on the walls of their homes, and hang their plaques out front for others to see. This will help to inspire the other families of the barrio to work harder to achieve the MFF goals themselves.

All the activities of the recognition day program reflect the MFF slogan, "Every farm family a model farm family." The program should be interesting and festive, for it marks a milestone for all the families actively involved in the program, and for the barrio as a whole. It should serve to deepen everyone's interest in attaining model status for the barrio, and in working unceasingly for the larger goal of building the Philippines into a nation of prosperous and independent people.

CHAPTER 22 MODEL VILLAGES

One of the major problems the PRRM field staff has faced in working in the barrios has been how to maintain a reasonably balanced development among the various parts of the four-fold program, not only within families, but also within entire villages. It is easy for the RRW, and for the barrio people, to become especially enthusiastic about some aspects of the program, and to devote their attention to them at the expense of other aspects. In the long run, this uneven development becomes self-defeating, because of the interdependence of advances in livelihood, education, health, and self-government.

PRRM has tried different approaches to the goal of balanced progress in the barrio. The program that has emerged, and been most successful to date, is that of the "Model Village." The model village is conceived of as a community in which the advances made in all four areas of the program are so outstanding that the community might well serve as a model for neighboring villages. In its effort to attain this status, each PRRM-aided barrio has a balanced over-all objective, and clearly defined goals in each of the four areas.

BACKGROUND

During the early days of the PRRM Movement, experiments aimed at achieving the goal of a model village were conducted in a number of barrios. In some, the desire to attain a model physical appearance led to vigorous activity in cleaning up streets and canals, constructing beautiful bamboo fences, and planting shrubs. These activities were highly desirable in themselves. But they tended to focus attention on beautification to such an extent that other important aims were partially neglected.

In 1960, PRRM formulated a set of criteria for the development of model villages in the separate phases of the four-fold program. In other words, a barrio might become a model barrio in livelihood, or a model barrio in health, or in education or in self-government. The criteria specified, for example, that a model barrio in livelihood must have a plant nursery, vegetable and flower gardens in homes, backyard piggery and poultry projects, and that the demonstration farmers in the barrio must each earn an additional net income of not less than ₱200 a year. Similarly, specific standards were set for model barrios in health, in education, and in self-government.

This program generated great enthusiasm. PRRM personnel working in the different areas entered into friendly competition with each other, and tried to advance their own projects in the barrios as far as possible. A large percentage of the barrios receiving PRRM assistance achieved model status in at least one phase of the program.

This approach afforded two distinct advantages: it stimulated enthusiastic efforts among PRRM field workers and the barrio people; and it was relatively easy to adopt, since there are usually important factors in any barrio favoring one type of development over another--such factors as readily available resources, and the people's interest and convenience.

But there was a serious drawback. In concentrating on one or another PRRM program in isolation, this approach did not take into account the _interdependence_ of the problems of poverty, illiteracy, disease, and civic apathy. Since it did not provide the means for an integrated attack on these problems, the vicious cycle in which rural communities are caught was left unbroken. For example, a barrio might achieve model status in health, with pure drinking water, blind drainage pits, and sanitary toilets. Its cleaned-up, attractive homelots might be impressive to the eye of the visitor. But if no projects had been undertaken in the area of livelihood, the people would remain in poverty. If left untouched, this basic condition would eventually undermine the progress achieved in health. Sooner or later the village would slide back to its former status.

PRRM experience has repeatedly shown that unchecked problems in one fundamental area tend to act as a drag on advances in all other areas. Fortunately, experience has also shown that balanced progress in all four areas results in mutual reinforcement and

MODEL VILLAGES

more stable continuous achievement. This was demonstrated by some of the early work done in the Model Village program. Some particularly energetic RRWs emphasized all four phases of the program at once. Their successes demonstrated that, with careful planning and a consistent effort to implement all parts of the four-fold program, a village could make exemplary advances not merely in one phase, but in all four phases of the program. This paved the way for a new approach to the Model Village program.

In 1963, the Senior Staff prepared criteria for model villages in eight parts: (1) general, (2) plant production, (3) animal production, (4) cooperatives, (5) supplemental income projects and public works, (6) health, (7) education, and (8) self-government. The criteria were tested over a one-year period and then revised, in consultation with barrio leaders, so they would apply to all kinds of rural communities. Further revisions may be expected as more experience is gained.

CRITERIA FOR A MODEL VILLAGE AND MAXIMUM ATTAINABLE SCORES

Below are the criteria, derived through trial and error, in the eight categories, showing the maximum points attainable on each item. Later in this chapter, a sample is given of a quarterly rating of one barrio, based on these criteria.

I. General

		Maximum Number of Points Attainable
1.	At least 25 per cent of all families are "model families," preferably spread throughout the barrio.	50
2.	Main streets and side canals are regularly cleaned.	20
3.	Plaza is well maintained and well utilized.	10
4.	Unwholesome activities are curtailed, and high moral standards are maintained.	20
	Total	100

II. Plant Production

1. At least 50 per cent of all farm families have an annual net or labor income of ₱700 from plant production.   30

2. At least 10 demonstration farmers have realized an additional net income of ₱130 from scientific plant production.   30

3. A plant nursery is well maintained.   15

4. At least 50 per cent of all homes have homelot vegetable gardens, and flowering and ornamental plants.   15

5. Farmers' classes are held regularly once a month and a farmers' seminar has been conducted.   <u>10</u>

                         Total   100

III. Animal Production

1. At least 50 per cent of all families have an annual net income of ₱240 each from animal production projects.   20

2. At least 10 demonstration farmers have each realized an additional net or labor income of ₱40 from animal production projects.   10

3. The following projects have been undertaken: (a) at least 10 families are engaged in hatching of purebred eggs; (b) all demonstration farmers have at least 2 capons each; (c) at least 2 farm poultry projects have been put up every year; (d) at least 50 per cent of all chickens are immunized during the semester.   30

4. The following piggery projects have been undertaken: (a) at least 1 purebred boar is present in the barrio; (b) there are at least 10 breeding sows in the barrio; (c) at least 50 per cent of all families are raising fattening pigs during each semester; (d) at least 50 per cent of all pigs in the village are immunized during the semester.   20

5. At least 50 per cent of all carabaos are immunized during each semester.   5

6. Training sessions for youths as auxiliary animal husbandmen have been held.   5

7. At least one animal production seminar has been conducted during the year.   5

8. At least 5 families have milking animals.   5

                                              Total   100

IV. Cooperatives

1. Following preliminary survey: (a) RRW, believing there is a great need in the barrio for a credit facility such as a credit union, has persuaded 4 or more barrio leaders to support it actively; (b) RRW is convinced that a competent, honest, and dedicated treasurer is available; (c) 50 or more barrio residents have paid their membership fees and made initial deposits of not less than ₱2 each.   15

2. Cooperative education:
(a) 6 or more village leaders have learned how to administer and manage the credit union.   20
(b) 50 or more members have each attended cooperative education classes 3 or more times.   10

3. Registration with the government: (a) the organization meeting and election have been held; (b) the articles of incorporation have been duly prepared; (c) the constitution and by-laws have been duly adopted.   5

4. Membership: the heads of at least 5 per cent of the village families have joined the society during the quarter.   5

5. Deposits and assets: average net deposits have amounted to ₱300 or more during the quarter.   5

6. The loans issued have totaled ₱1,000 or more during the quarter.   5

7. The average repayment on loans has been ₱300 or more during the quarter.   5

8. Net savings during the quarter have amounted to ₱200 or more.   5

9. Each borrower has realized ₱5 or more income from projects during the quarter.   5

10. Supervision: during the quarter (a) at least one audit has been made; (b) at least one analysis has been made; (c) at least one check-up of officers' performance has been made; (d) assistance in the preparation of records has been rendered at least once; and (e) at least one inspection of the books has been made.   20

                                        Total   100

V. Supplemental Income Projects and Public Works

1. At least 20 per cent of the barrio families derive a minimum net income of ₱100 per family per year from rural industries.   30

2. A training institute for rural industries and vocational arts has been conducted with a minimum of 10 participants.   30

3. An industry such as bamboocraft, fishing, or ceramics has been introduced or maintained for at least 10 families in the village.   20

4. A community construction project serving at least 10 families has been completed.   20

                                        Total   100

Authorized alternative projects for items 3 and 4:

    a. Building a feeder or village gravel road at least one kilometer long.

    b. Construction of a standard public school classroom.

    c. Building a bridge valued at ₱200 or more in labor and materials.

    d. Construction of a multipurpose concrete

pavement.

e. Settlement of barrio boundary dispute.

f. Settlement of families in a new village site.

VI. Health

1. Barrio health center is adequately supplied with medicine, is regularly visited by rural health unit (RHU), and has a regular schedule according to which trained auxiliary health workers are assigned to the management of the center.   20

2. At least 50 per cent of all homes have sanitary toilets.   20

3. At least 50 per cent of all homes have well-maintained blind drainage systems.   10

4. At least 50 per cent of all houses have adequate fences.   10

5. 100 per cent of all houses in the barrio have clean and well-kept surroundings.   10

6. At least 50 per cent of the susceptible population of the barrio are immunized against communicable diseases.   10

7. Special projects:

   a. The barrio has had a special course for the training of auxiliary health workers, or a special training class for mothers.   10

   b. There is an ongoing project in de-worming or vital statistics being conducted in the barrio.   <u>10</u>

                                                      Total   100

VII. Education

1. At least 80 per cent of the teachable illiterates in the barrio have completed the basic literacy course.   30

2. There is an ongoing literacy class or

classes, with at least 5 pupils attending regularly. 10

3. There are at least 3 active auxiliary literacy teachers. 15

4. The reading center is used regularly by the people of the barrio; it is kept clean, with reading materials in good condition and well arranged. 10

5. The reading circle is well supervised, and has at least 20 members. 5

6. At least one folk dance is presented during the quarter. 10

7. There has been a folk song presentation during the quarter. 10

Note: A wholesome recreational activity undertaken during the quarter may be substituted for either item 6 (a folk dance) or item 7 (a folk song presentation).

8. At least one PRRM-sponsored play is presented during the year. 10

Total 100

VIII. Self-Government

1. Barrio council: (a) the barrio council meets regularly once a month; (b) at least 4 ordinances and/or resolutions were passed during the quarter; (c) the barrio council is engaged in at least 3 community projects during the quarter. 25

2. Barrio associations: (a) the 3 people's rural reconstruction associations meet regularly once a month; (b) each of the 3 people's associations is engaged in at least 3 community projects; (c) the membership of each of the people's associations has increased by 5 or more during the quarter; each association has a strong group feeling and requires little help from the RRW; the officers and members of the associations carry out most of the work of the projects. 60

3. Barrio hall or multipurpose hall:
(a) cleanliness is maintained; (b) surroundings are well-kept, with adequate fencing; (c) it is equipped with necessary facilities; (d) it is used for group activities by the barrio council and by the people's associations.   15

                                Total   100

                          General Total   800

IMPLEMENTING THE PROGRAM

The socio-economic survey conducted by the RRW when he begins his work in a barrio (see Chapter 4) is the chief source of organized information on the barrio--its strengths, weaknesses, assets, and needs --and is essential to intelligent planning of the Model Village program.

Gaining the Support of the People

The "model village" concept becomes meaningful when it reflects the conscious hopes and aspirations of leaders in a rural community. This does not happen automatically. Before a development program is started, there may be in the community an acute awareness of some needs, but only a limited awareness of others. There may be a strong desire for some types of development, but little or no desire for others. The reason for this may be, chiefly, a lack of firsthand experience. Most of the people in a barrio, for example, may not know how much more they could be earning, or how useful literacy could be to them in their efforts to improve their levels of agricultural production. They may not realize that they could better the health of every family in the community by learning and adopting sanitary practices. And they may never have experienced the self-respect and dignity that would be theirs with a demonstration that they can themselves conduct the business of government at the barrio level.

In planning projects and activities with the barrio leaders, the RRW gives full attention to the needs which they feel to be most pressing. Experience has shown that, as a rule, it is best for him not to contradict their choices when they select the first projects for implementation. Their enthusiasm and active involvement are more valuable than a schedule of activities planned with only technical considerations in mind. After the initial projects are well started, the RRW can begin directing attention to other projects that he believes would be practical and beneficial to the barrio, making use of facts obtained in the socio-economic survey.

One of the RRW's fundamental tasks--which provides a real test of his initiative, sensitivity, judgment, and persuasiveness--is to help the barrio people to expand their horizons, and to acquire a realistic awareness of what they can attain through their own efforts. When this is well done, over a period of months, the barrio people almost invariably respond with awakening interest and a growing desire to develop their capabilities in all areas of their lives. The vision and enthusiasm of the RRW become, in a real measure, the vision and enthusiasm of the people. When this happens, it is a sign that the RRW is doing a good job. The goal of a "model village" is no longer a private goal of PRRM personnel; it is equally the goal of the barrio people who, alone, can achieve it.

Gaining the Support of Barrio Leaders and Organizations

Much of the RRW's effort, as he strives to reach this stage, is with the influential leaders in the barrio and with the principal barrio organizations. Their active cooperation and support are essential. Members of the barrio council, the officers of the three people's associations, the principal members of credit unions and other organizations, and other respected citizens, including the local school teachers, can be invaluable allies. And the various village institutions can play a vital role in promoting the objectives of the Model Village program in the areas of their special interests and responsibilities.

The RRW thinks out, and then discusses carefully with others, therefore, what the individual leaders and what each of the organizations might be able to do to forward the Model Village program and to give it a dynamic quality. This helps him to pinpoint the responsibilities that individuals and groups may be asked to assume in promoting the various parts of the program.

Then comes the crucial task of enlisting the cooperation and active leadership of the individuals and organizations concerned. For this, the RRW will need to employ his best judgment, and the skills of persuasion and leadership that he has learned. In each important step, he tries to work in close collaboration with one or more of the key leaders in the barrio, and to get them to assume gradually increasing responsibility for the leadership and promotion of the Model Village program.

Gaining the Support of Public and Private Agencies

Because of its inclusive aims, the Model Village program provides an ideal framework, within a barrio, for the coordination of many valuable resources and services that may be available from all PRRM departments and from government and private agencies working in the rural areas. The RRW, by working effectively with the members of the barrio council in helping to coordinate such outside aid, can be of real help to each agency, and thereby magnify the efforts of all who are working for better conditions in the barrio. He endeavors to share with the representatives of the agencies, and to have the members of the barrio council share with them, the aspirations of the barrio people toward achieving all-round progress and model status for their village.

There are many specific ways in which various governmental and private agencies have given a big boost to progress in the barrios, and to everyone's morale; and the barrio councils, with the cooperation of RRWs, have done much to facilitate such assistance. Municipal and provincial governments, for instance, have given free gravel and sand for the construction and maintenance of barrio roads. The Philippine Charity Sweepstakes has extended help in the construction of community health centers. Municipal rural health units have visited the barrios in a more systematic way to give free consultations and treatment, knowing that the people needing their services, in the PRRM-aided barrios, would be ready and waiting. Some private physicians have also cooperated in providing needed medical counsel and service. The Bureau of Animal Industry has given free vaccine for animal immunization. Other agencies have contributed in other ways.

The real value to the barrio of assistance from outside sources depends greatly on the people's cooperation in using the resources made available, and in helping to conduct the various organizational campaigns. The RRW and the village leaders play an important role in bringing about a high level of cooperation.

Whenever outside aid is given to the barrio, the criteria of the Model Village program again serve a useful purpose: The assistance rendered can be registered in terms of points the village has gained in the model village rating. Everyone who has worked on the program, including the representatives of the agencies, should be aware of the improvements in the barrio's rating. Credit should be given where credit is due. Real, measurable progress toward a broadly-conceived goal acts as a great incentive to further efforts, and stimulates even more fruitful cooperation.

RECORDING AND RATING OF PROGRESS ACHIEVED

Communities that have achieved the status of model barrios illustrate the fact that the Model Village program can be introduced successfully under widely differing local conditions. Typical examples are (a) San Fabian, Sto. Domingo, Nueva Ecija, where 93 per cent of the residents are farm families whose major source of income is rice and secondary crops; (b) Tagangao, Batangas, Batangas, a fishing village; (c) Pasajes, Concepcion, Tarlac, a hacienda barrio where all the families are laborers on the sugar cane plantation. These model villages are evidence that any type of rural community can be developed into a model when its people are sufficiently awakened, and when a certain flexibility is applied in implementing the program.

In order to follow the progress of a village in achieving model status, and to illustrate the method by which the RRW keeps track of the extensive data involved, let us examine a single case in some detail.

Manaois barrio is located in the eastern part of Paniqui municipality, Tarlac province. It is connected to a national road by a dirt road about three kilometers long. Its residents include farm families as well as wage earners on a sugar cane plantation.

When the PRRM was just starting the Model Village program here, in 1963, some of the basic data about Manaois, as determined by the socio-economic survey, read as follows: There were 86 families in this barrio, and a total population of 562. Twenty-six families derived their income from rice and sugar cane production, 12 were regular employees of the sugar central, and the rest--more than 50 per cent--had no permanent, year-round work. During the sugar cane planting and milling seasons, they were, however, hired by the sugar central on a temporary basis. There were no homelot gardens and it was not a common practice for the farmers to plant a secondary crop. Few engaged in poultry and swine-raising, due to rampant animal diseases. There was no health center in the barrio.

There were 6 sanitary toilets, 6 blind drainages, and 10 homes with homelot fences. Of the 51 illiterates found during the socio-economic survey, 29 were "teachables," while the rest were found to be unable to learn the fundamentals of reading and writing due to poor eyesight and old age. There was a barrio council, but no barrio hall at which to hold meetings and transact official business.

Sample Progress Report

The record of development in Manaois, achieved during two years of PRRM assistance, is shown in the following progress report, prepared on a standard form used by the RRWs in compiling data and evaluating over-all progress.

PROGRESS REPORT FOR MODEL BARRIO

Barrio   Manaois   Municipality   Paniqui
Province   Tarlac   First Quarter 1965 (as of March 17, 1965) Start of PRRM Assistance   April 17, 1963

I. General

Basic Data: Population   593   Total Families   92
Farm Families   26   Houses   83

1. No. of model families   46
2. Streets and canals cleaned: (check one)

           a. once a month   x
           b. once in two months   ___
           c. once in a quarter   ___
    3. Plaza maintenance and utilization:
           a. landscaped: yes   x   no ___
           b. landscaped with playground: yes x no ___
           c. with stray and grazing animals:
              yes ___ no x
           d. maintained cleanliness: yes x no ___
           e. used properly: yes x no ___
    4. Occurrence of the following:
           a. robberies: yes ___ no x
           b. organized gambling: yes ___ no x
           c. drunkenness   yes ___ no x
           d. unwholesome activities deterrent to high
              moral standards and decency: yes ___ no x

                   II.   Plant Production

    1. No. of farm families with an annual net or
       labor income of ₱700 from plant production: 20
    2. No. of demonstration farmers who have realized
       ₱130 or more additional income from scientific
       plant production in the current or previous year:
        20
    3. Status of plant nursery: (check one)
           a. has a site set aside   ___
           b. with initial development   ___
           c. is partially developed   ___
           d. is fully developed   x
    4. No. of houses with:
           a. homelot garden   46
           b. flowering and ornamental plants   75
    5. Farmers' classes are held regularly once a month:
       yes x no ___ and a farmers' seminar conducted
       this year: yes x no ___

                  III. Animal Production

    1. No. of families with an annual net income of ₱240
       each from animal projects: 45
    2. No. of demonstration farmers who have realized an
       additional net or labor income of ₱40 each from
       animal projects: 20
    3. Poultry projects:
           a. no. of families engaged in hatching purebred
              eggs: 5
           b. no. of demonstration farmers having 2 capons
              each: 10   (total demonstration farmers:
               20)

                              376

c. no. of farm poultry projects put up during year: __1__
   d. no. of chickens immunized during semester: __450__ (total chicken population: __500__)
4. Piggery projects:
   a. no. of purebred boars in barrio: __none__
   b. no. of breeding sows: __20__
   c. no. of families raising fattening pigs during semester: __60__
   d. no. of pigs immunized during semester: __130__ (total pig population: __130__)
5. No. of carabaos immunized during semester: __105__ (total carabao population: __105__)
6. Training of youths as auxiliary animal husbandmen has been held: yes ___ no __x__
7. No. of animal production seminars conducted during year: __3__
8. No. of families who have milking animals: __3__

IV. Cooperatives

1. Economic survey:
   a. no. of barrio leaders willing to give active support to the society: __15__
   b. availability of competent, honest, and dedicated treasurer: yes __x__ no ___
   c. RRW convinced that there is great need in barrio for credit facility such as a credit union: yes __x__ no ___
   d. no. of barrio residents who have paid membership fees and initial deposits of not less than ₱2 each: __30__
2. Cooperative education:
   a. no. of barrio leaders who have learned how to administer and manage a credit union: __5__
   b. no. of members who have attended cooperative education class 3 or more times: __80__ 2 times: __60__
3. Registration:
   a. organization meeting and election held: yes __x__ no ___
   b. articles of incorporation duly prepared: yes __x__ no ___
   c. constitution and by-laws duly adopted: yes __x__ no ___
4. Membership:
   No. of barrio family heads who have already joined society: __30__
5. Deposits and assets:
   Average net deposits as of this quarter: __₱140__

6. Loans issued, amount __none yet__ (credit union newly organized)
7. No. of loans repaid __none__, total amount __none__
8. Net savings, amount __none__
9. Income from projects this quarter, amount __none__
10. Supervision conducted this quarter: no. of:
    a. audit __1__
    b. analysis __1__
    c. check-up of officers' performance __1__
    d. assistance in recording, etc. __1__
    e. book inspection __1__

V. Supplemental Income Projects and Public Works

1. No. of families in barrio who have derived a net income of ₱100 or more per year from rural industries: __20__
2. No. of participants in the training institute for rural industries and vocational arts: __20__
3. No. of families in barrio profitably engaged in:
    a. bamboocraft __none__
    b. ceramics __none__
    c. other rural industries ____, ____, ____
4. No. of families in barrio served by communal project: __92__ (free flowing artesian well)

    Substitute projects:
    a. length of feeder road constructed through self-help: __none__ km.
    b. no. of standard public school classrooms constructed through self-help: __none__
    c. no. of bridges built with a value of ₱200 in labor and materials: __none__
    d. no. of multipurpose concrete pavements constructed: __1__
    e. barrio boundary dispute settled: yes ___ no __x__
    f. families settled in new site: yes ___ no __x__

VI. Health

1. Barrio health center:
    a. adequately supplied with medicine: yes __x__ no ___
    b. regularly visited by RHU: yes __x__ no ___
    c. auxiliary health workers working regularly at health center: yes __x__ no ___
2. No. of homes with sanitary toilets: __60__
3. No. of homes with maintained blind drainage systems: __82__

4. No. of houses with adequate fences: __65__
5. No. of houses with clean and well-kept surroundings: __82__
6. No. of susceptible population immunized against communicable diseases: __350__
7. Special projects:
   a. no. of trained auxiliary health workers: __45__
   b. no. of mothers who have completed mothers' classes: __112__
   c. ongoing barrio project in de-worming or vital statistics: yes ___ no _x_

VII. Education

(Total no. of teachable illiterates: _____)
1. No. of teachable illiterates finished the basic literacy course: __24__
2. No. of pupils actively attending an ongoing literacy class: __5__
3. No. of active auxiliary literacy teachers: __3__
4. a. cleanliness of reading center maintained: yes _x_ no ___
   b. people go to reading center to read: yes _x_ no ___
   c. reading materials available in reading center: yes _x_ no ___
   d. a list of readers is available: yes _x_ no ___
5. a. reading circle is well supervised: yes _x_ no ___
   b. a list of reading circle members is available: yes _x_ no ___
   c. no. of reading circle members: __65__
6. No. of folk dances presented during quarter: __5__
7. No. of folk songs presented during quarter: __1__
   Note: A wholesome recreational activity undertaken during the quarter may be substituted for either a folk dance or folk song.
8. Drama:
   a. drama group organized: yes _x_ no ___
   b. no. of dramas rehearsed: __1__
   c. no. of dramas presented: __none yet__

VIII. Self-Government

1. Barrio council
   a. meetings: (check one)
      once a month   _x_
      once in two months   ___
      once during quarter   ___

    b. no. of ordinances and/or resolutions passed during quarter: __4__
    c. no. of community projects engaged in by barrio council during quarter: __3__
2. Barrio associations:
    a. meetings held (check one for each RRA)

	Monthly	Once in 2 mos.	Quarterly
RRMA		x	
RRWA	x		
RRYA	x		

    b. community projects engaged in (check one for each RRA)

	3 Projects	2 Projects	1 Project
RRMA	x		
RRWA	x		
RRYA	x		

    c. group growth (check one for each RRA)
       1) stability of membership:
       Number of members -

	Increased by more than 5	Unchanged	Decreased by more than 5
RRMA	x		
RRWA	x		
RRYA	x		

       2) group feeling (check one for each RRA)

	Strong group feeling	Some group feeling	Little or no group feeling
RRMA	x		
RRWA	x		
RRYA	x		

       3) initiative (check one for each RRA)

	Needs very little help from RRW	Shows some initiative	Too dependent on RRW
RRMA	x		
RRWA		x	
RRYA	x		

       4) distribution of work (check one for each RRA)

	Work mostly done by officers & members	Work mostly done by officers	Work mostly done by RRW
RRMA	x		
RRWA	x		
RRYA	x		

3. Barrio hall or multipurpose hall:
    a. cleanliness is well maintained: yes __x__ no___

   b. surroundings are well kept, with adequate fencing: yes _x_ no ___
   c. equipped with necessary facilities: yes _x_ no ___
   d. used for group activities:
      1) by barrio council: yes _x_ no ___
      2) by RRMA: yes _x_ no ___
      3) by RRWA: yes _x_ no ___
      4) by RRYA: yes _x_ no ___

Sample Rating Sheet

In addition to the progress report, the RRW completes another form, also on a quarterly basis, entitled, "Rating Sheet for Model Barrio Development." On this sheet, the level attained under specific detailed headings is rated in relation to the maximum number of points allowable for each item. When the scoring on individual items is completed, the rating of the village as a whole, in relation to the model village criteria, is derived.

To complete this form, the RRW makes use of (a) the maximum attainable rating points for each of the criteria, listed earlier in this chapter, (b) a rating guide prepared by PRRM, shown in the following section, and (c) the actual data he has recorded in the progress report.

To obtain the average rating of the village, the RRW adds the subtotals for all eight categories, and divides by eight. The barrio's classification depends upon its total score:

    Model Barrio   -   90 to 100 points
    Type A Barrio   -   80 to 89 points
    Type B Barrio   -   70 to 79 points
    Type C Barrio   -   69 and below

After the first half-year or more of effort, the people have generally accepted the rating of Class B Model Barrio as a sign of distinction, and this has provided an effective incentive to continued efforts on their part in the hope that, after a higher level of achievement has been recorded in all parts of the program, the community may be accorded the rating of Class A Model Barrio, and finally, Model Barrio.

Here is the rating sheet for Manaois, after two

years, when it attained an over-all rating of 93.13 per cent and became a "model barrio."

RATING SHEET FOR MODEL BARRIO DEVELOPMENT*

(For Manaois barrio, as of March 27, 1965)	Maximum Rating (Points)	Rating as of 1st Qrtr. (Points)	2nd Qrtr.
General:			
1. Model farm families**	50	50	
2. Streets and canals	20	20	
3. Plaza	10	10	
4. Moral standards	20	20	
Subtotal	100	100	
Type for general	Model	Model	
Plant production:			
1. Plant production net income	30	30	
2. Scientific plant production	30	30	
3. Plant nursery	15	15	
4. Homelot development	15	15	
5. Farmers' classes & seminars	10	10	
Subtotal	100	100	
Type for plant production	Model	Model	
Animal production:			
1. Animal production net income	20	19.56	
2. Demonstration farmers' net income	10	10	
3. Poultry projects	30	17.50	
4. Piggery projects	20	15	
5. Carabao immunization	5	5	
6. Auxiliary animal husbandmen	5	0	
7. Animal production seminar	5	5	
8. Milking carabaos	5	3	
Subtotal	100	75.06	
Type for animal production	Model	B	

---

*Complete form provides additional space for ratings in third and fourth quarters.

**For an explanation of this and all subsequent items on the rating sheet, see the earlier section entitled "Criteria for a Model Village."

Cooperatives:
1. Economic survey   15   11
2. Cooperative education   30   20
3. Registration   5   5
4. Membership   5   5
5. Deposits   5   3
6. Loans issued   5   0
7. Repayments on loans   5   0
8. Net savings   5   0
9. Income from projects   5   0
10. Supervision   20   20
                  Subtotal   100   64
         Type for cooperatives   Model   C

Supplemental income projects
  & public works:
1. Rural industries   30   30
2. Vocational arts   30   30
3. Other industries   20   20
4. Communal projects   20   20
                  Subtotal   100   100
         Type for projects
           and public works   Model   Model

Health:
1. Barrio health center   20   20
2. Sanitary toilets   20   20
3. Blind drainage   10   10
4. Home fencing   10   10
5. Yard cleanliness   10   10
6. Immunization   10   10
7. Special projects   20   10
                  Subtotal   100   90
         Type for health   Model   Model

Education:
1. Basic literacy course   30   30
2. Literacy classes   10   10
3. Auxiliary literacy teachers   15   15
4. Functional reading center   10   10
5. Reading circle   5   5
6. Folk song activities   10   10
7. Folk dance activities   10   10
8. Drama   10   7
                  Subtotal   100   97
         Type for education   Model   Model

Self-Government:
1. Barrio council   25   25
2. Barrio associations   60   55

383

3. Barrio hall or
   multipurpose hall   15   15
              Subtotal   100   95
   Type for self-government   Model   Model

General Total   800   721.06

Average Rating
   (general total divided by 8)   90.16

Barrio Type   Model   Model

Standard Rating Guide

In order that the scoring may be as objective as possible, and also according to uniform standards, PRRM has prepared the following standard guide to be used by the RRWs in making the quarterly ratings of their respective barrios.

RATING GUIDE FOR MODEL BARRIO DEVELOPMENT

(Based on the Criteria and Progress Report)

General:

1. If at least 25 per cent of all families are model families, preferably spread in the barrio, give the maximum rating of 50 points. Model families refer to both farm and non-farm families. If less than 25 per cent, prorate, using the formula:

   $$\frac{\text{No. of model families developed}}{25 \text{ per cent of total no. of families in the barrio}} \times 50 = \text{rating of barrio in MFF points}$$

2. When the main streets and side canals are regularly cleaned:
   a) once a month, give the maximum rating of 20 points
   b) once in two months, give 15 points
   c) once in a quarter, give 5 points

3. When the plaza is well maintained and well util-

ized:
   a) landscaped, give 2 points
   b) landscaped with playground, add 2 points
   c) no stray or grazing animals in plaza, add 2 points
   d) cleanliness maintained, add 2 points
   e) used properly, add 2 points

4. When high moral standards are maintained, and unwholesome activities curtailed:
   a) without robberies, give 5 points
   b) no organized gambling, add 5 points
   c) no drunkenness, add 5 points
   d) no unwholesome activities deterrent to high moral standards and decency, add 5 points

Plant production:

1. When 50 per cent of all farm families have an annual net or labor income of ₱700 from plant production, give the maximum rating of 30 points.

2. When at least 10 demonstration farmers have realized an additional net income of ₱130 from scientific plant production, give 30 points.

3. If the plant nursery: (maximum points = 15)
   a) has a site set aside, give 2 points
   b) is in an initial stage of development, add 3 points
   c) is partially developed, give 10 points
   d) is fully developed, give 15 points

4. If 50 per cent of all homes have:
   a) homelot gardens, give 10 points
   b) flowering and ornamental plants, give 5 points

5. When farmers' classes are held regularly once a month and a farmers' seminar has been conducted, give 10 points.

Animal production:

1. When at least 50 per cent of all families have an annual net income of ₱240 each from animal projects, give the maximum rating of 20 points.

2. If at least 10 demonstration farmers have each realized an additional net or labor income of ₱40 from animal projects, give the maximum rating of

10 points.

3. If the following poultry projects are undertaken:
   a) at least 10 families have undertaken the hatching of purebred eggs, give 10 points
   b) all demonstration farmers have at least 2 capons each, give 10 additional points
   c) at least 2 farm poultry projects have been put up every year, give 5 points
   d) immunization of at least 50 per cent of all chickens has been accomplished during each semester, give 5 additional points

4. If the following piggery projects are undertaken:
   a) there is at least 1 purebred boar in the barrio, give 5 points
   b) there are at least 10 breeding sows in the barrio, give 5 points
   c) at least 50 per cent of all families are raising fattening pigs during each semester, give 5 points
   d) immunization of at least 50 per cent of all pigs has been accomplished during each semester, give 5 points

5. If at least 50 per cent of all carabaos are immunized during each semester, give 5 points.

6. If a training course has been held for youths as auxiliary animal husbandmen, give 5 points.

7. If at least one animal production seminar has been conducted during the year, give 5 points.

8. If at least 5 families have milking animals, give 5 points.

Cooperatives:

1. Economic survey (maximum points = 15)

   a) If the RRW has convinced 4 or more barrio leaders to give active support to the society, give 2 points.

   b) If the RRW has convinced 2 or 3 barrio leaders to give active support to the society, give 1 point.

   c) If the RRW is convinced of the availability of

a competent, honest, and dedicated treasurer, give 2 points.

d) If the RRW is convinced that there is a great need for a credit facility in the barrio such as a credit union, give 1 point.

e) If 50 or more residents of the barrio have paid their membership fees and their initial deposits of not less than ₱2 each, give 10 points.

If 40 to 49 residents of the barrio have paid their membership fees and initial deposits, give 8 points.

If 30 to 39 residents of the barrio have paid their membership fees and initial deposits, give 6 points.

If 20 to 29 residents of the barrio have paid their membership fees and initial deposits, give 4 points.

If 10 to 19 residents of the barrio have paid their membership fees and initial deposits, give 2 points.

2. Cooperative education (maximum points = 30)

a) If 6 or more barrio leaders have learned how to administer and manage a credit union, give 20 points.

b) If 3 to 5 barrio leaders have learned how to administer and manage a credit union, give 10 points.

c) If 1 or 2 barrio leaders have learned how to manage and administer a credit union, give 5 points.

d) If 51 or more members have each attended cooperative education classes 3 or more times, give 10 points.

If 41 to 50 members have each attended cooperative education classes 2 times, give 8 points.

If 31 to 40 members have each attended cooperative education classes 2 times, give 4 points.

If 15 to 20 members have each attended cooperative education classes 2 times, give 2 points.

3. Registration with the government
   (maximum points = 5)

   a) If the organization meeting and election are held, give 3 points.

   b) If the articles of incorporation are duly prepared, give 1 point.

   c) If the constitution and by-laws are duly adopted, give 1 point.

4. Membership (quarterly basis) (maximum points = 5)

   a) If 5 per cent of barrio family heads join the society, give 5 points.

   b) If 4 per cent of barrio family heads join the society, give 4 points.

   c) If 3 per cent of barrio family heads join the society, give 3 points.

   d) If 2 per cent of barrio family heads join the society, give 2 points.

   e) If 1 per cent of barrio family heads join the society, give 1 point.

5. Deposits and assets (quarterly basis)
   (maximum points = 5)

   a) If the average net deposits amount to ₱300 or more, give 5 points.

   b) If the average net deposits amount to ₱200 to ₱299, give 4 points.

   c) If the average net deposits amount to ₱100 to ₱199, give 3 points.

   d) If the average net deposits amount to ₱50 to

₱99, give 2 points.

e) If the average net deposits amount to ₱20 to ₱49, give 1 point.

6. Loans issued (quarterly basis)
   (maximum points = 5)

   a) If loans issued amount to ₱1,000 or more, give 5 points.

   b) If loans issued amount to ₱750 to ₱999, give 4 points.

   c) If loans issued amount to ₱500 to ₱749, give 3 points.

   d) If loans issued amount to ₱250 to ₱499, give 2 points.

   e) If loans issued amount to less than ₱250, give 1 point.

7. Repayment on loans (maximum points = 5)

   Give points on the same basis as for deposits.

8. Net savings

   a) If net savings amount to ₱200 or more, give 5 points.

   b) If net savings amount to ₱150 to ₱199, give 4 points.

   c) If net savings amount to ₱100 to ₱149, give 3 points.

   d) If net savings amount to ₱50 to ₱99, give 2 points.

   e) If net savings amount to less than ₱50, give 1 point.

9. Income from projects (maximum points = 5)

   a) If each borrower realizes ₱5 a quarter or more, give 5 points.

   b) If each borrower realizes from ₱3 to ₱4 a

quarter, give 4 points.

    c) If each borrower realizes from ₱2 to ₱3 a quarter, give 3 points.

    d) If each borrower realizes from ₱1 to ₱2 a quarter, give 2 points.

    e) If each borrower realizes less than ₱1 a quarter, give 1 point.

10. Supervision   (maximum points = 20)

    a) If 1 audit is made each quarter, give 6 points.

    b) If 1 analysis is made each quarter, give 5 points.

    c) If 1 check-up of officers' performance is made each quarter, give 4 points.

    d) If 1 assistance in the preparation is made each quarter, give 3 points.

    e) If 1 inspection of the books is made each quarter, give 2 points.

Supplemental income projects and public works:

1. If at least 20 per cent of the families derive minimum net income of ₱100 per family per year from rural industries, give 30 points.

2. If a training program for rural industries and vocational arts has been conducted with a minimum of 10 participants, give 30 points.

3. If an industry such as bamboocraft, fishing, or ceramics is introduced or maintained for at least 10 families in the barrio, give 20 points.

4. If a community construction project has served at least 10 families in the barrio, give 20 points.

    Note: Substitute projects for items 3 and 4:

    a) building a feeder or barrio gravel road at least 1 kilometer long
    b) construction of a standard public school

- c) building a bridge valued at ₱200 in labor and materials
- d) construction of a multipurpose concrete pavement
- e) settlement of a barrio boundary dispute
- f) settlement of families in a new barrio site

Health:

1. Barrio health center (maximum points = 20)

    a) If it is adequately supplied with medicine and regularly visited by the RHU, give 10 points.

    b) If trained auxiliary health workers are assigned by a regular schedule to the management of the center, give 10 points.

2. If 50 per cent of all homes have sanitary toilets, give 20 points.

3. If 50 per cent of all homes have maintained blind drainage systems, give 10 points.

4. If 50 per cent of all houses have adequate fences, give 10 points.

5. If 100 per cent of all houses have clean and well kept surroundings, give 10 points.

6. If 50 per cent of all susceptible population in the barrio are immunized against communicable diseases, give 10 points.

7. Special projects:

    a) If the barrio has trained auxiliary health workers or a mothers' class, give 10 points.

    b) If there is an ongoing project on de-worming or vital statistics in the barrio, give 10 points.

Education:

1. If 80 per cent of the teachable illiterates have finished the basic literacy course, give 30 points.

2. If a literacy class or classes are under way, with at least 5 pupils, give the maximum rating of 10 points. If there are less than 5 pupils, give 2 points per pupil.

3. If there are at least 3 active auxiliary literacy teachers, give the maximum rating of 15 points. If there are less than 3, give 5 points per auxiliary literacy teacher.

4. a) If the reading center is clean and the reading materials are well kept and arranged, give an additional 2 points.

   b) If people go there and read, give an additional 4 points.

   c) If there are sufficient reading materials, give 2 points.

   d) If there is a list of readers, give 2 points.

5. a) If the reading circle is well supervised, give 2 points.

   b) If there is a list of members, give 2 points.

   c) If there are at least 20 members, give 1 point.

6. If at least 1 folk dance is presented during the quarter, give 10 points.

7. If a folk-singing program is presented during the quarter, give 10 points.

   Note: A wholesome recreational activity undertaken during the quarter may be substituted for either a folk dance or folk singing.

8. A PRRM-sponsored drama:

   a) If a drama group has been organized, give 4 points.

   b) If there has been at least a drama rehearsal, give 3 points.

   c) If a drama has been presented, give 3 points.

Self-government:

1. Barrio council   (maximum points = 25)

   a) Meetings

   If held once a month, give the maximum 5 points.

   If held only once in 2 months, give 3 points.

   If held only once during the quarter, give 1 point.

   b) Ordinances and resolutions

   If 4 ordinances and/or resolutions were passed during the quarter, give the maximum 5 points.

   If only 2 to 3 ordinances and/or resolutions were passed, give 3 points.

   If only 1 ordinance and/or resolution was passed, give 1 point.

   c) Community projects

   If the barrio council was engaged in 3 community projects during the quarter, give the maximum 15 points.

   If the barrio council was engaged in 2 community projects, give 10 points.

   If the barrio council was engaged in 1 community project, give 5 points.

2. Barrio associations   (maximum points = 60)

   a) Meetings held:

	Monthly	Once in 2 Months	Quarterly
RRMA	3 points	2 points	1 point
RRWA	3 "	2 "	1 "
RRYA	3 "	2 "	1 "

b) Community projects engaged in:

	3 Projects	2 Projects	1 Project
RRMA	9 points	6 points	3 points
RRWA	9 "	6 "	3 "
RRYA	9 "	6 "	3 "

c) Group growth:

1) Stability of membership

	No. of members increased by more than 5	No. of members unchanged	No. of members decreased by more than 5
RRMA	2 points	1 point	0
RRWA	2 "	1 "	0
RRYA	2 "	1 "	0

2) Group feeling

	Strong group feeling	Some group feeling	Little or no group feeling
RRMA	2 points	1 point	0
RRWA	2 "	1 "	0
RRYA	2 "	1 "	0

3) Initiative

	Needs very little help	Shows some initiative	Too dependent on RRW
RRMA	2 points	1 point	0
RRWA	2 "	1 "	0
RRYA	2 "	1 "	0

4) Distribution of work

	Work done mostly by officers & members	Work done mostly by officers	Work done mostly by RRW
RRMA	2 points	1 point	0

RRWA	2 points	1 point	0
RRYA	2 "	1 "	0

3. Barrio hall or multipurpose hall
   (maximum points = 15)

   a) If cleanliness is well maintained, give 4 points.

   b) If surroundings are well kept, with adequate fencing, give an additional 3 points.

   c) If it is equipped with necessary facilities, add 4 points. These facilities must include an office desk or table, 7 chairs (or 1 chair, and benches which can seat 6 persons), and a bulletin board.

   d) If used for group activities:

      1) by the barrio council, add 1 point
      2) by RRMA, add 1 point
      3) by RRWA, add 1 point
      4) by RRYA, add 1 point

Modified Rating Guide for Hacienda Barrios

In the hacienda barrios, modified instructions are needed for one main section. This is because these barrios do not have the same legal status as other barrios and are, consequently, without barrio councils. It would be unfair, therefore, to use for them the standard rating procedure in the section on self-government. For the other sections, the rating procedure remains the same as for other barrios. Under self-government, increased points are given for the performance of the barrio associations, to compensate for the inability to earn points through the performance of barrio councils. The modified rating guide follows.

MODIFIED MODEL BARRIO RATING GUIDE
FOR HACIENDA BARRIOS

Self-Government:

1. Barrio associations   (maximum points = 84)

    a) Meetings held:

	Monthly	Once in 2 Months	Quarterly
RRMA	6 points	4 points	2 points
RRWA	6 "	4 "	2 "
RRYA	6 "	4 "	2 "

    b) Community projects engaged in:

	3 Projects	2 Projects	1 Project
RRMA	14 points	10 points	5 points
RRWA	14 "	10 "	5 "
RRYA	14 "	10 "	5 "

    c) Group growth

    1) Stability of membership

	No. of members increased by more than 5	No. of members unchanged	No. of members decreased by more than 5
RRMA	2 points	1 point	0
RRWA	2 "	1 "	0
RRYA	2 "	1 "	0

    2) Group feeling

	Strong group feeling	Some group feeling	Little or no group feeling
RRMA	2 points	1 point	0
RRWA	2 "	1 "	0
RRYA	2 "	1 "	0

3) Initiative

	Needs very little help from RRW	Shows some initiative	Too dependent on RRW
RRMA	2 points	1 point	0
RRWA	2 "	1 "	0
RRYA	2 "	1 "	0

4) Distribution of work

	Work done mostly by officers & members	Work done mostly by officers	Work done mostly by RRW
RRMA	2 points	1 point	0
RRWA	2 "	1 "	0
RRYA	2 "	1 "	0

2. Barrio hall or multipurpose hall
   (maximum points = 16)

   a) If cleanliness is well maintained, give 3 points.

   b) If surroundings are well kept, with adequate fencing, give an additional 3 points.

   c) If it is equipped with necessary facilities, add 4 points.

   d) If it is used for group activities:
      1) by RRMA, add 2 points
      2) by RRWA, add 2 points
      3) by RRYA, add 2 points

PROJECTION OF GOALS FOR MODEL VILLAGE DEVELOPMENT

   PRRM's experience has demonstrated the value of projecting goals under the Model Village program. It is now standard operating procedure for the RRW, in consultation with appropriate village leaders, to project these goals one year in advance, with subgoals for each quarter, as a means of establishing balanced targets toward which planned progress can be achieved.

This projection of goals serves to ensure even development in the four-fold program from quarter to quarter. It also translates the larger goals of the Model Village program into practical steps that can be achieved through steady effort. And it enables the RRW, in his daily work, to give his full attention to the matter at hand, without having to keep every aspect of the program "in his head" at all times.

In projecting quarterly and annual goals, the aim is to plan projects and activities on a scale that is realistic as well as ambitious. This means that the RRW must think carefully about the particular circumstances of his barrio, and take them into account. These include such factors as material resources available for development, seasonal demands, the receptivity and quality of human resources in the barrio, and his own capacity to provide leadership and guidance.

How Goals and Activities are Projected

PRRM has developed a form for the RRW's use in projecting quarterly goals for a barrio. On this form, he enters present data on the barrio (taken from the progress report) and rating points (taken from the rating sheet). This information is taken as "baseline data," since it shows the present level of development, against which future goals are planned.

In planning activities for the year ahead, the RRW projects goals for each quarter in terms of number, where applicable--such as the number of families he expects to start homelot gardens--and in terms of the corresponding rating points.

By averaging the projected rating points in each of the eight categories, he derives the classification he expects the barrio to attain at the end of each quarter. For example, if he has projected goals that, if achieved on schedule, will give the barrio an average rating of 71, he can state that the barrio's goal is to reach the status of Model Barrio Type B at the end of that quarter.

Corresponding to the projections by numbers and points are the projected general activities which the RRW spells out on this form. For instance, an entry of this kind might read: "to increase by 15 the number of model families." Thus the form provides a common-sense statement of objectives as well as a capsule projection in terms of the rating system.

It is important to note that if the "model" rating is reached in any line of activity, this does not mean there should be any slowing down of efforts in that activity. On the contrary, the momentum of the effort should be maintained. The scoring is only a device to help stimulate, and measure, progress toward goals that are of value to the people, irrespective of the scores attained. If the people of a barrio keep progressing beyond the minimum requirements for "model" rating in any activity, this can be a basis for satisfaction and pride among them.

Sample Projection of Goals and Activities

Following are the goals and activities actually projected for Manaois barrio, at the end of the first quarter of 1965, for the remaining three quarters of 1965.

PROJECTED GOALS AND ACTIVITIES: GENERAL

Goals

	Maximum Rating	Baseline Data as of 3/27/65	1965 Goals as of		
			2nd Quarter	3rd Quarter	4th Quarter
	No. Pts.	No. Pts.	No. Pts.	No. Pts.	No. Pts.
1. 25 per cent are model families	23 50	46 50	61 50	76 50	86 50
2. Streets and canals clean	20	20	20	20	20
3. Plaza maintained	1 10	1 10	1 10	1 10	1 10
4. Moral standards maintained	20	20	20	20	20
Subtotal	100	100	100	100	100
Rating (for General)	Model	Model	Model	Model	Model

Activities

2nd Quarter	3rd Quarter	4th Quarter
1. Develop 15 additional model families.	Develop 15 additional model families.	Develop 10 additional model families.
2. Maintain cleanliness of streets and canals.	Barrio council request municipal government to fill holes in streets with gravel and sand.	Barrio council pass ordinance requiring families to maintain cleanliness of streets opposite their homes.
3. RRYA further beautify plaza by planting ornamental plants.	Maintain upkeep of plaza and further improve utilization.	Committee on recreational activities schedule games at least twice a week.
4. Maintain high moral standards.	Initiate wholesome activities for out-of-school youth, to prevent juvenile delinquency.	

PROJECTED GOALS AND ACTIVITIES: ANIMAL PRODUCTION

Goals	Maximum Rating No. Pts.	Baseline Data as of 3-27-65 No. Pts.	1965 Goals as of 2nd Quarter No. Pts.	1965 Goals as of 3rd Quarter No. Pts.	1965 Goals as of 4th Quarter No. Pts.
1. 50 per cent of all families have ₱240 net income	46 20	45 19.56	45 19.56	49 20	60 20
2. 10 demonstration farmers have ₱40 MAC	10 10	20 10	20 10	20 10	26 10
3. Poultry projects conducted	30	17.50	22.5	22.5	30
4. Piggery projects conducted	20	15	15	20	20
5. 50% of carabaos immunized	53 5	105 5	106 5	108 5	110 5
6. Auxiliary animal husbandmen trained	1 5	0 0	0 0	1 5	1 5
7. Animal production seminar conducted	1 5	3 3	3 5	4 5	4 5
8. 5 families have milking carabaos	5 5	3 3	4 4	6 5	8 5
Subtotal	100	75.06	81.06	92.5	100
Rating (for Animal Production)	Model	B	A	Model	Model

Activities

2nd Quarter	3rd Quarter	4th Quarter
1. 45 families have ₱240 net income.	4 additional families have ₱240 net income.	11 additional families have ₱240 net income.
2. 10 demonstration farmers have ₱40 MAC.	Same as 2nd quarter.	6 additional demonstration farmers have ₱40 MAC.

(continued)

3. (a) 5 additional families raise chicks from purebred hatching eggs.

    (b) 5 additional families have 2 capons each.

    (c) Maintain 1 farm poultry project.

    (d) Immunize 50 more chickens.

    (a) Maintain 10 families raising chicks from purebred hatching eggs.

    (b) Same as 2nd quarter.

    (c) Same as 2nd quarter.

    (d) Auxiliary animal vaccinator immunize increased chicken population.

    (a) 40 additional families raise chicks from purebred hatching eggs.

    (b) 11 additional demonstration farmers have 2 capons each.

    (c) Carry out 4 additional farm poultry projects.

    (d) Auxiliary vaccinator conduct mass immunization of chickens.

4. (a) Convince 1 family to purchase boar.

    (b) Maintain 20 breeding sows.

    (c) 5 additional families have fattening pigs.

    (d) Immunize increased pig population.

    (a) RRW and 1 demonstration farmer canvass and buy good breed of pig to be raised as boar for service.

    (b) Increase breeding sows by 5.

    (c) Same as 2nd quarter.

    (d) Start mass immunization of pigs at end of quarter.

    (a) Healthy boar about ready for service.

    (b) Maintain 25 breeding sows.

    (c) Same as 3rd quarter.

    (d) Conduct mass immunization of pigs.

5. Immunize increased carabao population.

    Same as 2nd quarter.

    Conduct mass immunization of carabaos.

6. Train youth as auxiliary animal husbandmen.

    Auxiliary animal husbandmen help pig raisers to maintain healthy stock.

    Same as 3rd quarter.

7. Conduct seminar on animal production for RRWA.

    Conduct seminar on animal production for RRYA.

    Conduct seminar on animal production for RRMA.

8. 1 additional family has milking animal.

    Same as 2nd quarter.

    2 additional families have milking animals.

402

PROJECTED GOALS AND ACTIVITIES: PLANT PRODUCTION

Goals

	Maximum Rating		Baseline Data as of 3-27-65		1965 Goals as of					
					2nd Quarter		3rd Quarter		4th Quarter	
	No.	Pts.	No.	Pts.	No.	Pts.	No.	Pts.	No.	Pts.
1. 50 per cent of farm families have ₱700 net income	13	30	20	30	22	30	24	30	26	30
2. 10 demonstration farmers have ₱130 MAC	10	30	20	30	20	30	20	30	26	30
3. Plant nursery maintained	1	15	1	15	1	15	1	15	1	15
4. 50 per cent of homes have gardens	42	15	46	15	59	15	79	15	83	15
5. Farmers' classes & seminars conducted	25	10	28	10	31	10	34	10	38	10
Subtotal		100		100		100		100		100
Rating (for Plant Production)		Model		Model		Model		Model		Model

Activities

2nd Quarter	3rd Quarter	4th Quarter
1. 2 additional farm families have ₱700 net income.	Same as 2nd quarter.	Same as 3rd quarter.
2. 20 demonstration farmers have ₱130 MAC.	Same as 2nd quarter.	6 additional demonstration farmers have ₱130 MAC.
3. RRYA & RRMA propagate planting materials in plant nursery.	Same as 2nd quarter.	RRAs jointly collect high quality seeds for seed bank.
4. 13 additional homes have homelot gardens.	12 additional homes have homelot gardens.	12 additional homes have homelot gardens.
5. Conduct 3 farmers' classes.	Same as 2nd quarter.	Conduct 3 farmers' classes and 1 farmers' seminar.

PROJECTED GOALS AND ACTIVITIES: COOPERATIVES

Goals

		Maximum Rating		Baseline Data as of 3-27-65		1965 Goals as of					
						2nd Quarter		3rd Quarter		4th Quarter	
		No.	Pts.	No.	Pts.	No.	Pts.	No.	Pts.	No.	Pts.
1.	Economic survey		15		11	13		15		15	
2.	Cooperative education		30		20	30		30		30	
3.	Registration		5		5	5		5		5	
4.	Membership		5	30	5	40	5	60	5	70	5
5.	Deposits	₱300	5	₱140	3	₱200	4	₱1000	5	₱3000	5
6.	Loans issued	₱1000	5	0	0	0	0	₱900	5	₱2800	5
7.	Repayments on loans	₱300	5	0	0	0	0	₱300	5	₱500	5
8.	Net savings	₱200	5	0	0	0	0	₱50	2	₱200	5
9.	Income from projects	₱5	5	0	0	0	0	₱6	5	₱10	5
10.	Supervision		20		20	20		20		20	
	Subtotal		100		64		77		97		100
	Rating (for Cooperatives)		Model		C		B		Model		Model

Activities

2nd Quarter	3rd Quarter	4th Quarter
1. President of credit union convince 10 additional residents to give it active support.	Increase active supporters of credit union by 10.	Increase active supporters of credit union by 15.

2.	Train 2 additional members to administer and manage credit union.	Same as 2nd quarter.	Train 1 additional member to administer and manage credit union.
3.	Submit credit union registration papers to Cooperative Administration Office.	Credit union registered with Cooperative Administration Office.	
4.	Officers of credit union get 10 additional residents to become members.	20 new members join credit union.	10 new members join credit union.
5.	Increase deposits to ₱200 or more.	Increase deposits to ₱1,000 or more.	Increase deposits to ₱3,000 or more.
6.	No loans issued yet.	Issue initial loans of ₱900 or more to members.	Issue loans of ₱2,800 (expected) to members.
7.	No repayments on loans yet.	Receive repayment on loans of ₱300.	Receive repayment on loans of ₱500 (expected).
8.	No savings yet.	Savings total ₱50 or more (expected).	Increase savings to ₱200 (expected).
9.	No income from projects yet.	Income from projects total ₱6 each (expected).	Income from projects total ₱10 each (expected).
10.	Conduct audit, analysis, check-up of officers' performance, assistance in preparation of books, and inspection.	Same as 2nd quarter.	Same as 3rd quarter.

PROJECTED GOALS AND ACTIVITIES: SUPPLEMENTAL INCOME PROJECTS AND PUBLIC WORKS

Goals

	Maximum Rating		Baseline Data as of 3-27-65		1965 Goals as of					
					2nd Quarter		3rd Quarter		4th Quarter	
	No.	Pts.	No.	Pts.	No.	Pts.	No.	Pts.	No.	Pts.
1. 20 per cent of families engaged in rural industries	18	30	20	30	25	30	25	30	30	30
2. Vocational arts undertaken	10	30	20	30	20	30	30	30	30	30
3. 10 families engaged in other industries (substitute projects)	1	20	1	20	1	20	10	20	10	20
4. 10 families served by communal projects	10	20	92	20	92	20	92	20	92	20
Subtotal		100		100		100		100		100
Rating (for SIP and Public Works)	Model		Model		Model		Model		Model	

Activities

2nd Quarter	3rd Quarter	4th Quarter
1. 5 additional families engage in rural industries.	Maintain 25 families engaged in rural industries.	5 additional families engage in rural industries.
2. Vocational arts graduates undertake income-producing projects.	Train 10 more women in vocational training.	All 30 vocational arts graduates undertake income-producing projects.
3. Conduct training in bamboo-craft for 10 participants.	Continue training while producing articles for sale.	10 families engage in bamboocraft as source of supplemental income.
4. Maintain communal projects.	Same as 2nd quarter.	Maintain multipurpose pavement.

PROJECTED GOALS AND ACTIVITIES: HEALTH

Goals	Maximum Rating No. Pts.	Baseline Data as of 3-27-65 No. Pts.	1965 Goals as of 2nd Quarter No. Pts.	3rd Quarter No. Pts.	4th Quarter No. Pts.
1. Barrio health center actively administered		20	20	20	20
2. 50 per cent of homes have sanitary toilets	42 20	60 20	65 20	70 20	83 20
3. 50 per cent of homes have blind drainages	42 10	82 10	82 10	83 10	83 10
4. 50 per cent of homes have adequate fences	42 10	65 10	70 10	75 10	83 10
5. 100 per cent of homes have clean yards	83 10	83 10	83 10	83 10	83 10
6. 50 per cent of susceptible population is immunized		10	10	10	10	10
7. Special projects undertaken	20	10	10	20	20
Subtotal	100	90	90	100	100
Rating (for Health)	Model	Model	Model	Model	Model

(continued)

407

Activities

	2nd Quarter	3rd Quarter	4th Quarter
1.	Request RHU to make regular visits on permanent basis.	RRWA take responsibility as permanent principal supplier of medicines.	RRYA auxiliary health workers take permanent responsibility for administering first aid treatment.
2.	5 additional homes have sanitary toilets.	5 additional homes have sanitary toilets.	13 additional homes have sanitary toilets.
3.	RRWA officers campaign for repair and maintenance of blind drainages.	Same as 2nd quarter.	Same as 3rd quarter.
4.	5 additional homes fence homelots.	5 additional homes fence homelots.	8 additional homes fence homelots.
6.			RHU conduct immunization against preventable diseases.
7.		Start de-worming project.	

PROJECTED GOALS AND ACTIVITIES: EDUCATION

Goals	Maximum Rating No. Pts.	Baseline Data as of 3-27-65 No. Pts.	1965 Goals as of 2nd Quarter No. Pts.	3rd Quarter No. Pts.	4th Quarter No. Pts.
1. Literacy course completed by 80 per cent of teachable illiterates	23 30	24 30	24 30	24 30	29 30
2. 5 pupils attend literacy class	5 10	5 10	5 10	5 10	0 10
3. Auxiliary literacy teachers trained	3 15	3 15	3 15	3 15	3 15
4. Functional reading center	10	10	10	10	10
5. Active reading circle	5	5	5	5	5
6. Folk dancing undertaken	1 10	5 10	6 10	7 10	8 10
7. Folk singing undertaken	1 10	1 10	2 10	5 10	10 10
8. Active drama group	1 10	1 7	1 7	1 7	1 10
Subtotal	100	97	97	97	100
Rating (for Education)	Model	Model	Model	Model	Model

(continued)

409

Activities

	2nd Quarter	3rd Quarter	4th Quarter
2.	Intensify teaching of literacy pupils.	Same as 2nd quarter.	5 literacy pupils finish basic literacy course.
3.			Give certificate of recognition to literacy teachers.
4.	Councilman on education take charge of maintenance of reading center, and encourage new literates to read.	Solicit additional reading materials for reading center.	
6.	Rehearse and present one folk dance.	Same as 2nd quarter.	Same as 3rd quarter.
7.	Rehearse and present one folk song.	Same as 2nd quarter.	Same as 3rd quarter.
8.			Present one drama.

PROJECTED GOALS AND ACTIVITIES: SELF-GOVERNMENT

Goals

	Maximum Rating No. Pts.	Baseline Data as of 3-27-65 No. Pts.	1965 Goals as of 2nd Quarter No. Pts.	3rd Quarter No. Pts.	4th Quarter No. Pts.
1. Active barrio council	25	25	25	25	25
2. Active barrio associations	60	55	55	60	60
3. Barrio hall or multipurpose hall maintained	15	15	15	15	15
Subtotal	100	95	95	100	100
Rating (for Self-Government)	Model	Model	Model	Model	Model

Activities

	2nd Quarter	3rd Quarter	4th Quarter
1. Give barrio council absolute discretion in conduct of barrio affairs.	Minimum guidance by RRW.	Same as 3rd quarter.
2. Give barrio associations maximum liberty in contributing to progress of community.	Minimum guidance by RRW.	Same as 3rd quarter.

Notes on Completing Projection-of-Goals Form

   1. In the case of a criterion with sub-items, such as "poultry-raising" in the Animal Production category, list all the sub-items on a separate paper and prorate the remaining number and corresponding points downward by quarter. The totals are the projected points per quarter for the criterion.

   2. Plan for continued achievement in every phase of a project even after no more rating points are to be gained in this area. Project numerical goals in excess of the minimum requirement, maintaining the maximum rating points throughout.

Continued Planning

   Every quarter, the RRW has the opportunity to check his projected goals against the actual progress the barrio is making. He does this simply by comparing the results recorded on the quarterly progress report with the figures previously entered on the projection-of-goals form for that quarter. If the progress has been less than expected, he must revise, realistically, the goals for the remaining quarters. Similarly, if progress has exceeded his expectations, he will revise his goals upward for succeeding quarters.

   As time goes on, the RRW takes into account a natural tendency for a barrio that has been making good initial progress to slow down, and then, gradually, to revert to its former state. He realizes that, to be truly meaningful, the Model Village program must depend less and less on him, and more and more on the ability--and determination--of the barrio people to sustain and carry to new levels the progress they have been making.

   With this in mind, he plans, with the village leaders, projections of goals which include more leadership training for them, and their acceptance of more and more responsibility for the management and continuity of all programs and projects, including those under the supervision of the barrio council, and those being conducted by the RRMA, RRWA, RRYA, and other organizations in the barrio. The goals projected for barrio Manaois illustrate this approach.

Turning over to others the responsibilities of initiative and leadership, then backing them up strongly until they demonstrate their own capacities for self-reliant and sustained leadership, is not easy. The RRW who succeeds in doing this while he is living in a barrio not only helps to plant the vision and hopes of PRRM in the hearts of the people. He also instills in them a new confidence, born of experience, that they can go forward on their own to new and greater achievements.

APPENDIXES

APPENDIX A   IIRR AND PRRM PERSONNEL
WHO PARTICIPATED IN
PREPARING THIS MANUAL

INTERNATIONAL INSTITUTE OF RURAL RECONSTRUCTION

Y. C. James Yen, President

Gregorio M. Feliciano
Chairman, Committee on Technical Training

SENIOR TECHNICAL STAFF

Eduardo E. Agustin
Technical Expert, Health

Enrique L. Claudio, Jr.
Technical Expert, Self-Government

Juan M. Flavier
Training Director

Rufino B. Gapuz
Technical Expert, Animal Production

Pablo N. Mabbun
Technical Expert, Economics and Research

Angel P. Mandac
Technical Expert, Cooperatives

Mrs. Josefa Jara Martinez
Technical Expert, Model Farm Family

Arcadio G. Matela
Technical Expert, Education

Harry B. Price
Director, Technical Cooperation and Publications

Ernesto L. Rigor
Technical Expert, Plant Production

PHILIPPINE RURAL RECONSTRUCTION MOVEMENT

as of September 1, 1966

Gregorio M. Feliciano*, President

Juan M. Flavier*, Executive Assistant
to the President

SENIOR STAFF

Jess L. Banguis
Public Relations

Enrique L. Claudio, Jr.*
Self-Government and Deputy Field Director

Juan M. Flavier*, M.D.
Health

Rufino B. Gapuz*
Animal Production & Fisheries

Pablo N. Mabbun*
Economics & Research

Angel P. Mandac*
Cooperatives

Arcadio G. Matela*
Education & Model Farm Families

Ernesto L. Rigor*
Field Director, Plant Production, & Rural Industries

---

*Members serving concurrently on the staff of IIRR.

FIELD OPERATIONS ASSISTANTS

Menandro S. Pernito - Senior Field Assistant
Francisco Velasco - Pilot (Nueva Ecija) District
Gerardo Tumaneng - Northern Luzon District
Jaime R. Cruz - Southern Luzon District

TECHNICAL ASSOCIATES

Damaso P. Cabacungan - Education
Dr. Jacinto C. Gotangco - Health
Mrs. Maria M. Reyes - Self-Government
Jose B. Totaan - Model Farm Families
Mrs. Julita B. Sicat - Personnel & Training

TECHNICAL ASSISTANTS

Plant Production	- Laurito Arizala Felino Cinense Casiano San Jose Santiago Abesamis
Animal Production	- Bartolome Rebollido Eduardo Bumagat
Cooperatives	- Rogelio Bañas Mariano Florendo Amparo Alvarez Miguel Ponce
Rural Industries	- Reynaldo de la Torre Anselmo Pagay
Vocational Arts	- Lilia Soriano Avelina Fronda Carolina Cabansag
Education	- Perla Castro Norma Callanta
Health	- Ciriaco Balajadia Vicente Mactal Prosperina Cabantac
Self-Government	- Menardo Ballestar Raquelito Pastores Josefina Romero Quintin Yatar

Model Farm Families — Carolina Supnet

Model Barrio Research — Julieta Atendido

Personnel & Training — Venerio G. Florendo

Specialized Workers

Housing & Public Works — Eblas Blancas
 Domingo Buenaventura
 Antonio Melliza

Rural Industries — Radigundis Agsalud
 Enrique Floresca

Research Group

Research — Jesusito Amores
 Luciana Arandia
 Brigido Cabantac
 Milagros Solitario
 Rodrigo Villanueva

TEAM CAPTAINS

Alfredo Volante	Olegario de Leon
Franklin Fermin	Cipriano Ramos
Urcolano Llegado	Romeo Bilaw
Manuel Calairo	Adriano Capinding
Juan Goroza	Adonis Convalecer

GROUP LEADERS

Hilario Ibarra   Gil Dacasin

RURAL RECONSTRUCTION WORKERS

Abenoja, Febe	Backeng, Elena
Aggalot, Lolita	Bautista, Rebecca
Antaran, Carmen	Bautista, Rosario
Arellano, Alejandria	Batoom, Medina
Arenas, Arturo	Baylon, Rosario
Arenas, Rosie	Blanche, Rosa
Arizala, Nenita	Bolisay, Salvador
Abrina, Flordeliza	Buenavista, Yvonne

APPENDIX A

Cabico, Armenio
Cachero, Editha
Camangeg, Abraham
Cañenero, Erlinda
Capito, Maximino
Caseñas, Tomas
Castillo, Angelina
Castro, Eduardo
Castañeda, Perla
Comia, Dolores
Concepcion, Felicidad
Cortez, Paz
Cruz, Remedios
Cueto, Apolinaria
Cucio, Manuel
Cucio, Nerina
Dacapias, Basilisa
Dacapias, Ismael
Daenos, Ebedesto
Diaz, Francisco
Diaz, Pio
Divina, Azucena
Domingo, Marcela
Duque, Corazon
Esguerra, Pastor
Falcon, Casilda
Figueros, Angel
Florendo, Teresita
Fontillas, Carlina
Franco, Gloria
Fronda, Eleno
Fronda, Rufino
Gallego, Juanito
Galvez, Victorino
Gaspar, Catalina
Giao, Nonida
Gonzales, Marietta
Guzman, Milagros de
Honquilada, Quirino
Ibañez, Alfredo
Imana, Candido
Inobe, Nelian
Izon, Pacita
Lachica, Felix
Lavidez, Flordeliz
Lamug, Felix
Ligot, Teresita
Llacuna, Felicitos
Lomboy, Francisco
Manalang, Concepcion
Martinez, Deogenes
Marquez, Florencio
Medina, Luzviminda
Mejia, Carmelita
Melliza, Luningning
Mendoza, Esteban Jr.
Nejal, Nazarena
Ordonio, Virginia
Osuna, Erlinda
Panganiban, Maxima
Pulanco, Aida
Quiapo, Leticia
Quimosing, Abundio
Rabara, Rodrigo
Ramil, Manuel
Ramos, Frances
Ramos, Herminigildo
Rebollido, Carolina
Revilla, Araceli
Rosa, Manuel de la
Rosa, Dioscoro de la
Rosos, Flor
Sanchez, Leticia
Sacro, Monica
Santos, Julita
Sermonia, Teresito
Simon, Adelino
Soriano, Agustin
Tabada, Delia
Tanyag, Pedro
Tesoro, Irenea
Totaan, Remedios
Veniegas, Gloria
Vidallo, Leticia
Villacrusis, Alfredo
Villarta, Dionisio
Villaroya, Leticia
Visaya, Laurinda

APPENDIX B FILIPINO AND TECHNICAL TERMS

ampalaya — an annual or perennial tendril climbing herb with rounded leaves, yellow flowers and, in cultivated form, ribbed, wrinkled, cylindrical fruit 15 to 25 cm. in length and pointed at both ends.

balagtasan — a debate in verse.

barrio — as commonly used in the Philippines, a village; not, as in some Latin American countries, a section of a city or town.

batao — hyacinth bean, a smooth, twinning annual vine with tri-foliolate leaves, pink-purple or nearly white flowers, and oblong flattened pods.

buri — a fiber gathered from unopened leaf-stalks of the talipot palm tree.

dama — a Filipino version of chess.

duplo — a literary joust recited or sung in beautiful verse.

gabi — taro, an aroid grown for its edible starchy tuberous rootstocks.

garmamela — hibiscus plant.

ipil — a tree having a dark, very hard, durable wood, and yielding a valuable brown dye.

katurai — a pea tree yielding a gum used as a substitute for gum arabic.

kaukauati — a smooth, deciduous tree which reaches a height of 3 to 10 meters, with pink flowers and oblong pods.

kondol	— a gourd producing an elongated, white, edible fruit.
kulitis	— a stout, erect, smooth herb which attains a height of 0.4 to 1 meter; grows wild and abounds along sandbars and margins of streams; young leaves are eaten as vegetables.
lodge	— in agriculture, a verb meaning fall or lie down, as rice stalks beaten to the earth by wind or rain.
malungay	— a horseradish tree, so named from the pungent taste of the root, which is sometimes eaten; fruit also edible; seeds, called bennuts, yield an oil which may be used in art products.
moromoro	— a play portraying a conflict between Moslems and Christians, in which the Christians always emerge as victors.
mungo	— a bush-type legume.
municipality	— administrative division of a province, comprising a number of barrios.
palay	— rice in the husk.
panicle	— a cluster, as of rice grains.
patadyong	— one-piece attire, in colorful design, which serves as either a long or short skirt and is paired with a loose blouse having a wide neckline.
patani	— Sieva bean, a slender, climbing vine with greenish or pale yellow flowers and oblong pods containing seeds somewhat smaller than Lima beans.
patintero	— a dodging and tagging game played between competing teams of 4 to 8 members each, making use of 4 adjoining squares drawn on the ground.

APPENDIX B

patola — a type of gourd which is eaten green or cooked.

pechay — green, soft-leaved annual with compact, elongated leaves, the inner sides of which are blanched; grown chiefly as a late autumn or winter vegetable and now frequently referred to as "Chinese cabbage," or "celery cabbage."

San Francisco — a plant of the croton genus. One type yields croton oil; other types yield aromatic resins.

sarswela — a dramatic presentation with songs.

saya't kimono — two-piece attire consisting of a skirt and a loose blouse with wide neckline, made of finely woven material.

seguidillas — a rooted tropical herb with an edible tuberous root, also prized for its edible young pods.

sipa — a game involving the kicking of a ball made of rattan strips.

sitao — long-podded variety of the cowpea.

sungka — Filipino version of the ancient, intriguing game of kalah, which requires as equipment only a narrow board with two parallel rows of 7 shallow round holes each, and 2 deeper end holes; and 98 small pebbles, marbles, or fruit seeds. There are two competitors. At the outset, 7 small pebbles (or marbles or seeds) are placed in each shallow hole. One player starts by picking up all the pebbles in any hole in his row and dropping them, one at a time, clockwise, in the 14 shallow holes and the deeper hole at his left, which is his "bank." If the last pebble in his hand falls in a shallow hole containing one or more pebbles, he picks up all the pebbles in that hole and continues the process. The first player's turn ends when his last pebble falls in an empty hole. The other player then takes his turn in the same way, after which the turns alternate. The player who accumulates the most pebbles in his "bank" wins the game.

tiller — in agriculture, a verb meaning put forth new shoots or tillers.

upo — a coarse vine, with somewhat rounded leaves and large solitary white flowers, which bears a club-shaped or egg-shaped fruit that is green, mottled with gray or white.

violeta — violet plant.

DATE DUE